BREAKDOWN

SEX, SUICIDE,

AND THE

HARVARD

PSYCHIATRIST

EILEEN McNAMARA

POCKET STAR BOOKS

New York   London   Toronto   Sydney   Tokyo   Singapore

A Pocket Star Book published by
POCKET BOOKS, a division of Simon & Schuster Inc.
1230 Avenue of the Americas, New York, NY 10020

ISBN: 0-671-79621-6

First Pocket Books paperback printing May 1995

10 9 8 7 6 5 4 3 2 1

POCKET STAR BOOKS and colophon are registered
trademarks of Simon & Schuster Inc.

Cover photo by Grant Peterson Photography

Printed in the U.S.A.

"Real Love in Imaginary Wagon" from *Anne Sexton:
A Biography,* reprinted by permission of Sterling Lord
Literistic, Inc., copyright © 1991 by the Estate of
Anne Sexton.

To Margaret Rodgers Feuer

Acknowledgments

No book is ever written alone. I am indebted to a great many people, especially those whose memories gave life to this narrative and those whose expertise provided it with context.

Few professions are at once more revered and more reviled than psychiatry. I am grateful to its practitioners, of all philosophical stripes, who overcame an innate suspicion of journalists to speak with me and to direct me to the relevant literature. In particular, Drs. Ralph P. Engle, Thomas G. Gutheil, Edward J. Khantzian, Carol C. Nadelson, Malkah Notman, Miles Shore, Jay Silberger, and Larry H. Strasburger offered varying views and much insight. In addition, Dr. Sanford Gifford exposed me to the history of psychoanalysis in Boston.

Many other psychiatrists shared a wealth of knowledge and acknowledged the reservoir of ignorance about mood and personality disorders with the understanding that they would not be identified in the text. Their anonymity does not preclude my gratitude.

My conversations with Joseph T. Coyle, chairman of the Consolidated Department of Psychiatry at Harvard Medi-

ACKNOWLEDGMENTS

cal School; James I. Hudson, staff psychiatrist at McLean Hospital; W. Barry Gault, staff psychiatrist at Newton-Wellesley Hospital; and Paul R. McHugh, chairman of the Department of Psychiatry at the Johns Hopkins University School of Medicine, presage a brighter future for American psychiatry, one grounded less in trendy theory than in confirmable science. My acquaintance with Carolyn Moore Newberger provided the model of the sort of sensible, compassionate therapist vital to the recovery of any child who really has been abused.

There are few worlds more private than that of a family. A sanctuary of shared secrets and intense loyalties, it is a place where soiled linen is washed with the shades drawn. Marcos and Epifania Lozano and their children, Norma, Mark, Martha, Pilar, and Abel, earned my appreciation by abandoning the pretense of perfection to discuss their vulnerabilities as well as their achievements. They tolerated a level of intrusiveness that sometimes bordered on impertinence, knowing they would have no control over the conclusions I drew.

I am grateful as well to Paul Lozano's friends, classmates, and fellow psychiatric patients who, trusting that I would honor their requests for anonymity, shared memories of Paul.

The assistance of many individuals helped turn an idea into a book. I am grateful to Julie Michaels and Jennifer Josephy, for pushing me off this cliff; to Judith Regan, senior editor and vice-president of Paramount Publishing, for catching me; to my agent, Colleen Mohyde, and to my editor, Danelle McCafferty, for their skill and extraordinary sense of humor and perspective; to Leslie Jones and Anne Cherry for their attention to detail; to Robert H. Phelps, for his careful reading, and for everything he taught me; to Theresa Burke, Lillan Byrne, Lisa Driscoll, Janet Knott, Kelly Macdonald, Michele McDonald, and Matt Roshkow for their supportive contributions, which allowed me to concentrate on writing.

I am indebted to John S. Driscoll, the editor of *The Boston Globe,* and Ande Zellman and Fiona Luis, editors of

ACKNOWLEDGMENTS

its magazine, who freed me from my duties there to pursue this project; to Gerry O'Neill, Al Larkin, and the late Bob Anglin, three among many fine *Globe* editors who trained me to do it; to the colleagues who encouraged me throughout, especially David Warsh and Joe Kahn, and the unlicensed therapists who were always on call: Bella English, Sally Jacobs, Kate McMahon, Susan Trausch, and Joan Vennochi.

For reasons that extend beyond this book, I am indebted to the women of *The Boston Globe,* especially Muriel Cohen and Nina McCain, who years ago made room for me at the table and fed me on their wisdom and experience.

The book itself owes much to the influence of the late Daniel J. McNamara, who taught me to distinguish fact from opinion; to Frances T. McNamara, who taught me the danger of rash judgments; and, not incidentally, to Maureen, Danny, and Nancy, who crossed Mass. Ave. first, making my own passage so much the easier.

It could not have been written without the generosity and patience of Peter May and the sustaining presence of Timothy, Patrick, and Kate, who have given fresh and wondrous meaning to the idea of family in my own life.

And finally, I am indebted to Margaret Rodgers Feuer, to whom this book is dedicated, for the gift of Barnard College, which changed everything, forever.

"Real Love in Imaginary Wagon"

by Anne Sexton

Well Doctor—all my loving poems
write themselves to you.
If I could channel love,
by gum, it's what I'd do.

And never pen another
foolish freudian line
that bleeds across the page
in half assed metered rhyme.
[. . .]
If all this bother and devotion
is not, in truth, for you—
(since you're the expert on emotion)
tell me Doctor—who?

All's misalliance.
Yet why not say what happened?

—Robert Lowell

BREAKDOWN

Prologue

The recovery room at Providence Memorial Hospital was filled with the morning's postoperative cases when Pilar Williams was called to the telephone from a patient's bedside.

A maid employed by the apartment complex that Pilar's parents managed was on the line. "You need to come—right now," Maria said in Spanish, her voice high pitched and her tone insistent.

"Why? What for? I'm busy. I'm taking care of patients," Pilar protested.

Before Maria could explain, Epifania Lozano picked up an extension and Pilar heard not urgency but dread in her mother's voice: "Something is wrong. Ambulancia. Policia."

"Mom, that's a senior citizens' complex. Probably one of the elderly people got sick. That's all," Pilar said. But even as the words were forming her stomach began churning. *Oh, my God,* she thought. *It's Paul.*

Her hand shaking, she dialed the number of her brother's apartment in the complex. When her father answered the telephone, Pilar's heart sank. "Your brother is dead," Marcos Lozano told Pilar. Just like that: "Your brother is dead."

A nimble colleague sent the secretary's chair sailing across the polished linoleum in the nurses' station just in time to catch Pilar as her knees buckled, her body taking in what her mind would not. "No, you're wrong; you're confused. He must be unconscious. Dad, we need to get help."

"You don't understand, the police are here. We do have help. Paul is dead."

Listening but not hearing, Pilar demanded to speak to the officer in charge. "Hello? I'm a registered nurse. My father is the manager there. He tells me that something has happened but I can't understand a word."

"Well, yes. We have a male here in his midtwenties. Looks like an overdose. He's dead."

"Are you sure?"

"Lady, I'm sure. He's probably been dead for ten or twelve hours."

Pilar walked dry-eyed toward the locker room to retrieve her purse and to call her husband. "I have to leave. My brother is dead," she told her supervisor. Waving away condolences, she insisted on giving a report on the condition of every one of her patients before leaving. "Maybe you could write this down," she urged another nurse. "My hand is shaking."

Waiting outside the hospital for her husband, Hal, to arrive, Pilar Williams considered the policeman's words. Ten or twelve hours? *No, that's not right,* she thought. *Paul has been dead a hell of a lot longer than that.*

Pilar was quiet for the ten-minute drive along the familiar route to the Nell Gardner Pilot Homes on that April afternoon in 1991. After all the words between them about Paul over the past few years, she and Hal found themselves strangely silent in the face of his death.

Hal maneuvered the car past the Tower Motel and around the yellow police tape cordoning off the driveway to Pilot Homes. Pilar saw the ambulance. The police cars. The apartment door ajar. Most of all, she saw the absence of bustle, a sign of death here as surely as on any hospital floor when help arrives too late.

"Please, I need to see my brother," she told the policeman standing sentry at number 15. "I need to know before you take him away what happened. I'll believe what you tell me if you just let me look at him."

A more senior officer waved her into the darkened room. Paul was leaning back in his chair, his feet propped up against the desk, a text on internal medicine open in front of him. Beside the book lay a lab report, dated the day before, April 1, declaring his blood and urine free of illicit drugs. An empty syringe was on the floor. Blood stained his arm near a visible puncture wound.

He wore only clean Jockey underwear. A bottle of Calvin Klein cologne, his favorite, stood open. He must have splashed it on just after his shower, just before his death, Pilar thought. His skin had begun to mottle; rigor mortis was setting in. His bed had not been slept in; the blanket was pulled smooth and tight across the mattress—the military precision of a West Point man.

Her survey of the scene took no more than a minute. Pilar Williams then bent and placed a kiss on her brother's forehead. Across the room, her father began to weep. Together they walked outside into the too bright sunshine to wait, while the men from the coroner's office lowered the corpse from the desk chair onto the stretcher.

The sound of the men's laughter spilled into the gravel courtyard from the small studio apartment where Paul's body had stiffened into death. How many times had she done that? Pilar Williams wondered. How often had she and another nurse made lunch plans or a movie date as they sponged and wrapped the dead while loved ones lingered within earshot?

Now she was the next of kin, standing helpless outside her brother's room while familiar postmortem rituals were performed by strangers trading mindless predictions about NCAA basketball. It was more defensive than insensitive, this chatter about point spreads and championship prospects, she knew. How could you cruise El Paso in that long black hearse, transporting the remains of old men felled by heart attacks or young men dead of drug overdoses, if you didn't distance yourself?

As police officers rolled the gurney bearing Paul's body into the back of the coroner's van, they saw only what the medical examiner's report would clinically define as a twenty-eight-year-old "well-developed, well-nourished Latin male." But in the few seconds it took for those steel doors to slam shut behind him, Pilar Williams saw it all: her baby brother's brilliant ascent into manhood and his sudden collapse into madness.

She watched with her father as the hearse pulled onto Alameda Avenue and passed the patrol cars ringing the apartment complex for the elderly that her parents had managed for the last ten years. She leaned against a rough white stucco wall for support and thought about the brother Paul once had been, the young man changed unalterably during what was to have been his time of greatest glory, his years at Harvard Medical School. The preschooler who used his "Sesame Street"–acquired printing skills to order a set of Dr. Seuss books by mail. The precocious pest, eight years her junior, peering over her shoulder to calculate the answers to her algebra homework while, befuddled, she chewed the yellow sheen off her number 2 pencil. The teenage boy who introduced her to Vivaldi as well as 10,000 Maniacs. The med school lab rat who could make hyperthermia research sound like a night on the town.

More recent images of her brother she would force back for now. She could not survive his death without imposing a kind of temporary amnesia. She remembered only too well the horror of that rainy night six months earlier when she discovered the box of letters, baby books, and toys in Paul's attic apartment in suburban Boston. All the love notes from "Dr. B." All the cards from "Mom." All the instructions to Paul that made no sense: "You are sometimes still my baby, very, very tiny, with tiny, tiny fists and a mouth that loves to suck on things and I'm still your Mom and you can feel this way and we are really close and love each other." All of them written in the same scrawled script that also filled page after lined notebook page with detailed female fantasies of rape and sodomy, bondage, and sexual degradation. All of them in the handwriting of Paul's psychiatrist.

No. Pilar would bury the accomplished brother she knew, not the crippled child who had come home from Boston clutching a baby blanket, hugging a stuffed toy dog, and cowering in the corner of his bed, mumbling the name of the Harvard psychiatrist he was alternately convinced was his mother or his lover.

Margaret. She could not bear the sound of that name. Margaret Bean-Bayog could wait. She would see Margaret in court.

Chapter

The house on the edge of Huffman Farm was a hive of activity the August afternoon in 1962 when Marcos and Epifania Lozano brought Paul Anthony home from Wyandot Memorial Hospital.

Their five older children had spent the morning making preparations: changing bed linens; setting in place the half-screens their mother had bought at Pfeifer Hardware to open the house to the breezes that wafted across the wheat fields; hanging sheer white curtains that billowed when they caught a draft of air blowing through the shade trees that shielded the house from the summer sun; stuffing plump feather pillows into those smooth cotton pillowslips their mother had sewn from old flour bags, the faded logos of the local mills still imprinted on one side.

The children would not be able to see their mother and baby brother from the yard. The corn was so high that State Road 182 seemed to cut like a narrow river through the Huffman and Fleeman fields. But from the bedroom windows on the upper floor, they could catch the first sight of the red Ford pickup truck carrying their parents and their new brother home.

Only the second of the Lozano children to be born in a hospital, Paul Anthony was the first to arrive up north, in the western Ohio heartland, where the Lozano family of Monterrey, Mexico, had settled after embarking on its immigrant journey.

Leaving behind family in Mexico and odd jobs in the Texas border towns of Laredo, Alice, Kingsville, and Corpus Christi, Marcos and Epifania Lozano had packed their five children and a few belongings into their secondhand pickup and headed north in search of a better life.

In one sense, there was nothing new about their journey. Mexicans had crisscrossed the border for generations in the same search for better wages. Epifania herself had been born in Gonzales, Texas, during one of her father's tours as a tenant farmer on the better-paying American side of the river.

But Ohio was nowhere near the Rio Grande. And only migrant farmers traveled so far north into the United States, not bricklayers like Lozano. He had no talent for farming, and caution kept him out of the fields as well. He had lived through enough modern Mexican history to doubt the belief, so firmly held, that land meant wealth. That was true only for the most privileged and politically connected, he knew.

Marcos Lozano had been born in 1922 in the big house of his maternal grandfather at Rancho Ortegon, the eighth of eleven children of Maria del Ortegon and Monico Lozano. He was six years old when most of his grandfather's ranch was redistributed under the post-Revolutionary government's land reform policies.

Some of the family stayed to raise cattle on the remaining land, but like so many others from the countryside, his parents migrated to Monterrey, the third largest city in Mexico. Here the older children found factory work, and young Marcos entered the first of what were to be his six years of formal schooling.

The same political currents that reconfigured the Ortegon Ranch would also eventually bring the Coronado family to Monterrey. Epifania was the youngest of nine children of

Paublo Coronado and Antonia Tapia, for whom her own youngest child (Paul Anthony) would one day be named. She had grown up contented on a succession of small farms where, as the youngest, she tended the chickens and helped harvest the corn and the beans.

She did not see a city until 1939, when she was nineteen and the family moved into an apartment next door to the Lozano family in Monterrey. Epifania apprenticed herself to her older sister, Alicia, a seamstress of impressive talents, and soon the two were sewing beads on fine dresses at the shop most favored by Monterrey's moneyed class.

With her raven hair and cinched waist, Epifania immediately caught the eye of young Marcos Lozano, who was himself learning his trade as a stonecutter while working on the assembly line of the big furniture manufacturer Rocha-Salinas. He courted her for a year before they married in 1942. Through tears at the altar rail she confessed that she was really twenty-two years old, not twenty, as she had led him to believe. Her abject admission, made in fear that their union would be void if entered under false pretenses, would become the source for more than fifty years of familial laughter at the expense of the "old lady" and "cradle robber" who had duped a man two years her junior into marriage.

When a strike closed the Rocha-Salinas production line, Lozano found work at the stone quarries around Monterrey, but labor troubles there and the birth of his first child, Norma, in 1943 set him thinking about opportunities in the United States. Epifania and Norma went ahead to stay with relatives in Laredo while Marcos waited for his immigration documents to clear. The Christmas holiday delayed the paperwork and he arrived in Laredo to begin his new life on December 26, 1946.

In the early years he took what work came the way of *peones,* day laborers. Some ranching. Some construction. One dry summer, he regularly took along Epifania and the children—Martha, Mark, and Pilar had followed Norma in quick succession—and hoisted one after the other into the branches of a leafy shade tree while he set about his work burning the needles off a field of nopal cactus to provide a source of water for the cattle.

By the time Abel was born, in 1959, Lozano's belief that he would become prosperous in the United States was fading, and he crossed back into Mexico to see if he might do better at home. But his children were unhappy in Mexico, and within a year, the Lozanos returned to Texas.

For all of Marcos Lozano's mistrust of farming, it was the migrant farmworkers who first planted the idea in his mind to move north. When the seasonal work ended in Ohio and the migrants returned to Texas, they told tales of masons like Lozano earning a hundred dollars for every thousand bricks laid, twice the wage he was earning in West Texas.

With no more than their reports and his own ambition to guide him, Lozano and his family set out for Ohio the year America was turning for leadership to a young Harvard-educated senator from Massachusetts, whose vision of a New Frontier had captured the country's imagination. The Lozano family would be part of John F. Kennedy's advance forward.

It was late fall when they left for Ohio. Accustomed to southwestern winters, they packed their trunks with cotton sheets and sweaters, not wool blankets and overcoats. The pickup, with its jerry-rigged roof above the flatbed to create sleeping quarters, was as unpredictable as the weather. All that worked for certain was the cigarette lighter, and Epifania tossed that out the window somewhere east of Arkansas after two-year-old Abel wrested it from its dashboard niche and pressed it against her skin. The loss of the lighter did nothing for Marcos's mood, normally mellowed by the nicotine he would now be denied.

The Ford was fickle, but it held together until the family reached the rich farming belt near the headwaters of the Sandusky River in Ohio. In the migrant camps of Seneca County, Lozano sought out Mexican farmhands for advice as to where he might find work. Since he spoke very little English, he relied on his oldest, Texas-schooled, children to translate for him at the farms to which he was referred.

Farm work would feed his family until he could make connections at the nearest brickyard.

In Upper Sandusky, the family was offered a small shack near the roadside on a large farm, thick with apple orchards, grape arbors, and pear trees. The house was small and lacked indoor plumbing, but their landlords were kind. It was a place to begin.

Lozano soon found masonry work through the union hall in neighboring Bucyrus and more comfortable accommodations in the two-story rented house on a farm owned by the Huffman family. He knew he had made the right move. Work was plentiful and, within a year, he was earning $5.35 an hour, at a time when the minimum hourly wage was $1.15.

His children made friends with the Fleeman kids across the road and quickly reestablished the sibling pecking order. Abel's squalls could be heard outside the house the afternoon Pilar conned him with a tale about a little black fox who poisons bananas. Sitting on the second-floor landing, she explained how she *had* to eat his share of bananas to keep him from getting sick. By the time she had dissolved into giggles and he into tears, the bananas were gone.

The children were doing well in the public schools. Epifania had pulled them from St. Peter's, the local Catholic school, the day the first report of corporal punishment crossed her threshold. It was one thing for her to smack her children for playing one too many games of paratrooper on the fine sofa that Thelma Fleeman had passed along; it was quite another to tolerate it from the nuns.

With Spanish spoken exclusively at home, the younger children had only a rudimentary command of English. They would have to sink or swim in class, and they were imbued early with a special obligation to swim. Epifania had told her children that more would be expected of them than of the blond, blue-eyed descendants of the German farmers who settled this level plain on the banks of the Sandusky River. If nature dictated that they would stand out with their black hair and cinnamon-colored skin, they would, through hard work, distinguish themselves by conspicuous achievement.

Pilar, for one, wrapped her difference around her like a mantle. Her classmate Kate Reed remembered Pilar's arrival in fourth grade in Eden Elementary School. "There were a few other Mexican kids in the class, migrants, and in those days we would say a prayer before lunch. Well, the Mexican kids were Catholics. The rest of us, like most of the town, were Protestant. The Mexicans were too shy to make the sign of the cross. Well, when Pilar arrived she got them together and told them, 'We most certainly *will* make the sign of the cross!' And they did from that day forward."

That spring, the annual assembly to choose the May queen from the crop of fair-haired sixth-graders was distracted by the sight of little Pilar Lozano arriving in the auditorium with her fourth-grade class, a dark beauty in her pale pink dress. The audience of parents and teachers uttered an audible, collective sigh.

Marcos, too, was winning applause for his skill as a mason. He supplemented his construction work by designing and building fireplaces for local farmers. He had more work than he could handle, enough that within two years, he was able to buy a Civil War–era home in town on Fourth Street.

The house was run down but beautiful. A bridal staircase graced the foyer and hand-carved moldings crowned the formal, high-ceilinged parlor. Under the stairs was a closet where Paul and Abel sometimes played, holding the door shut to see who could stay inside the longest without succumbing to a fear of the dark. Lozano paid $24,000 for it. Realtors had shown him the house without hesitation. Whether this was from an absence of racial bias or because his pale skin could pass for white and his accent was sometimes mistaken for German has long been the subject of family conjecture.

The neighborhood, like the town itself, was designed for the simple pleasures of childhood. There was no movie house, but the Star Players staged musicals at the community theater. There was swimming at Harrison Smith Park and exploring to be done at Turtle Mound and the burial grounds of the Wyandot Indians.

When William Brown laid out the broad straight streets in 1843, he could not have had bicycles and roller skates in mind, but the flat roadways seemed made for boys and girls riding shiny two-wheelers or racing on gleaming silver wheels.

Every summer, the main street staged its own show. Columns of large trucks hauling grain rumbled out of the fields, past the Romanesque courthouse on the town square, filling the air with snowlike seeds from the freshly harvested wheat that was stored in the huge silos at the western end of town where Wyandot Avenue runs straight into the Chesapeake & Ohio railroad line.

Every fall, the high school football stadium spilled over with Rams fans. For thirty years, Evie Hall has stood at the front counter in the principal's office, her white hair in recent years pulled back into a ponytail and her blunt-cropped bangs brushing the top of her wire-rimmed glasses, distributing season tickets. She is careful always to assign the townspeople the same seats that were first selected a generation or two earlier and are reclaimed by the same families year after year.

The Lozano children had their impromptu games, too. Playing hide-and-seek with Martha's little dog, Mustafa. Staging Vietcong-style guerrilla raids, like those featured on the evening news, in the apple orchards behind the retired sheriff's house. And maybe, with enough nagging, luring their father to the old Indian Mill Dam with their bamboo poles. There was nothing Marcos Lozano hated quite so much as fishing, but there he would sit, above the Sandusky, trying to satisfy his children's longing for an American dad in the mold of Robert Young or Carl Betz.

However, there was no mistaking the Lozanos' lives for the fantasies the children watched on television situation comedies. Always there was an awareness that their pleasures came at the cost of their parents' hard labors. Their father left the house each day at dawn, returning only when the sun had set. Abel and Paul would be waiting when he came through the back door, smelling of sweat and stone dust. He would sit at the big kitchen table while Abel applied iodine to the fresh gashes in his rough hands, discolored by the mortar he slopped between hard red bricks all day. Paul, flinching at his father's pain, would wait his turn to apply a soothing topcoat of Cornhusker's Lotion to the fresh calluses.

Marcos's sores were visible, but the adjustment to Ohio was hardest on Epifania, whose Indian features could never be mistaken for Caucasian and whose social isolation was all but assured by the language barrier. She missed her sisters and the company of women she had known as a seamstress in Monterrey. She wanted to return to work, but Marcos would not hear of it. Each time Epifania brought up the subject, Marcos would retreat behind the Spanish-language newspapers that arrived each week by post from Monterrey.

She nodded politely to all her neighbors but, unable to speak English without embarrassment, she did not make friends. "I was lonely sometimes but I had the children and school functions," she said, both sad and proud in the remembering. Her children, exhausting and draining for a woman who was forty-two when her last child was born, gave her plenty of cause for pride. Mark, the oldest boy, struggled with schoolwork but distinguished himself on the football field, excelled at all things mechanical, and served as a page one year in the Ohio House of Representatives. Paul, the youngest, astounded his family by teaching himself to read at age three. He skipped kindergarten and wrote in his elementary school scrapbook at age five that he intended to be a "star."

Norma married in 1969, the same year Martha, the family's first college entrant, set off for Ohio State. Paul was eight that year, when the Lozanos found themselves attracting unwanted attention after Pilar, a sophomore at Upper Sandusky High, became pregnant.

The boy was a senior, a popular basketball player. When marriage was ruled out, the Lozanos pulled close, less from embarrassment than from fear for their daughter's future. After the school system informed them, in keeping with policy, that Pilar would be unable to continue her studies, the family paid a call on the superintendent. He was told that teachers could forward her lessons and Pilar would complete the work at home. After the baby's birth, Pilar would resume her place alongside her classmates. Unprecedented, he said. Nonnegotiable, they replied. Erick was born on December 26, 1969, and Pilar returned to school the following fall to graduate with her class in 1972.

With their new grandchild in tow, the Lozanos moved in 1970 to 404 Center Drive, a ranch-style house they had built themselves, one of the first projects of the newly launched Lozano Construction Company. A house for Norma and her husband, Mike Grossman, went up right behind. And, two years later, when Hal Williams married Pilar and adopted Erick, yet another Lozano house went up on the vacant lot next door. Mark would survey the sites, Marcos lay the foundations, Hal and Mike lend their labor, and young Abel try his hand at landscaping. Paul was too young to do much more than watch.

For the first time, Abel and Paul had separate bedrooms. Since their rooms were on either side of a big family room in the basement they had their own private domain where Paul was able to experiment, to his heart's content, with his chemistry set. However, one night, his chemistry experiment exploded, and smoke poured into the hall upstairs. The whole family came running. Paul finally surrendered the chemistry set to his mother after his experimentation with various chemical combinations resulted in a rash covering both his hands.

Friends remember the house on Center Drive most for the aroma of blended red chili peppers and beef that issued from the always busy kitchen. With children, grandchildren, in-laws, and coworkers, a dozen people for dinner was not uncommon. Epifania cooked her Chili Colorado in army surplus cauldrons to accommodate the crowd, which always swelled on the nights she prepared her handmade corn tortillas.

Bethany Foltz was Pilar's supervisor at the Wyandot County Social Service Department, where she got a job after high school investigating child abuse cases. Bethany was a frequent dinner guest. "Mrs. Lozano is the type of hostess who would prop you back and feed you peeled grapes all day long if you let her," she remembered. "There were always lots of laughs at her table."

In turn, her kitchen was Epifania's refuge, the place where she felt most secure. Epifania's children were becoming Americanized faster than she could process the changes in them. All but Paul still spoke to her in Spanish, but they babbled to one another in what was to her the incomprehensible lingo of American slang.

Language became the preadolescent battleground between her and her youngest son. Eager to be like other families and embarrassed by the obvious differences, Paul feigned ignorance of Spanish and spoke only English in his mother's presence. He once called Pilar's office, shouting, "What is this woman saying to me?"

In truth he had taught himself Spanish years before, listening to family chatter and scanning the back editions of *El Norte* that piled up beside his father's living room chair. During a visit from his grandmother when he was twelve, Paul had to choose whether to reveal his competence in Spanish or to lose perhaps his last chance to speak with the old woman, then in failing health. They whispered conspiratorially to each other for hours in Spanish during her stay, while the rest of the family looked on, amazed.

At East Elementary School, the natural desire of a child to blend into his surroundings was thwarted for Paul, less because of his race than because of his obvious intellectual gifts. Always an exceptional student, his astuteness pleased his teachers but provoked some of his classmates. His defiant response to their taunts merely escalated the teasing. "If you were saying something bad to him, he would say, 'What makes you treat me like this? Do I look stupid?' That was a real big thing of his: 'Do I look stupid?'" Abel remembered. "People would reel back from him like, 'Who in the hell do you think you are?'"

Paul's playground scrapes were so common that Abel took to positioning himself at the schoolhouse door as his class spilled out for recess and Paul's poured back in. Paul would name his tormentor, and "as the kid came in, I'd nab him."

Most children his own age bored Paul, but older kids, with whom he wanted to spend time, teased him. One boy regularly mocked his curly hair, calling him Hereford Head. Longing to fit in but unable to find a niche, he retreated to his family and his books. He applied himself so intently to his studies that he would ask for aspirin tablets to carry with him when he had a cold rather than risk marring his perfect attendance record. He wanted to be the best, and when he felt he let himself down, he could be temperamental. "I don't think he handled stress well," said Debra Amos, who attended school with Paul, "and it's stressful to want to be the best, to reach that goal."

Cultural differences also stood in the way of the integration he so craved. When Abel proposed that they both join the Cub Scouts in elementary school, their father was appalled to learn that this particularly American experience would involve his sons sleeping in tents with boys he did not know, supervised by men he had never met. "If you want to go camping, pitch a tent in the backyard where I know you'll be safe," Marcos told him.

They camped out often. In the middle of the night the boys would slip out of their tent and make for the school playground around the corner. Lying on their backs on the summer grass, the brothers would marvel at the stars. They taught each other the constellations and timed their playground visits to monitor Orion's movement through the night sky.

If his family set Paul apart, it also harbored him when the world dealt disappointment. When he did not make the high school basketball team, he and Abel poured a concrete pad behind the house, welded a piece of eighteen-foot steel tubing in place, and added a hoop. Having a court of their own was, in some way, more important than using it. In time, their nephews Erick and Tyler played on it more than they did.

Basketball was one of Paul's few failures in high school. He excelled at his studies and impressed Ralph Young, his track coach, with both his determination and his character. "If you had a son, you would want him to be like Paul Lozano. He was a hardworking individual, well liked by everyone. He came to practice, put his head down, and fulfilled every requirement. Paul was a wonderful young man."

Shy socially, he was popular enough among his classmates to be elected to Student Council and Boys State, a statewide mock government for Ohio teenagers. From junior high school on, he was selected each summer for special academic programs sponsored by Ohio State and Purdue. In his senior year, he wrote an essay on philosophy that won him an award from Bowling Green University. He was named to Mensa and the National Honor Society and listed in *Who's Who Among American High School Students* in 1978–79.

"There were few honors available to high school students that did not come Paul Lozano's way. And never was there a nicer boy who deserved them more," Charlotte Leeth, a favorite English teacher of Paul's, remembered.

Paul's achievements were a balm to his parents, whose initial success in the construction business had eroded in the face of high interest rates and a downturn in the economy. While his older brothers helped retool the business from building houses to constructing packing crates, Paul was relegated to the sidelines. His job was to study, his family told him repeatedly. Older heads would wrestle with the family's future.

"If he suffered from anything in those years, it was from the boy-genius syndrome. We doted on him," said Pilar, the sister closest to him in age, who helped her mother with the daily tasks of caring for the two younger boys.

But there was no denying his sensitivity. "My brother was always plagued with self-doubt from the time he was in high school," Pilar recalled. "No matter how much I reassured him and my family reassured him that we thought of him as being so gifted and special, he always told me that when he would walk into a room he would have the sense of not being as good as the other people there. He always said that he felt someday he would wake up and that they would find out that he wasn't as bright as everyone thought he was. He always felt like that."

As Abel, only three years his senior, got more involved in the business, Paul felt left behind. It was sometimes literally true. When he would join Abel jogging, his older brother would shoot ahead, leaving Paul to run alone. "None of this was done with evil intent," Abel said, his guilt exaggerated in the light of Paul's later troubles in life. "I was just a stupid teenager, overly impressed with myself, and I went from treating him like my best friend to [treating him like] a pesky kid."

Paul would say later that he felt inadequate during this period because everyone else was making a contribution, trying to get the folks back on their feet, while he was merely studying. Schoolwork seemed trivial next to the challenge the family faced, and he felt he had nothing to offer.

While Paul produced papers on DNA that even his teachers could not decipher, the rest of the family was getting an education of its own in three converted chicken coops Marcos had bought on the edge of town. They raised the ceilings, bought an old forklift, and went to work making packing crates and pallets. One coop was used for storage of raw materials, a second for the cutting operation, and the third for assembly. Marcos would take Pilar to the bank with him to help negotiate loans. Her husband, Hal, an instructor in business at the high school, helped set up flow patterns and production schedules.

What began as a seat-of-the-pants operation grew to eighty employees. But trouble loomed. Abel was too taken with his role of inspecting timber and negotiating lumber contracts and too possessive of his father, eventually driving Mark and Hal away. Interest rates continued to climb, and competitors sprang up overnight, some from the ranks of former employees. The death knell sounded two hundred miles away in Detroit. The Lozanos' biggest customer was a local manufacturer of windshields whose own best customer, Chrysler, had just gone belly-up.

There was enough warning for the Lozanos to shut down small purchasing orders but not enough to cancel contracts with their lumber wholesaler. Still carrying a heavy debt from its earlier housing ventures, Lozano Construction Company followed Chrysler into bankruptcy. The family lost everything, including the house on Center Drive.

The business failure was devastating. At fifty-nine Marcos was faced with a return to bricklaying and his family with relocation. Mark and Norma, who were employed by the local Westinghouse plant, both had been offered transfers to El Paso to help train Mexican workers to staff a new plant in Juárez. Marcos and Epifania decided to follow their children south.

Paul did not have to go. Pilar and Martha would be staying in Upper Sandusky long enough that he would be able to finish his senior year of high school there. But he was worried about his parents, Paul confided to Charlotte Leeth. They had done so much for him; he wanted to be with them now when they needed him. "He was torn," she recalled. "He had made an effort to see what classes were available at the high school in El Paso. He'd done his research. He felt, in the end, that he did not want to leave his family at a difficult time. It was clear he loved them very much."

The family left in stages. Mark and Norma were already in Texas when their parents, with Paul and Abel, reversed the route they had taken nineteen years before that had brought them north to Ohio, to new opportunities and ultimate disappointment. They would start over, yet again, in El Paso.

"It was very hard. We were all pretty stressed out. It was such a change to have to leave town and move someplace else and start all over again. And to leave behind all those things that you've grown up with. It was a heartbreak," said Abel. "Leaving in stages was hard on us emotionally. My dad has always been a real trouper, though, and we took our cues from him."

Martha, Pilar, and their husbands followed. The family was reunited in a new city to face new challenges. "We do much better together than we do alone. We get strength from each other, from the family," said Martha. "There was no question we would all end up in El Paso, wandering in and out of each other's kitchens."

Transitions are rarely easy, and the move to Texas was no exception. Norma was going great guns at her new job with Westinghouse, setting an exhilarating pace for her co-workers only to crash when she came home. Martha began teaching in the local schools but often was weighed down by the same type of self-doubts that plagued Paul. Arguments were common; Norma's and Martha's marriages began to fray. Both marriages would soon end in divorce.

Marcos went back to laying brick, and his wife took her culinary skills out of her kitchen and into a day care center where, at sixty-one, to her husband's humiliation, she held her first job since she had been a young woman in Monterrey. Abel repossessed jewelry until Pilar, who was working for an employment agency, sent him on a successful job interview for a sales position. In time, Pilar went back to school to finish the training she had begun in Ohio, and became a nurse.

By all accounts, Paul adjusted well to Coronado High School, where he was shocked on his first day to be asked for his green card by an administrator who took him to be a Mexican national and needed to document his immigrant status. With twenty-five hundred students, Coronado was five times the size of Upper Sandusky High School. But he soon found friends and schoolwork to engage him.

He, Corey Knight, and Armando Castellanos formed a troika of bookworms. "We kept to ourselves. We were our own clique. We'd go to concerts, stuff like that. Some parties, but we were pretty much into our studies. I guess you'd call us timid, nerds even," recalled Castellanos.

Paul "was smart and happy" that year, he said. If the move got him down, his friends did not see it. "He was close to his family and I think he was just happy they were all together." Coronado High had the drug problems common to border towns but, Castellanos said, "We never even drank in high school. We were clean-cut American youth, I guess you'd call us."

In fact, Paul was so "clean-cut" and so bright that he had been recommended to West Point by Ohio Senator John Glenn. Colonel James L. Hayden, who interviewed Paul for West Point, remembered "just being so impressed with this kid. He was a brilliant young man, quiet and serious."

"The family was very, very concerned about Paul getting through school and being able to go to college," Abel said. There were other scholarship offers, including an eight-year deal from Case Western Reserve that included medical school, but none had the luster for the Lozanos of the U.S. Military Academy. The Fleemans, who had been so kind to them when they first arrived in Upper Sandusky, had sent their son to the U.S. Naval Academy at Annapolis, and he had been a source of great pride.

"My parents wanted him to go because they felt that he would be set for life. The Fleemans' son was very well respected and very cultured and carried himself real well. And when he got out of the service he went into teaching and had a job. You would be established as a professional," Abel recalled. "My father admired the military. He is a patriot, the way only an immigrant can be."

Paul was less certain, even though his friend Armando Castellanos had also been accepted. "We were both excited. It was an honor," Castellanos said, but Paul saw West Point as a ticket to medical school, not the start of a military career. He did not hide his feelings. "When I interviewed him he wanted to be a doctor; I remember that clearly," said Hayden. Still, even on that first meeting, Hayden knew that Paul would be accepted to the academy.

The night before he was to leave for West Point, Paul's brothers and sisters, nieces and nephews pitched camp on the floor of his parents' apartment in order to be there for the dawn send-off. There were balloons and kisses and hugs all around and not a few tears as the baby of the family set out for New York.

Once he began at West Point, however, it was clear that Paul was not prepared for military training. He bristled at the discipline, at the rules, at the hierarchy and the hazing that were the lot of plebes.

In a letter to his former teacher Charlotte Leeth, he complained of an atmosphere he found humiliating and unjust. "He could not accept the unfairness, the cruelty. That was not the way he had been raised. He was a gentle boy. I also had the feeling that at West Point he felt like a Mexican, a minority, deeply, for the first time," she said.

He chose punishment over conformity. He spent hours walking the yard during his plebe year, although Castellanos said that he himself got many more demerits that year than Paul. Resistance cost Paul academically as well. For the first time in his life, he was not only a discipline problem but a marginal student. His first-year grades reflected his unhappiness: a 2.3 grade-point average, including a D in computer science and four C's. The only course in which he earned an A was psychology.

"It's a hard place for a guy used to getting all A-pluses. You say to yourself, 'I could get A-pluses if they gave me time, but they don't give me time. I've got to polish brass, clean my rifle, shine my shoes, parade, and go to the doggone football game.' It's not for everybody," said Colonel Hayden. In fact, 25 percent of every entering class quits before graduation.

Reports filtered back to Hayden that concerned him. Paul was a loner; he didn't mix well; his classmates felt he had a chip on his shoulder. "Anyone that smart, sometimes they are a little harder to break into the system," said Hayden. "They start to tangle with the chain of command. A lot of things they do up there at the Point can seem silly and unnecessary. Humiliation is built in. He probably said, 'I'm tired of this Mickey Mouse stuff.' He wanted to be a doctor. It probably seemed like a distraction from his goal. Nothing to be embarrassed about, if you ask me."

It was learning how unlikely his prospects were for attending medical school if he remained at West Point that pushed Paul to consider resigning his commission after sixteen months. No more than 2 percent of any class are recommended for medical school at Fort Sam Houston in

Texas. In addition to top grades, candidates must have excelled in their military training, an unlikely achievement for Paul Lozano.

When he could not secure a commitment from the academy to send him to medical school, Paul resolved to leave. "We tried to talk him out of it, but you had to respect the guy's decision. He wanted to be a doctor," said Castellanos, who graduated from West Point and went on to graduate studies in space systems operations.

Paul called Abel to break the news and ask his advice about the inevitable consequences—their parents would be crushed and his return home would be a financial burden for them. Abel was sympathetic. He was on the outs with the folks at the time, too, having eloped with Sandy, an El Paso girl, against their wishes. Pilar had tried to discourage the marriage by showing Sandy snapshots of Abel's former girlfriends, but Sandy was not so easily dissuaded. Abel and Sandy moved to Albuquerque for Abel's sales job. He was doing well, although he was keeping up the same sort of frenetic pace, with the attendant deflation, that characterized Norma's performance at Westinghouse.

Paul declined Abel's offer to put him up, and he returned to El Paso, worried about money and anxious about getting his education back on track. He felt like a failure, and his parents' obvious disappointment at seeing him working at a minimum-wage job in a Farah slacks factory further eroded his self-esteem.

He enrolled at the University of Texas at El Paso for the spring term in 1982, and his grades soared immediately to their previous heights. "One point I wish to mention in case the subject not appear anywhere else in Paul's pre-med applications concerns his rather poor academic performance at the Military Academy at West Point," James E. Becvar, a UTEP assistant professor of chemistry, wrote in a medical school recommendation for Paul. "Because I was curious about Paul's moderate overall GPA in view of his performance here at UTEP, he mentioned that he was not at all happy at the Academy and was quite aware that this had a severe effect there on his performance academically. I believe him because of his subsequent straight A work here."

He finished three years of academic courses in two and a half, in addition to his work in biomedical research in Becvar's chemistry lab. He impressed his professor as much for his personal as for his academic qualities. In his recommendation letter, Becvar cited Paul's "sensitivity in regard to personal relationships with other people" and the "good rapport" he formed with the students he tutored. Paul graduated with honors in microbiology. He hoped to find a joint program where he could earn both his Ph.D. and his medical degree. "I only wish this institution had a doctoral program so that I did not have to see him leave," Becvar wrote in another letter of recommendation.

In his essay accompanying his Harvard Medical School application, Paul Lozano wrote that "working in research has introduced me to a level of creative and independent thinking unlike anything I have experienced in the classroom.

"Considering the tremendous underrepresentation of minorities in medical research, I feel this is where I could make a small but unique contribution to society. Major advances in the early detection and treatment of such conditions as cancer and coronary disease have saved thousands of lives. Obviously, there are still many contributions to be made. I would like to use my training to further medical knowledge and to someday touch the lives of others."

Offers from medical schools poured in but, despite his obvious academic talents, Paul was gripped with self-doubt. Maybe he wasn't as smart as everyone said; maybe he was being recruited as a minority; maybe his reach would exceed his grasp. Shy and still awkward socially, he worried aloud to his sister and confidante, Pilar, that he would be friendless in a strange city far from his family's support. Sensing Paul's fears, his UTEP adviser told him Harvard might not be the right choice for him. Maybe he would do better closer to home.

But Harvard was the best, wasn't it? To choose anything less would be to embrace what he hated most, mediocrity.

He had to go. Harvard was the one place where he could regain his self-esteem by erasing what he considered the embarrassment of washing out of West Point. If only he did not have to go alone.

In his chemistry lab at UTEP, Paul had been drawn to another aspiring medical student, equally shy and uncertain of herself. He and Evelyn Susan Burlingham, who was known as Susan, were soon spending all their time together, studying, hiking, and backpacking. Sam Favela was a classmate whom Paul tutored in organic chemistry. He remembers the quiet, inseparable couple.

"Paul was a supersmart guy, and shy; one of those people so smart they lose interest in other things. When we were applying to medical school most of us were looking at Texas. Deep inside we all knew Paul would end up at Harvard. He did not throw it in anyone's face when he got in. He wasn't that kind of guy," said Favela, now an ophthalmologist in El Paso.

When Paul and Susan, without a word to either set of parents, slipped off to City Hall and married on January 27, 1984, his classmates were not surprised. "He and Susan got married to get her to Harvard," Favela said without hesitation. "That was the understanding I had back then. We all did. When you are trying to get into med school you'd do anything. They were very close, affectionate, happy. It was clear they cared for each other. But they also thought Harvard would take both of them if they were married."

After the wedding ceremony, the couple drove to Albuquerque for the weekend. Abel and Sandy were stunned to see them coming up the drive.

The desert stretched out for miles to the east behind Abel and Sandy's home. Soon after the newlyweds arrived, the brothers took Abel's dogs and set out across the prairie. They walked and talked for hours. "I thought it was pretty impulsive. I didn't know how realistic he was being because he was so financially dependent on the family. I didn't know how realistic it was for him to think that it would make it any easier for him to get through medical school. Because I think that is what he was aiming for," Abel said.

Despite his misgivings, Abel took an optimistic view of the marriage. He himself had married against the family's wishes and was doing well. "Go for it," he said to Paul. "Stay here, you can go to the medical school here. You guys have the grades for it. You'll have to work and feed yourselves, but you won't be hurting for a place to stay."

But, as the visit wore on, Abel sensed an ambivalence in both Paul and Susan. Sitting on the front porch one night, Paul turned to his brother and announced, "I think I'd rather get through medical school and then try to find out if I want to settle down."

Sandy was having equally confusing conversations with Susan inside the house. Susan was worried about holding Paul back, concerned that their families would be furious. "This leap of faith into marriage was tentative at best. They went into it still not having ironed out a lot of the specifics. Once they were married, it was just very overwhelming to them," Abel said.

When the newlyweds drove south to El Paso, Abel and Sandy were unsure what the future held for Paul and Susan.

Paul had not come around that weekend, so Epifania Lozano was relieved when her son showed up, unannounced, for dinner one night. Stirring the evening stew of pork, zucchini, and corn, she caught sight of the gold band on his left hand as she ladled the *quisado* into serving bowls. "Are you married?" she sputtered. "You do such a thing and tell your family nothing about it?"

There were tears and recriminations. Impulsive, immature, he was called. The Lozanos' fear was born, in part, of the strains then showing in their other children's marriages. They urged Paul to rethink his decision. Pilar, whose opinion Paul always sought and seldom dismissed, was appalled. Was he trying to sabotage his own future? Had he taken leave of his senses?

The marriage lasted six days. News of the annulment enraged Abel almost as much as the marriage had angered his parents and Pilar. He drove into El Paso, breathing fire. "I was sure he'd been forced into this, and I was furious," he said. "Talking to Paul, it really wasn't so much the case. Oh, they told him to end it all right, but I think in the end Paul and Susan mutually decided that maybe they had overstepped."

It was a painful lesson, but in a few months, Susan would pack her bags for medical school in Houston and Paul for Harvard. They would remain friends for the rest of his life. In a birthday note to him that August, she expressed the affection she would always feel for him. "I think you have come a long way in your first twenty-two years, and who knows what will come your way in all the years to come. I hope you always remain open-minded and continue to grow throughout your life—you've got some really beautiful qualities. It would make me very happy many years from now that you never settled for less than your full potential and that you never settled for less than you really wanted. It will always be a privilege to call you my friend."

Paul knew that Boston would be lonely without Susan, without his family. But Harvard was an opportunity not to be missed, a chance to learn medicine from the best minds the nation had to offer. Packing his trunk, the socks and ties pinned neatly to their coordinating shirts by Pilar, Paul Lozano might even have wondered whether Harvard would offer him another opportunity, as well: the chance to grow up at last.

Chapter

2

Harvard Medical School occupies a tight, square parcel on the west side of a noisy two-lane artery, congested during daylight hours with buses, cars, and taxis shuttling both the ill and their healers into the heart of Boston's hospital district.

The winding paths, the white-steepled chapel, and the ivy-covered bricks that Paul Lozano associated with the nation's oldest university are laid out along the banks of the Charles River in Cambridge, miles away from the medical school dormitory that he would call home. Vanderbilt Hall, its windows tinted a soot gray from the relentless traffic on Longwood Avenue, was as far from his imaginings of Harvard as Boston was from El Paso.

Across the avenue, Harvard Medical School, its gleaming white marble facade a nod to architectural elegance, anchors a block of otherwise nondescript research and hospital buildings whose inner workings have earned Boston its reputation for medical excellence. Administration and classroom buildings, laboratories and libraries ring a tree-lined quadrangle, where Frisbees fly on the first warm day of spring and the occasional stethoscope-draped snowman breaks the bleakness of a Boston winter.

Paul Lozano arrived at Harvard in the summer of 1984, a participant in a program for minority students with an interest in basic science research. His airless room in Vanderbilt was bleak but convenient. It was just a three-block walk to his summer lab job at the Dana Farber Cancer Institute and right next door to Sami's open-air international food carts—the burritos were something short of authentic but a welcome break from cafeteria fare.

One of the first faculty members Paul met that summer was Dr. Alvin F. Poussaint, a prominent black psychiatrist gaining wider national notice at the time for his role as a consultant to "The Bill Cosby Show." At Harvard Medical School, Dr. Poussaint was an informal adviser to minority students. He found the young man from El Paso one of the more serious of the new group. "He was quiet but friendly. One had to bring him out in conversation," Dr. Poussaint recalled, "but he seemed within the normal limits of a quiet person. I didn't pick up any problems, but then, I was not on the lookout either." Dr. Poussaint's lasting impression was that of a conscientious young researcher.

Despite the evident pleasure Paul took in the laboratory, there were problems. It was not an easy landing at Harvard. He discovered that being smart did not count for much. Everyone was smart. The 165 people in his class had been chosen from 3,600 applicants, 1,000 of whom were good enough to be granted interviews. That made many of his classmates feel like the elite, but it had an unnerving effect on Paul's more fragile ego. Maybe his admission was a fluke, he felt, a concession to cultural diversity and affirmative action. He was one of five Mexican-Americans, two Puerto Ricans, 18 blacks, and 22 Asians in an overwhelmingly white class.

Harvard had worked to diversify its faculty and its student body. In the twenty years between 1952 and 1972, Harvard Medical School had 18 minority graduates. In the next twenty years, it had 530. But statistics do not speak to the experience of being black, brown, or yellow in a predominantly white world.

Students of color on campus banded together, forming the Black Health Organization, the National Chicano Health Organization, the Boricua Health Organization, the Third World Caucus. In addition to their professional aims, such groups were a source of support and identification for minority students.

Paul Lozano joined the National Chicano Health Organization and attended monthly scientific meetings for minority students interested in medical research. Dr. Harold Amos, professor emeritus of microbiology and molecular genetics and the former dean of the Medical Sciences Division, usually sat next to him during those evening lectures. Paul came often to his office as well, to discuss scientific interests they shared.

"I knew him to be a bright young person. He was inquisitive; he always asked questions at the talks," Dr. Amos recalled. "I would not have said he was a happy person. I always found him to be a quiet person, maybe with something on his mind. But he was engaging, a pleasant, nice guy. People here felt a lot of affection for him and knew him to be bright, very bright."

It was less the academic skills than the social ease of his classmates that unnerved Paul Lozano at Harvard. The faculty was chockablock with research giants and Nobel laureates. While he was trying to negotiate his way from awe to simple intimidation, his classmates seemed unaffected by the rarefied atmosphere.

Even the security guards, in their ersatz Brooks Brothers uniforms, seemed to fit in better than he. In crisp navy blazers, gray trousers, white shirts, and red striped ties, they were stationed at the entrance to the MEC, the Medical Education Center, attentive at their work even when their noses were in their books (they were forbidden to read newspapers on duty: in training they had been taught that newspaper reading looked intellectually lazy).

The need for all that security was disconcerting as well. It was true that the medical area abutted one of Boston's largest public housing projects. But what crime was spawned by poverty and drug trafficking was mostly inflicted on the residents of Mission Hill, not the students who skirted the periphery. Still, bulletin boards that regularly advertised used textbooks for sale and film times for *Casablanca* also carried flyers for the school's free taxi escort service: 8 P.M. to 2 A.M. seven days a week, within a one-mile radius of campus.

The University of Texas in El Paso had been so unpretentious and safe by comparison. Not to mention warm and sunny. Even in summer, the Boston sky could turn a dull gray and stay that way for days. It reminded Paul of the Hudson River Valley and his unhappy tenure at West Point. He did not want Harvard to be another West Point. He knew how much the military academy had meant to his parents, how proud they had been of his admission, and how disappointed by his decision to withdraw. But there was a crucial difference, he told himself. He had not wanted to be a soldier; he wanted nothing more than to be a doctor.

Then why couldn't he get accustomed to this place? Why was he so depressed when he was finally on the verge of accomplishing what he and his family had dreamed of for so long? Once classes began in September, he bought notebooks but did not fill them. He lost assignment sheets. He lacked the energy to walk from his room to lectures right across the street in the MEC. When he did attend class, it was clear he could master the work, but morning after morning he just stayed in bed.

He resisted the temptation to call Pilar about his adjustment problems. He was still angry at her about the family's role in his breakup with Susan. One of his goals at Harvard was to begin making decisions for himself. He had always leaned on his older sister too much, even when he was a kid, and she pampered him as though he were *her* baby. The surrogate-mother role was not fair to either of them; it burdened her and kept him from growing up.

Besides, he knew that if he told her, Pilar was likely to dismiss his depression as homesickness and urge him to tough it out. He had always admired the dogged persistence that saw his sister through her own personal and professional troubles. But he felt he was not as strong as Pilar. Toughing it out was not working.

Didn't the student handbook acknowledge that "there are times when the pressures of medical school, personal conflicts, and other disturbing situations can get even the most stoic types down"? Hadn't the University Health Service posted a list of therapists who would see medical students confidentially for a free consultation? Hadn't the two staff psychiatrists told the class during orientation week that too few students availed themselves of the counseling services, especially those who suspected they might have a problem with alcohol or drugs? After all, psychiatry was medicine, wasn't it?

A list of consulting psychiatrists was posted in the health service; copies were stacked in the student affairs office and tacked on bulletin boards. It couldn't hurt to talk to someone, could it? The first name on the alphabetically ordered list was that of Dr. Margaret Harvey Bean-Bayog.

He looked up her credentials in a directory of Massachusetts physicians in the Countway Library. She was a specialist in alcoholism, a past president of the American Society of Addiction Medicine. That was good. He thought he drank too much at West Point. His brother Abel had reassured him that he drank no more or less than most college students, but having been such a straight arrow in high school, he worried about the change he had undergone when he left home for the first time.

He saw that Dr. Bean-Bayog was not a full-time faculty member at Harvard. Hers was a part-time, or clinical, appointment, an arrangement that allows more than six thousand Greater Boston physicians to claim the prestigious Harvard affiliation in exchange for an occasional lecture or the supervision of medical students and postgraduate interns and residents in a hospital setting.

Dr. Bean-Bayog primarily supervised Harvard trainees at Cambridge Hospital, where she was a staff psychiatrist, he learned. Her rare appearances on the Longwood Avenue

campus were occasioned by an annual lecture or two about
alcoholism. Infrequent though they were, her classes were
always well attended because of her reputation as a charis-
matic speaker.

Dr. Bean-Bayog did not get bogged down on research data
about the genetic or behavioral origins of alcoholism; she
talked about individual suffering and the importance of
treating people, not merely their disease. Maybe it was
because her topic was human behavior and not the fine
points of anatomy, histology, and cell biology that dominate
the early years of medical studies, but even students settled
into the upholstered seats for a catnap in the choice rear
rows of Amphitheater E would begin to stir at the sound of
such words as *empathy* and *compassion.*

It is hard to overstate the appeal of such a personal
approach to medicine. Even with concerted efforts in recent
years to emphasize the social and ethical context of medicine, training in its initial years is still less like a colloquium
than like a trade school, where memorization and mastery
of detail are key. Until the third year, when students come
into regular contact with patients, technical competence is
stressed over the philosophical issues Dr. Bean-Bayog was
admired for raising.

Impressed as Paul Lozano was by Dr. Bean-Bayog's
reputation, once he made up his mind to see her on
September 24, he had to force himself to hop on the free
shuttle that left every ten minutes for Harvard Square from
the front door of his dorm. Dr. Bean-Bayog's office was a
few blocks outside the Square in a row of old brownstones
rented by Harvard-affiliated psychiatrists.

Sitting across from this stranger, Paul was quiet for a long
time. At forty-one, Margaret Bean-Bayog was an attractive
woman with an open manner and an engaging smile. Her
straight hair, colored a shade lighter than its natural brown,
was cut in bangs across her forehead and blunt where it
brushed the top of her shoulders. She relied on reading
glasses when she consulted her notes.

Like so many of Paul Lozano's classmates, she looked
right at home at Harvard. A third-generation physician,

from Radcliffe College by way of a private boarding school, she was just the sort of person comfortable in academic medicine's most hallowed halls, among the busts of Oliver Wendell Holmes and the oil paintings of long-dead deans. Just the sort of person Paul Lozano could not help but envy.

Given her background, could she understand the pressure he felt to succeed, Paul wondered, not just for himself but for his family and his race? He had not been born to white Anglo-Saxon Protestant professionals or gone to an Ivy League college, as she and so many of his classmates had. Half the class came from the same ten schools, it sometimes seemed to Paul. Could she really understand the conflict between his working-class, Chicano background and the largely white world of privilege he encountered at Harvard?

Beyond such worries, he simply felt awkward. He had never sought psychiatric help before. Where was he supposed to begin? Maybe he should have called his sister Martha. She had gotten counseling when she and her husband, David, were having marital problems, and even though others in the family teased her about it, Paul admired her for recognizing that she needed some help. They were so much alike, he and Martha—the two Lozanos who were the hardest on themselves. They were always pushing and striving to achieve, setting standards for themselves that were sometimes unrealistically high and then flagellating themselves if they fell short of perfection.

Paul began on a positive note, telling Dr. Bean-Bayog about the research presentation he had made that summer at the Dana Farber Institute. How hard he had worked and how much satisfaction he found in the lab. But ever since medical school classes had begun, he felt empty, he said. His loneliness was sometimes overwhelming.

He mentioned that his girlfriend had not been admitted to Harvard, that they had broken up, and that he felt guilty about the way he had treated her. He could transfer to the University of Texas to be with Susan, he knew, but how could he leave Harvard? Others "would give their right leg" to be in his place, he told the psychiatrist.

On his second visit, he confessed that Susan was more

than a girlfriend. Their brief marriage the previous winter had been a bad idea, he could see that now. She was twenty-seven; he was twenty-two. They had thought—erroneously, as it turned out—that Harvard would offer her a place, too, if they came east as a couple. They simply had not done their research. He knew now that Harvard admitted spouses only as transfer students after the second year.

He feared that he had hurt Susan terribly. One minute she was reassuring, insisting she understood. The next she was crying, accusing him of deserting her. "Sure, I could transfer," he told Dr. Bean-Bayog, but "people here I meet I could read about in books. If I leave this place, I'll lose that." Besides, he said, his family would be furious if he blew this opportunity.

It had not been simply romance and the comforting idea of a study partner through medical school that had prompted the marriage. He longed for a lasting relationship. He envied his five siblings their marriages and their children. When his family was so adamant in opposing his deepening friendship with Susan, he went forward with the marriage as much to spite them as to please her and himself. It was the first time he had ever really stood up to his parents. Defying them had always been unthinkable; they were so supportive of him, so proud. "I could always turn to them," he told Dr. Bean-Bayog.

Eloping had been impulsive, he realized now. Stupid, even. Marriage was not a game. Part of what he hoped to learn in therapy, if he kept coming, was how to separate from his family. He needed to define himself independently, as an adult. As he told Dr. Bean-Bayog, "They can't jump on a plane and spank me."

In fact, if he could really acknowledge that, he said, maybe he didn't need therapy. Maybe his problem was as simple as overcoming his loneliness and breaking his dependence, a habit common to so many Chicano families he knew back home. Even Norma, at age forty, was still asking their parents' advice before making a decision. He would just be more independent. That was a matter of will, wasn't it? After two sessions, Paul Lozano wrote to thank the psychiatrist for her time:

> Dear Dr. Bean-Bayog,
> I just wanted to let you know that I appreciated the time you took to listen. It helped me through a rough period of adjustment. Thank you.

It would be two years before Paul Lozano and Margaret Bean-Bayog would meet again. They were full years for both student and doctor.

Once engaged in classes, Paul pursued his studies with the vigor that had characterized his academic pursuits since childhood. He passed his courses, except for Anatomy, and received grades of "Excellent" in Surgery and Preventive Medicine and Epidemiology. He took a makeup exam for Anatomy, the course most likely to trip up students in the first year, and easily passed it.

Margaret Bean-Bayog, meanwhile, was adjusting to married life and stepmotherhood. Just three months before she met Paul Lozano, she had married Dr. Rogelio Bayog, a psychiatrist from a prominent Filipino family, whose wife, Antonia, a physician herself, had died of cancer four years before at age thirty-eight. Margaret moved from her apartment in Brookline to the elegant Lexington home Bayog shared with his two children: Franz, then nine, and Ruby, then seven.

The wedding of Rogelio Bayog, known as Roger, who was a psychoanalyst at a Harvard-affiliated veterans' hospital, and Margaret Harvey Bean was a blend of both their family traditions. In deference to his Catholicism, the ceremony was performed in the chapel at Boston College, but her uncle, the Rev. George Bean, an Episcopal priest, also officiated. One of the guests was Corazon Aquino, who had lived in exile in suburban Boston with her husband, Philippine opposition leader Benigno Aquino, before his assassination in 1983.

Margaret Bean wrote about that period of her life in the

Twenty-fifth Anniversary Report of the Harvard-Radcliffe class of 1965: "I didn't expect when I was at Radcliffe that I would be a happy woman. I certainly wasn't then. I got into medical school and made it through it. I discovered psychiatry, which I love, and which gave me access to psychoanalysis, which transformed my inner and outer opportunities. For nearly fifteen years I saw patients and taught and wrote and participated in various organizations. We hoped every doctor could learn to work gently and skillfully with alcoholic and addicted people. It was wonderful, and I had time to change myself so I could, finally, to my family's surprise and relief, marry. My husband was a widower with two children. I plunged into family life and discovered new dimensions of delight and fatigue. We are all thriving now, despite various losses, and the repeated surprise of getting older."

Among those losses was a series of miscarriages. But Roger's children proved a source of delight more than exhaustion, according to those who witnessed Dr. Bean-Bayog's headlong dive into parenthood. Dr. Carol C. Nadelson, a Boston psychiatrist and past president of the American Psychiatric Association, remembers a chance encounter with the Bayogs when her family and theirs were both vacationing in Mexico.

"I had heard that she married Roger and I thought, 'Oh that's really nice. This poor guy has these two little kids. It must be awful.' Then we met them on a trip to Cancún, and they wound up in the same hotel we were in with the kids. And I remember thinking about how courageous she was to take that on. And she was incredibly good with the kids," Nadelson recalled.

"We were on the beach together. I think the thing that most struck me about it was seeing how warm and giving she was and how devoted she was to the kids. I mean, she really was into it. I don't think anybody there would have dreamed they weren't her kids. She paid a lot of attention to them.

"And I remember a discussion with her about baby-sitters and she said she wasn't quite sure about getting a babysitter, so they would all go out to dinner together. They were together all the time. That part really stuck in my mind because my husband and I both talked about it. And talked about it in terms of the fact that she really got into this and took on a very difficult task. And that was characteristic of a lot of the things people said about her. That she would take on a challenge. She wasn't afraid of challenges the way a lot of people are."

She was certainly not afraid of the depressed young medical student who reappeared at her office after a two-year hiatus on the eve of the July Fourth holiday in 1986.

Paul Lozano had been carrying her card in his wallet for two years. In the past, his dark moods had lifted as the weather brightened, but in the summer between his second and third years in medical school he seemed burdened by constant depression. He called Pilar to say he thought therapy might be a good idea. Despite his best efforts, he could not help but lean on his sister. He had gotten into the habit at Harvard, just as he had at West Point, of calling her two or three times a week for support. If he saw a psychiatrist, it would certainly take the pressure off Pilar. She had her own life to worry about. And his collect calls were adding up; she and Hal did not have endless resources to deal with his loneliness. They had their son to raise.

Paul Lozano had plenty of company as a medical student dealing with depression. A study by Chicago researchers, reported in 1988 in the *Journal of the American Medical Association,* found that at least 12 percent of medical students studied exhibited signs of depression during the first three years. The largest fraction, 25 percent, was symptomatic near the end of the second year—just when Paul sought out Dr. Margaret Bean-Bayog. A separate study found that 76 percent of all medical student suicides occur during the sophomore and junior years.

At Harvard, medical leaves are rare but most occur during the first year. Dr. Edward M. Hundert, Associate Dean for Student Affairs, finds it is an especially vulnerable year for students who may be away from home for the first time. A genetic predisposition to depression often manifests itself then, when a student is separated from his family support system, said Dr. Hundert, a psychiatrist.

That might explain Paul Lozano's adjustment problems at West Point, problems that prompted him to drink too much in his first year and, finally, to quit in his second. "I had reached my limit, drunk, looking out of windows, thinking about jumping," he would tell Dr. Bean-Bayog of his months at the military academy. "I think people who kill themselves don't see options. Somehow, I always manage to land on my feet. I told myself maybe the option is I could leave."

When he did leave, he felt a mixture of relief and defeat. But the depression he experienced at the academy subsided on his return home to El Paso, where he spent the next two years living with his parents and excelling at his studies.

His depression returned at Harvard and had deepened in the two years since he had seen her last, Paul told Dr. Bean-Bayog. "Maybe it's my perceptions, not the situation," Paul told her on his July 3 visit, but he felt like a failure even when his professors told him he was doing just fine. To all appearances, medical school was going well. His work in the Intensive Care Unit reminded him of his boyhood dreams of becoming a world-class soccer goalie: a way of stopping death from scoring the winning goal. Even the routine clinical work pleased him: coaxing children into ear exams by telling them Mickey Mouse was hiding in there; dropping in on patients just to say hi. They appreciated it and let him know. He thrived on that kind of feedback. Maybe too much so. He did fine when praised but, in its absence, he felt like a failure.

He worked hard on his job as a lab assistant on a research project to determine the effects of hyperthermia on anesthetized beagles. But the work only increased Paul's sadness. He was responsible for giving fatal injections to the dogs after the experiments, which he hated; the beagles were so cute and defenseless. His supervisors warned him not to pet the dogs, but he could not help himself.

His clinical rotations were beginning, and if he felt this

bad about dogs, how would he cope with patients? he wondered. They sometimes died, too. His anxiety made him think of a college adviser who had warned him he might be too sensitive for clinical work. Maybe he belonged in the lab. He had felt the tug between clinical medicine and research since those first stimulating years in Dr. Becvar's lab at UTEP. As the time approached when he would be working with patients, Paul's ambivalence and self-doubt increased.

His personal life depressed him as well. He had not made many friends at Harvard, besides his roommate, Victor Gonzalez, a Chicano from California. And even his relationship with Victor was problematic. Paul was jealous of Victor's Princeton education and his many friends. Paul almost always ate his lunch alone; he would cringe when he saw a group of classmates sit down together in the cafeteria or when Victor's Princeton pals filled their apartment with laughter.

Paul interpreted his envy of Victor as more evidence of his worthlessness: here this fellow had befriended him, and Paul's gratitude was tainted with jealousy. Victor tried to coax him out of his depression, but it was no use.

Paul "seemed unhappy the majority of the time. I believe this reflected his state of depression," Victor recalled, noting that Paul "would have brief episodes where he was happy and then would unexpectedly revert to his unhappy, depressed state. He would be doing well for periods of time and appear upbeat. However, the majority of the time, he would be his usual somber self. At times his downswings were severe enough that he would begin to contemplate suicide."

Just after they had moved in together in January, Paul had been hit by a car while crossing the street near their apartment. He was just distracted, "inattentive," Paul would tell his psychiatrist. "It came around the corner and smacked me." He banged up a knee, interrupting a routine of bicycling and jogging that usually had an ameliorating effect on his depression.

Reinforcing his mood, the New England spring lived up to its reputation that year: it was raw and cold into May, when his romance with a classmate seven years his senior ended because she had begun dating someone else. He took the breakup badly. Women found him attractive, his five-foot, eight-inch frame taut from regular exercise and his dark good looks softened by a disarmingly boyish charm. He was an attentive date. He sent flowers and had the rare and valued gift of being a good listener. But he was emotionally needy, too, and his intensity often scared young women off, leaving him even more lonely and isolated.

The truth was, he had always felt like an outsider, Paul told Dr. Bean-Bayog. Academic giftedness had set him apart when he was young. He was teased on the playground for being weird; he thought he was probably the only kid in America who hated recess. He definitely had not belonged at West Point; he drank there to "get anesthetized." He said he still had an occasional beer with friends, wine with dinner, or a few drinks when he was feeling anxious. But Victor recalled later that he never saw Paul Lozano drunk.

His academic talents were not unusual at Harvard, but there were other reasons to feel alien here, Paul told Dr. Bean-Bayog. His skin color. His need to paste together part-time jobs to pay for living expenses while more free-spending classmates took off on ski vacations.

Would he ever fit in? Would he always feel so hopeless, so worthless even in the face of his obvious achievements?

On July 11, his second visit, Dr. Bean-Bayog scribbled a note on the lined paper she used to record her impressions during his sessions, tentatively diagnosing depression and alcohol abuse and questioning whether Paul Lozano was a suicide risk. Had that accident in January been a quasi-suicidal gesture? Had he walked into the path of an oncoming car deliberately?

She prescribed Imipramine, an antidepressant. But the drug had so little effect that a visit to a Van Gogh exhibit at the Boston Museum of Fine Arts put Paul in mind of a popular song about the Dutch painter's suicide. "Starry, starry night, paint your palette blue and gray/Look out on a summer's day, with eyes that know the darkness in my soul." The song became one of his favorites.

As his depression deepened, Paul told his psychiatrist that he had always been unhappy, even as a boy. He endured the taunts of his brothers and sisters, he said. He was teased, locked in a closet, screamed at, and told repeatedly by his straight-haired siblings that his curly locks were proof that he had been adopted. He would take the long route home from school, talking to himself, he said. On his seventh visit to Dr. Bean-Bayog, he recalled once having chased his brothers and sisters with a knife in retaliation for their relentless teasing.

"My sister Pilar was nice. She took it away, hugged me, read to me," Paul told his psychiatrist. "She's seven years older. I thought she was my mom."

During that session, according to Dr. Bean-Bayog's office notes—986 pages that offer a rare public glimpse into the most private of relationships—the psychiatrist who had neither met nor spoken to Paul Lozano's family concluded flatly: "You were abused."

As the summer of 1986 progressed, Paul spoke more and more of his worthlessness, despair, and self-loathing. "For the past twenty-four years, I realize I've managed to be a failure," he told her, confiding his fear that his success had been a fluke, that he would be unmasked at Harvard.

He lost seven pounds in one week, could not sleep, did not eat. He bought potassium chloride and thought about injecting it. "It doesn't matter if it's sterile if you are using it to check out," he told her. He went jogging through the park late at night, hoping to attract the attention of muggers. He went to the library and read veterinary journals to learn painless ways to kill large animals. "There is a defect in the machinery. It's important to be logical about this. Some people just aren't going to make it. When a computer shorts out no one makes a fuss," he said.

"I've been telling myself I didn't feel this way, but it's a relief to admit that I *do* feel it. What has fueled me for years is that I was going to show them. Medical school is very important. Without it, there would be no reason to go on being."

In late September, Paul confided to Dr. Bean-Bayog that

he had taken the elevator to the thirteenth floor of the Harvard School of Public Health building, opened a window, and calculated the time it would take to hit the ground. "Skulls break in very characteristic places," he told her. "It would be a bad one or two seconds, but pain is short."

His preoccupation with suicide alarmed Dr. Bean-Bayog. She urged her patient to hospitalize himself voluntarily for his own safety. He balked initially, citing the importance of keeping up in medical school and expressing the fear that if Harvard knew of his troubles it could "stop Chicanos from getting in."

But "increasingly dependent [and] able to accept my judgment," she noted, he agreed to be admitted on September 24 to McLean, a private psychiatric hospital famous for such celebrity patients as singers James Taylor and Ray Charles, and poets Sylvia Plath and Robert Lowell.

The hospitalization was humiliating for Paul. Reminders of Harvard were everywhere. The 328-bed hospital and research center on 240 acres in suburban Belmont is a major teaching facility for Harvard Medical School. He was even assigned to the ward named for Henry P. Bowditch, a former dean.

He refused to grant permission to notify his family of his hospitalization, a refusal that concerned the staff because of Dr. Bean-Bayog's opinion that childhood abuse was central to Paul's depression. Amy Stromsten, the social worker intern assigned to the case, had similar concerns after interviewing Victor Gonzalez, Paul's roommate.

"The patient is very bitter toward his family, and Victor states that the patient remembers being locked in a closet repeatedly as a child and mistreated," Amy Stromsten wrote in his chart. "Paul was scapegoated by the family and appears to have suffered emotional abuse."

When she interviewed Paul himself, however, Amy Stromsten said she saw another dimension to Paul's relationship with his family—how protective of them he was; how responsible he felt for them. "He didn't want me to tell his family he was in the hospital because there was that

Hispanic thing about shaming your family. He had a lot invested in protecting them. He said, 'If they know I'm in a mental hospital they'll be upset. My mother will be so upset. She has hypertension. I don't want to worry her.' He was wanting to protect them from the fact that he was hurting. Because I wasn't allowed to see his family, I spent much more time with him. I came away feeling that he felt pressured but extremely close to his family, too. It was obvious to me that he loved them very much. I was not sure whether they were pressuring him to succeed or if he was pressuring himself on their behalf."

However problematic his relationship with his family, it was clear to the staff that this was a seriously depressed patient. He talked often about being teased as a boy. He would curl up on his bed in a fetal position. He told a nurse he wanted to be a puppy and cuddled. He would lapse into baby talk or speak in a soft, childish voice.

"As the depression lifted and his vegetative signs cleared, he became less needy and more able to discuss with some tolerance his history of depression and social isolation," Dr. Frances R. Frankenberg, the psychiatrist in charge of his hospital care, wrote in his chart.

The childish behavior frightened him, though. He took it as a sign of mental deterioration and feared his illness would derail his plans to be a doctor. The staff took pains to explain that hospitalization itself often has a regressive impact on patients, whose meals and bedtime are regulated as in childhood. His neediness, they explained, was caused by his depression in much the same way that his sleep disturbance was. Depression can also distort memory, causing patients in the midst of a depressive episode to recall their childhoods in much bleaker terms than after their depression lifts.

This was a very different message, however, from the one Paul Lozano was hearing from Dr. Bean-Bayog. According to Amy Stromsten, Dr. Bean-Bayog's long visits with her patient were attracting staff attention, and her fixation on the psychological roots of Paul's distress was raising eyebrows among the members of the hospital treatment team who early on had concluded that this was a classic case of biological depression.

Paul was seen several times at McLean by Dr. Harrison G. Pope, Jr., a staff psychiatrist whose research into the biological causes of mental illness has earned him a national reputation. He agreed with the team's diagnosis of a "major affective disorder, depressed, with melancholia, and without psychotic features, probably recurrent." He prescribed desipramine, an antidepressant, and Paul improved immediately. Paul's caregivers were cautiously optimistic, their reserve born of the knowledge that drugs sometimes have only a short-term placebo effect. Even with that caveat, Dr. Pope thought that Paul could resume his medical studies successfully, with strict monitoring of his drug regimen.

In a detailed report written on October 8, Dr. Pope laid out his recommendations. If the desipramine proved ineffective, he suggested alternative medications and, failing that, a course of electroconvulsive therapy. Noting that the short-term memory loss associated with ECT, or shock therapy, as it is more commonly known, "would be quite a nuisance for a medical student, given the large amount of memorization required in medical school," Dr. Pope urged a fair trial period for the antidepressants, with the expectation that they would suffice.

The different approaches of Dr. Pope and Dr. Bean-Bayog mirrored a long-standing debate in psychiatry about the causes and treatment of mental illness. The topic is often referred to, simplistically if not entirely accurately, as the "nature versus nurture" or "mind versus brain" debate. The dispute pits those psychiatrists grounded in the analytic tradition of Sigmund Freud against those schooled in empirical research. As modern science began to establish the physiological basis of many mental disorders, the Platonic view of the mind and the body as distinct entities came under challenge.

It is not an idle philosophical point. A patient's treatment can be determined by whether a doctor subscribes to the view that depression is the result of a chemical imbalance in the brain or a consequence of unconscious inner conflicts having their roots in childhood. There are few psychiatrists today who do not acknowledge the efficacy of psychotropic drugs in treating many forms of mental illness. Sigmund Freud himself might well have shared in the excitement of biopsychiatry, having recommended psychoanalysis only for neurotics, or "the worried well." For more seriously disturbed patients, he wrote, "the future may teach us how to exercise a direct influence by particular chemical substances."

To frame the tension in psychiatry, then, simply in terms of a polarized struggle between adherents of "drugs" versus "talk" misses a more subtle point about empiricism. That the two views are not mutually exclusive has been demonstrated by studies showing that psychotherapy itself causes physiological changes in the brain. The issue is not whether drugs or psychotherapy is the answer to people's mental health problems. The more central questions are: What works best and when? and, Where is the proof?

Even as medication was proving ever more effective in the treatment of such mood disorders as depression, most of Freud's disciples in the 1980s still viewed drugs as symptom relievers, ancillary to the more fundamental work of "talk therapy."

Research was leading in the opposite direction, however, establishing that chemicals known as neurotransmitters send electrical signals between cells, which in turn trigger neural reactions that impact on behavior and mood. One such neurotransmitter, serotonin, has been tied to sleep and mood regulation. When the level of serotonin in a patient's system dropped, researchers documented a corresponding decline in mood and the emergence of classic depression symptoms: sleep and appetite disturbances, a diminished interest in sex, inability to concentrate, slowed speech, and an intrusive pattern of self-blaming and negative thoughts like those plaguing Paul Lozano. ("For the past twenty-four years, I realize I've managed to be a failure.")

By restoring serotonin levels to the normal range, the cycle of guilt and worthlessness could be stopped. Antidepressants were seen in the laboratory not as symptom relievers but as a sort of direct intervention like surgery, bringing the brain's metabolism back into balance.

Therapy was increasingly assigned an adjunct role—helping depressed patients cope with the behavioral and psychological fallout from their illness. For the treatment of depression, cognitive therapy, short-term and oriented to the present, was overtaking analytically oriented psychotherapy, which often consumes years in the effort to unearth childhood conflicts.

"Traditional, long-term psychotherapy with the goal of helping patients change their approach to life can even make things worse by putting too much responsibility for getting well on the patient," Dr. Francis M. Mondimore, a psychiatrist at Johns Hopkins University, concluded in his book *Depression: The Mood Disease.*

The changing view of depression was received with suspicion, if not outright hostility, by analytically oriented psychiatrists like Dr. Bean-Bayog, whose whole field was based on the theory that mood disorders were psychologically based and required talk therapy to be resolved. Far from viewing Dr. Pope as a collaborator on Paul Lozano's treatment, for instance, Dr. Bean-Bayog never even met her patient's psychopharmacologist. She did, however, continue Paul's medication.

Dr. Bean-Bayog's decision to operate under the rapidly vanishing practice of a T/A split—the *T* being the therapist and the *A* being the administrator or psychopharmacologist—relegated drugs to a secondary role in the treatment of Paul's depression. "One individual is the therapist who works entirely with the patient's inner life, and the second person is the administrator who works, in a certain sense, with the outer life," is how Dr. Thomas G. Gutheil, a psychiatrist and professor at Harvard Medical School, explained the arrangement that is still widely used among Boston analysts. "The therapist does the therapy. The administrator attempts to cope with the practical realities of the patient's life in a way that liberates the therapist from having to mess with those, and allows the patient to feel that they can talk more freely in some ways because somebody else is going to be deciding about hospitalization and medication and things that the patient may have some conflict about."

The separation of roles effectively precluded any real integration between Paul Lozano's medication management and his psychotherapy. During the years Paul was under their joint care, Dr. Pope says Dr. Bean-Bayog shared no details of her therapy with him, and he had no extended conversations about his medical management with Dr. Bean-Bayog.

It was as if they were treating two separate patients. Dr. Pope saw a classic biological depression that needed to be medically managed. Dr. Bean-Bayog saw a psychological mystery that needed to be unraveled. Because the therapists never met and rarely talked, their two approaches never jelled.

After eight weeks, Paul Lozano was discharged from McLean on November 19, 1986. Dr. Frankenberg noted that "Paul's depression responded very well to desipramine and he understands very clearly that he needs to remain on desipramine for at least six months, that the depression might recur, and that should this happen if he is not in touch with Dr. Bean-Bayog at that time, he should certainly consult a psychiatrist immediately."

Given that "Paul's depression was an extremely serious one with very lethal suicidal ideation," Dr. Frankenberg cautioned, ". . . should a depression occur again, without immediate assistance of a psychiatrist, this could have fatal consequences for him. Nevertheless, at the time of discharge, Paul was euthymic, enthusiastic about returning to medical school, and determined to continue in psychotherapy with Dr. Bean-Bayog."

The use of the adjective *determined* was not accidental. Amy Stromsten said she and others on Paul Lozano's treatment team at McLean had urged him to end his therapy with Dr. Bean-Bayog once he left the hospital. In their view, she said, the relationship seemed inappropriately intense and the therapist too involved. The psychiatrist visited too often and stayed too long when she did. Instead of encouraging his autonomy, her attentiveness was fostering Paul's dependence on her.

But Paul would have none of it. Margaret Bean-Bayog was the closest thing he had to a real friend in Boston. She cared about him. He thrived on her attention. He needed her. For once, the intensity he brought to a relationship with a woman was not only tolerated, it was rewarded. As soon as he was released, Dr. Bean-Bayog increased his therapy sessions to twice a week.

Although she would later describe this time as one of the most dangerous periods of Paul Lozano's illness, Dr. Bean-Bayog sounded a far more optimistic note in a letter to the associate dean of students at Harvard Medical School. "Fortunately, his disorder has responded beautifully to treatment and he is mending rapidly, in good spirits though naturally somewhat shaken by his experience, and looking forward to getting back to school," she wrote on October 23 to Dr. Daniel D. Federman.

After Paul's release from McLean, Dr. Bean-Bayog continued the medication Dr. Pope had prescribed but focused her attention on the childlike dimension to his personality that had emerged during his hospitalization. Who was this little boy curling up on his hospital bed who wished he was a puppy? What terrified child was hiding inside this medical student?

The psychiatrist clearly was intrigued, but her own notes reveal that her patient was "terribly ashamed of feeling like a three-year-old." His shame notwithstanding, Dr. Bean-Bayog devised what she would later describe as "unconventional" techniques to explore Paul's regressive feelings for the psychological source of his depression. "We invented a baby version of him who might have something on his mind. Maybe he could make friends with his three-year-old self," she wrote in her office notes.

Dr. Bean-Bayog consulted no colleagues before undertaking this approach, which she had never used before with a single patient, let alone one whose depression manifested itself in overwhelming feelings of shame and self-loathing. She did not consult with any experts on depression, who might have argued that such an infantilization could reinforce Paul Lozano's shame or who might have suggested that a therapeutic approach stressing his present status as a competent adult medical student might be more effective.

Instead, to reach Paul Lozano's inner child, Dr. Bean-Bayog devised a series of role-playing episodes in which she would be the mother and he would be her son. The doctor's voluminous notes make no mention of any discussion between patient and therapist of how this treatment would proceed, for how long it would continue, on what theories it was based, or what its prospects for success might be. The doctor would later say that those issues were addressed on a written sheet of "instructions for therapy" that she prepared and gave to Paul Lozano that fall. But, the Lozanos say, no such paper was found among his possessions after his death. Dr. Bean-Bayog says she did not keep a copy.

Her office notes reflect only that he was "the boy" or "the baby" or "the three-year-old" and she was "the Mom."

She explained her theory, through legal counsel, after Paul Lozano's suicide. "This role-playing was a form of supportive and cognitive therapy to counteract Lozano's depressive and suicidal thoughts. When Lozano felt panicked or suicidal, he would retreat to his three-year-old state and express the need for the concept of a protective mother figure to give him the comfort and support he needed to avoid committing suicide. When necessary, Dr. Bean-Bayog allowed Lozano to think of her as such a protective mother figure for this purpose. Her objective was to support Lozano's functioning as an adult while allowing the childlike part of his personality to mature and become integrated with his adult self."

Dr. Bean-Bayog reinforced her idea with concrete props. When Paul began clutching a small blanket on her couch during their sessions, she encouraged him to take it home for use as what analysts refer to as a transitional object. Patients sometimes use such items as tangible reminders of the support provided by the therapeutic relationship. Before long, he was bringing his "baby blanket" to sessions less self-consciously, she noted.

In the next year, Dr. Bean-Bayog and Paul began to use several such props, all of them designed to comfort the child in him. There was Pound Puppy, a stuffed dog dressed in satin pants and suspenders. It was a beagle, like the dogs he had killed in the lab. There was a small teddy bear, outfitted in green surgical scrubs, which Dr. Bean-Bayog said Paul originally gave to her as a gift and then reclaimed as a transitional object. They named it Dr. Bean Bear.

She gave him more than a dozen children's books as well, including *Charlotte's Web,* by E. B. White. "This is a favorite. I hope you like it. Love, Dr. B.," she wrote. On *Just So Stories* by Rudyard Kipling, she scribbled: "To my favorite elephant's child with his insatiable curiosity. Love, Dr. B." And, reinforcing their symbolic role-playing, Dr. Bean-Bayog gave Paul Lozano a copy of *Are You My Mother?* by P. D. Eastman and signed it: "Love, guess who?"

Dr. Bean-Bayog also read these children's stories to Paul during his therapy sessions and even made an audiocassette so that he could listen to her reading *Goodnight Moon* and other baby books at home.

This intense role-playing, confusing in and of itself, was immediately complicated by the sexual attraction Paul Lozano felt for Margaret Bean-Bayog. No sooner was he released from the hospital in November 1986 than he admitted to "having sexual feelings outside the office." He had difficulty discussing his "intoxication with me," his psychiatrist wrote, but she reassured him that "he didn't choose his feelings and they might bother him less if he talked about them."

Dr. Bean-Bayog found no conflict between her patient's sexual attraction to her and the therapy's aim of fostering the notion of her as Paul's symbolic mother. Indeed, when the classics of children's literature were insufficient to soothe her patient, Dr. Bean-Bayog says she and Paul Lozano collaborated on their own mother-and-son short stories.

One is called "Shots."

"Come on, Paul; we're going to the doctor."

"I won't go! I won't. He'll give me a needle." You glower.

"We have to."

"I won't—I'm scared."

"What's scary?"

"He'll give me a shot. It'll HURT!"

"Yes, it will, but only for a minute. And then we'll go by the pet shop to visit all the animals."

"Can I see the puppies?"

"Yes. AFTERWARD. Besides we'll play a game."

"What game?"

"YOU get to be the doctor."

"Oh. I still don't want to go."

You are not easily bought off.

"You don't have to want to but you do have to go."

"He'll hurt me. I'll cry. You'll get mad."

"I don't think so. I'll hold you."

We leave. You are nervous and talk fast all the way there. You count different things along the road.

You see the doctor. You do get a shot. I am holding you. You scream and try to hit me but it's over quickly.

Afterwards you take a doll. "This is the doctor." I have bought a 35 cc syringe, which I use as a turkey baster at home. You are going to give the doctor a shot. The needle is imaginary. It is big and long and VERY sharp.

The doctor begins to cry. He is scared. You scold him. "I didn't even give it to you yet. But I'm GOING to."

"No. No," shouts the doctor. "It will hurt."

"Yes, it will hurt a lot. But it will make you get well."

You grab the doll, hold it face down, and give it several shots. It howls every time. You have to give it a spanking for crying.

Then you turn on me. YOU need a shot, too, Mommy. "No. No. I'm not sick."

"No, you're not SICK; you're BAD. You let him hurt me. You TOLD me it wouldn't hurt."

"No, I didn't. I said you could cry."

"You STILL get a shot." You bend me over and give me a very big shot.

I shriek. "It hurts. It hurts. Stop, please, stop."

"No," you say. "You need another one."

"No, I'm scared." I begin to cry. You give me another shot. I try to run away but you catch me. You give me a spanking for running away. THERE.

We go to the pet shop.

Another is called "Fishing."

It is summertime. We are going fishing. The night before we pack a lunch. We put in cold chicken and apples and cookies. We take thermoses: one with milk, one with iced tea.

We get our poles ready. We dig some worms in the garden.

We leave early in the morning. It is cool and there is still mist on the lake. We get the dinghy, put the oars in the locks, put in our poles and picnic. We brought a book, too, in case the fish aren't biting.

We row out to the middle. The sun is burning off the mist. It will be a clear, hot day. There is some breeze out where we are. We put on hats and you get sunburn cream on your nose.

We fish.

It's a nice day.

Nothing much happens.

We aren't bored yet.

You wonder if something ate your worm. We check. It is still there.

We fish some more.

You get a little restless. We read the book, very

softly so it won't scare the fish. You are sitting in my lap, still holding your rod. It dips.

"A fishafishafish!"

It is bending the end of your pole over and swimming in all directions. You are winding it as hard as you can. You think you have caught a whale.

"It's a monster!" Actually, it's a catfish, not so little either. You bring it up beside the boat and I put a net under it and bring it over the side. It throws the hook and flops madly all over the boat. We get it into the pail of lake water.

We put our lines over again.

You are hungry and we have some lunch.

We fish.

You want to catch another whale. After a while, I catch a fish, another catfish. You are disappointed. You are fishing attentively, talking to the fish down there about your worm and how they would like it. We check your line. The worm is gone. Stolen. We bait your hook and throw it back in.

You really want another fish. To my relief, you get one, this time a sunfish, a real fighter. It drags the line all over creation and under the boat. You reel it in.

We go home. I kill and scale and gut the fish. You don't like that part, but you are very proud of having caught your dinner. We dip them in corn-meal and salt and pepper and fry them. We make hush puppies, too. You like the name and want to throw one to the dog. You do. The dog likes hush puppy.

We eat our catch.

Dr. Bean-Bayog's use of toys and dolls as therapeutic aids is not unprecedented in adult psychotherapy, but role-playing with adult patients has a far more controversial history. The psychoanalytic literature after World War II is filled with references to the notion of providing a "corrective emotional experience" for patients as a means of understanding their formative emotional life. The concept continues to have intellectual currency 50 years later in various forms of empathic therapy. But to most therapists it is a concept, not a concrete method of treatment. Lawsuits against misguided or ill-intentioned therapists have been one consequence of the oversimplified view that patients can be "reparented."

When Paul Lozano was in therapy, corrective parenting was very much in vogue in the United States. An association of such therapists, called Indepth, attracted 350 members when it was formed in the mid-1980s. A survey of 267 therapists in 1987 found spanking, bathing, and even breast-feeding of adults acceptable practice.

Psychiatry itself had opened the door to such bizarre therapies because of the lack of uniform standards for treating patients diagnosed as "multiple personalities" or victims of childhood abuse. Patients and the legal system are left struggling to distinguish legitimate techniques from foolish ones. At the same time Paul Lozano was role-playing as a three-year-old under Dr. Margaret Bean-Bayog's care, the Mid-America Treatment and Training Institute, in Kansas City, Missouri, settled two separate lawsuits initiated by former adult patients who claimed they were diapered as part of their "regression." The Institute denied any wrongdoing.

In 1991, a Tulsa, Oklahoma, woman who was diagnosed by her psychiatrist as a multiple personality sued Dr. Mark Kelley, challenging the legitimacy of his therapeutic techniques. His attempts to "reparent" his patient included having her suck his thumb, suck his breast nipples, nurse a baby bottle, and wear diapers. His aim, court papers assert, was "to cast himself in the role of her parents, and to have her experience childhood anew, this time in a more positive way, avoiding the traumatic events from her real childhood which had caused her alternate personalities to emerge." In court, Dr. Kelley did not disown his reparenting approach but denied the patient's charges that the "therapy" also included sexual contact. The case was still in litigation two years later.

Dr. Bean-Bayog was no trendy "reparenting therapist," however. The Harvard-trained psychiatrist based her mothering technique on the work of old-line analysts who theorized that major mental disorders could be traced to psychic wounds in infancy. Forty years ago, D. W. Winnicott, a British analyst, postulated that infants develop a "false self" in response to the deprivation of maternal love, and the analyst's challenge is to create a safe and nurturing "holding environment" to permit the "true self" to emerge.

Twenty years before that, Marguerite Sechehaye, a French analyst, devised a similar treatment approach, with a teenager who suffered from schizophrenia. Sechehaye concluded that the girl's illness could be traced to having had a cold and distant mother as a baby. To repair the damage, Sechehaye designed a therapy to fulfill her patient's presumed need for maternal love, with the analyst in the role of nurturing mother, bringing her patient dolls and gifts.

Sandor Ferenczi, a friend, colleague, and onetime patient of Freud, wrote in 1929 that what many patients in psychological distress need "is really to be adopted and to partake for the first time in their lives of the advantages of a normal nursery." In his pseudoparental role, Ferenczi was always available to his own patients, seeing them on weekends, even taking them on vacation with him.

Freud was not impressed, suggesting that Ferenczi was meeting his own needs, not those of his patients. Even while giving the eulogy for his old friend, Freud noted disapprovingly that "the need to cure and to help became paramount in him. From unexhausted springs of emotion the conviction was borne in upon him that one could effect far more with one's patients if one gave them enough of the love which they had longed for as children. He wanted to discover how this could be carried out within the framework of the psychoanalytic situation; and so long as he had not succeeded in this, he kept apart, no longer certain, perhaps, of agreement with his friends."

It was all interesting theory, but by the time Paul Lozano walked into Dr. Margaret Bean-Bayog's office, scientific research had gone a long way toward getting mothers off the hook. Even so eminent a Freudian as Arnold Cooper of the Cornell Medical School, a past president of the American Psychoanalytic Association, suggested to his colleagues in 1984 that by trying so hard to make depression and other mood disorders comprehensible psychologically, therapists actually could be harming their patients by not acknowledging that their suffering might have no childhood basis.

Paul Lozano's real family was unaware of the regressive nature of his therapy but was struck by the change in his behavior after he began seeing Dr. Bean-Bayog. Paul continued to call Pilar several times a week, but he said nothing of his hospitalization that fall or of the details of his therapy. However, he did talk about Dr. Bean-Bayog—Margaret, he called her. He spoke of her so often and with such reverence that his sister suspected that her brother was infatuated with his psychiatrist.

She was confused by Paul's reports that Margaret did not charge him for their frequent sessions and that she encouraged him to call her at home at any hour. Dr. Bean-Bayog had had Paul sign an agreement deferring payment until he completed his medical studies. But even Freud had insisted that his disciples charge their patients for each session, no matter how little, as a concrete way of establishing the impersonal nature of the relationship.

"I noticed almost immediately from the first treatment, from the first therapy session that he had with her, that he liked her very much, that he was very captivated by her. That alarmed me a little bit, because it's a doctor-patient thing. You could lose your sense of judgment," Pilar said. "But that was me speaking as a nurse. I held back because I didn't want to diminish his relationship with her. I was happy he thought she could help him."

Pilar was slower to pick up the change in the content of her conversations with Paul: their talks about medical ethics and the state of AIDS research had gradually given way to routine and often childish banter. "It was in his voice. But I was in denial. I was in constant denial about this, as a mother would be almost," she recalled.

It took Pilar's husband, Hal, and son, Erick, to point out that she spent hours on the telephone speaking as though she were soothing a distraught child. Paul was again the little boy whose tears she had dried more than twenty years ago, not the grown man, not the medical colleague she thought he had become.

"You know how little kids talk? 'Margaret said this and Margaret said that.' I mean it was like talking to a little boy." She recalled part of one such conversation she had had with Paul.

"But Margaret said I could do it if I wanted to," Paul said.

"Wait a minute," Pilar responded. "What is this? Where is this coming from? You know, Paul, I'm having a little problem here, because who is this person? What role is she playing in your life?"

"She's my doctor, she's my therapist."

"But why," Pilar persisted, "is she permitting you to become so dependent upon her?"

"Margaret says you're just jealous," said Paul. "Margaret says it's because I won't let you boss me around."

Pilar was more frustrated than jealous. If she was in denial about his regressed behavior, she was no less resistant to the very idea that her brother was mentally ill. She and her family were two thousand miles away from Paul, whom they knew only to be a young man plagued by pressure, self-doubt, and loneliness at Harvard. If there was more to his depression, no one had told them. Every time they asked Paul if they could speak to his psychiatrist, he told them that Dr. Bean-Bayog thought contact with the family would interfere with his therapy. They figured he was an adult and did have a right to privacy.

It is no wonder, then, that Paul Lozano told his psychiatrist that Pilar "would never believe that I was seriously suicidal until I was cold."

That the family was alarmed by the fact that Paul was taking psychotropic drugs is certain. They wanted him to just "snap out of it," in Pilar's words. "You are at Harvard

Medical School. Just do it," his sister told him. When he came home for the Christmas holidays, Pilar found his reliance on tranquilizers and antidepressants "embarrassing. I remember thinking this is what it must be like to work with handicapped children. With people always staring at them. And you're embarrassed but you're very strong and have nothing to be ashamed about. That was how I felt. I was embarrassed but I was ashamed of myself for being embarrassed."

His family's shame reinforced Paul's own. In his desperation to be normal, he discontinued his medication, triggering another bout of depression. Back at school, he pushed himself beyond his limits and then bemoaned the pressure he was under during his medical clerkship. After calling Dr. Bean-Bayog on a Saturday in January to complain about feeling overwhelmed, he wrote her a note, demonstrating the bind he was in. "If I wasn't going to comply with your request [that he take Saturday off from the hospital] I had no business calling, especially to say I'm upset," he wrote. "If I had a patient who would not comply with directions I think I would be much less tactful and simply ask him/her not to bother seeing me again until he could follow advice."

Dr. Bean-Bayog got him back on antidepressants and increased his therapy sessions to four times a week. The time commitment was both draining and angering him. "I spend a lot of energy on this—maybe that's why I'm so tired," he complained. "You made me believe it would get better."

But things only got worse. His clerkship required him to be on duty nights at the hospital, and he stopped taking his antidepressants again, concerned that the drugs would interfere with his work. The result was an even more erratic sleep pattern and deepening depression.

While she encouraged him to take his medication, Dr. Bean-Bayog saw the cause of his increasing despondency as being in his past, not his present. In his pediatrics training that April, Paul became attached to a critically ill baby named Stephen. In the nursery, he cradled Stephen in the rocking chair and cringed when he had to draw blood from his thin little arms. He could recognize Stephen's weak cry anywhere on the ward. The baby's suffering was agonizing for Paul Lozano either because, having discontinued his medication, he was suffering a relapse of depression or because, as Dr. Bean-Bayog interpreted it, suffering babies evoked memories in him of "a small boy with an inadequate, childlike and neglectful parent."

She had a similar explanation when Paul called her after midnight a few days later to discuss his distress about a homeless woman and young boy he had seen that night in the emergency room. Despite the lack of any hard evidence, Dr. Bean-Bayog was beginning to zero in on Paul's mother as the source of his depression.

Paul Lozano "discontinued his medication fifty or a hundred times over the course of treatment," Dr. Bean-Bayog estimates. However, Dr. Pope, her patient's psychopharmacologist, says that at no time did she seek a consultation with him about how to make Paul comply or whether to adjust his medication. Paul Lozano even reported to Dr. Pope that he had stopped his medication at Dr. Bean-Bayog's urging, an assertion she denies. Indeed, she contends, the only way to be certain that Paul took his desipramine was to dispense the 500-milligram tablets herself every day, which she says she did. If so, such a practice ran the risk of making Paul Lozano even more dependent on her and encouraging the idea that only she could save him.

That dependence was complicated by his attraction to her. He wanted to talk to her or see her all the time. That April, he often had appointments every weekend day and called her between sessions. On April 24, he told her with some pride in his self-restraint that he had wanted to call her the night before but settled for calling up her published work on his computer. "Very attached, gratified, seductive, flattering," Dr. Bean-Bayog wrote in her notes. She quoted Paul extolling the "incredible attention from you. I don't deserve it. But the more I get the more I feel better about myself."

Two days later, however, he reported that his sexual feelings for her were more troublesome than comforting.

"This feels like wanting to ask someone out but being anxious," he said. "'The boy' told him not to tell, but he's having 'those' feelings." The next day Dr. Bean-Bayog wrote in her notes, acknowledging that Paul Lozano was "afraid of me as though I'd make him choose between his integrity and the relationship."

Still, there is no record of her having sought any consultation about how to handle the mixed signals his sexual feelings and her maternal role-playing were sending.

Paul's need to be with Dr. Bean-Bayog constantly triggered panic when she was out of town. One weekend, in either a suicidal gesture or a play for his psychiatrist's attention, Paul injected himself with Trifalon, one of several drugs he had taken from the hospitals where he worked. He only told her about the incident days later when he called her at home, drunk and needy. At ten that night, she drove to her office to meet him and insisted he turn over the drugs and intravenous paraphernalia he had stockpiled. "He seemed amazed that I wanted him to give me his bag of drugs so badly, that it really mattered to me that he was alive," she wrote.

The less he took his antidepressants, the more he thought of suicide. He talked about dropping the emotionally draining pediatrics course or taking a leave of absence from medical school. Repeatedly he spoke of killing himself, relating fantasies of shooting himself and blowing his brains out all over his fastidious landlady's wallpaper. "My father has a gun. I keep thinking about it. I don't want to do a half-assed job. If you put a gun to your temple you may survive. But if you put it in your mouth . . ."

In late April, Dr. Bean-Bayog began to discuss hospitalizing him again, worried that his anxiety about his performance in his pediatrics course, his decision to take a leave from medical school, and her departure for an out-of-town conference could trigger another suicide attempt. When she suffered a miscarriage on the eve of her trip, the issue was moot. She would not be leaving town, she told Paul.

"What followed was a somewhat confusing discussion,

confusing because I was not feeling well and he was reacting to the change in plans. He was not totally relieved but felt better," she wrote. "I explained that while my leaving had been the precipitant for his depression, it might have a life of its own now. We had gone into the cave and kicked the sleeping bear."

Chapter

3

It was past midnight when Paul Lozano telephoned Margaret Bean-Bayog on May 3, 1987, from the thirteenth floor of the Harvard School of Public Health.

He had been sitting on a windowsill for fifteen minutes, he told her, dangling his legs over the ledge, thinking about jumping.

"I'll meet you at my office immediately," she said.

"We'll just talk?" he asked.

"We'll talk," she said.

Dr. Bean-Bayog did not call the police, an ambulance, or the rescue squad. Instead, she dressed quickly and drove from her Lexington home to her Cambridge office, where she found her patient waiting for her to arrive.

"Mercifully, he came, and mercifully he did not run out when I told him we had to go to the hospital," she wrote in her office notes.

On the five-mile drive to McLean Hospital, Paul told her he would have run if she had sent the police. At McLean, when a security guard got into the backseat to guide them across the darkened campus, Paul Lozano did run.

Two guards tackled him outside East House, the admissions building. Then, as he kicked and flailed, members of the hospital staff dragged him through the main foyer to a seclusion room. There they tied Paul Lozano's wrists and legs to a bed. He struggled against the restraints, screaming to be let "out of here" and thwarting attempts at a body search, routine for suicidal patients at admission.

"Mercifully, he was caught and put himself through a whole harrowing scene of being physically subdued, held and in four-point restraints," Dr. Bean-Bayog wrote.

To Dr. Frances R. Frankenberg, the psychiatrist in charge of the ward to which Paul Lozano was assigned, the scene was less about mercy than manipulation. "If you have a patient who is about to kill himself, I think that the safest thing to do is to involve the police and the community," Dr. Frankenberg would say later.

"To me, this had the air of something more interpersonal; that Mr. Lozano wanted Dr. Bean-Bayog to stop what she was doing and come down and rescue him. It was too personal. It sounded to me not like he was about to kill himself and wanted to be saved, but that he wanted Dr. Bean-Bayog to jump up and come down and save him. Quite a different message the way I heard it."

At his initial assessment that night, his chart noted that Paul was "an extremely agitated young man, hyperventilating." When he had calmed down sufficiently to be interviewed, Paul said, "I'm ashamed of being in the hospital and of how I've behaved." Significantly, he cited as the reason for his hospitalization not his risk of suicide, but the need to gain "insight into his dependent personality."

Dr. Frankenberg confronted Dr. Bean-Bayog with questions about her relationship with Paul Lozano. According to Dr. Bean-Bayog's office notes, Dr. Frankenberg "thought I was overinvolved (true) and suggested that I not see him while he's in restraints. I'll visit him briefly tomorrow as promised and let her take the heat—not see him for a few days." It seems to have been Dr. Bean-Bayog's notetaking habit to record her own thoughts or comments in parentheses. By writing the word *true,* she appears to be acknowledging Dr. Frankenberg's view of her as overinvolved.

Dr. Bean-Bayog did tell Paul, "We will have to 'cool down' what is happening between us while you are in the hospital," but she continued to call him and to visit him.

"They want you to stop seeing me. They're going to take you away from me," he cried. "I know I can't marry you, but someday I want to find someone like you and get married and have a family. That's why I didn't jump."

Confined to his room, he craved some physical contact with her. "It really helped the other night when you touched my hand when you left. I was so frightened I couldn't move," Paul told her.

"Even shaking hands is too confusing," she noted.

But Dr. Bean-Bayog did not "back off," as Dr. Frankenberg had urged. She continued to visit and even left Paul notes after her visits, assuring him she would always be there, promising to telephone when he was out of restraints and to return to see him. "I want you out of this room so I can see you in treatment," she wrote during his two days in restraints in the seclusion room.

Not only did Dr. Bean-Bayog continue to see Paul Lozano every day, but according to Dr. Frankenberg she saw him for so long that his nine-person hospital team of nurses, social workers, interns, and residents urged Dr. Frankenberg to speak with Dr. Bean-Bayog again.

"It was the impression of the treatment team and myself that, well, she was almost giving too much time to the therapy," Dr. Frankenberg recalled. "I knew that she had been doing things like driving down to the Harvard School of Public Health to pick him up, which struck me as a little unusual. I knew that she was seeing him without any fees being paid, which struck me again as a little unusual. So all of that, together with Mr. Lozano's complete dependence on her, had me somewhat concerned. . . . For example, there's a note in the chart somewhere that she had a session with him that lasted several hours, which is, I think, too long."

Even without knowing the details and the role-playing nature of Dr. Bean-Bayog's therapy with Paul Lozano, Dr. Frankenberg was alarmed. In a five-page letter to the hospital staff written at the time of Paul's admission, Dr. Bean-Bayog summarized their therapeutic work without ever mentioning a word about her unconventional regression techniques. Her methods were a mystery, but the results were obvious to Dr. Frankenberg.

"I worried that it was somewhat unrealistic, that he depended on her too much, saw her as sort of 'the' person who could save him. . . . I think the problem with depending on one person for your recovery is that, inevitably, that person will prove to disappoint you, so it's dangerous to be too dependent on one person," Dr. Frankenberg explained. She worried that the intensity of the therapy could do more harm than good.

"I think the conflictual feelings, his dependence on her and, I think, his shame about that and his longing to find, you know, one person in whom he could absolutely trust and rely on—that's a risky state of affairs."

Dr. Frankenberg did speak to Dr. Bean-Bayog again, three days after Paul was admitted to the hospital. Dr. Bean-Bayog's notes reflect her view of that conversation. "[I] met with Dr. Frankenberg who was concerned I was overinvolved, inappropriate and dangerous to the patient," she wrote.

"He is torturing you," Dr. Frankenberg told her. "How would you feel if he killed himself?"

"Upset, but I'd get over it," Dr. Bean-Bayog replied.

Knowing that Dr. Bean-Bayog had suffered a miscarriage only days before, Dr. Frankenberg asked if she did not blame this patient on some level for the stress she was under. "No. It hadn't crossed my mind. I was a little startled. No, I didn't think I was angry with him. Tired, yes. He was very hectic, panicking a lot, and with the blackmail of suicide in the background."

Summarizing the conversation with Dr. Frankenberg in her office notes, Dr. Bean-Bayog wrote: "She thought I was being conned. I thought she was unempathetic."

Margaret Bean-Bayog had been in analysis herself for the past ten years and relied on it to help her keep her personal issues out of her patients' sessions. "The better you know yourself, the more comfortable you will be with your own responses to patients, and the less you will be distracted by idiosyncratic or personal concerns," is how she would later explain the need for a therapist to engage in continual self-examination.

But Paul Lozano was an especially difficult case for her. She acknowledged as much in her letter to the McLean staff when he was admitted. "He is a mixture of fragile and incredibly tough, despite the battering he has had. I find it challenges everything I've got to keep my balance with him," she wrote. "I've learned a whole lot about myself in this process."

In fact, there were so many parallels, so many points at which the troubles in Paul Lozano's life came close to issues in her own, that it would be no wonder if he kept Margaret Bean-Bayog off balance. For one thing, she had crafted a therapeutic role for herself as a nurturing mother at the very time in her own life when she was in the midst of frustrating and ultimately unsuccessful fertility treatments.

Between 1984 and 1988, Margaret Bean-Bayog suffered nine miscarriages. She was taking the fertility drug Pergonal, whose side effects can include wide mood swings. How could she expect to keep her personal yearnings for motherhood out of a therapeutic process that cast her in the very role she craved? The handwritten children's stories found among Paul Lozano's belongings, while written by her, were collaborative efforts between patient and therapist, she insists. But the themes read more like a white middle-class woman's idea of an idyllic childhood than those of a Latino male. They make sugar cookies, for instance, not sopaipillas or empanadas.

And one cannot help wonder whose longings—the therapist's or the patient's—echo through the poignant vignette, written in Margaret Bean-Bayog's hand, called "Morning":

The sun is slanting through the bars of your crib. You are lying on your back, singing and talking away to yourself, waving your feet. You can chatter away like this to yourself for a long time. You are passing the time till you and I say good morning.

You hear me coming down the hall. "Mamma?" You swing to your feet. "Mamma!?" "Hi Baby. Good Morning! How's my Baby?" I pick you up. "Mamma!" We wrap ourselves around each other. We love each other VERY, VERY much.

Now the day can begin.

Whose needs are being addressed in the handwritten story called "Restless"?

You can't sleep. You are restless. I come. I never hit you. I pick you up and hold you. We walk up and down in the moonlight. You have a drink of water and we walk some more and read *Goodnight Moon,* twice. You are still restless. You have your legs around my waist. Your head is on my shoulder. You can feel my body, smell me. I am walking up and down, under you. You can hear me breathing, and my heartbeat. My body is soft and warm against yours. You like the feeling. You are calmer but you don't want to go to sleep. You are trying to stay awake. I keep walking back and forth, sometimes murmuring something to you. You are fighting sleep now. Gradually, you succumb. I don't put you to bed yet. I don't want to let you go. I walk up and down awhile more, carrying you. When I wake you in the morning you want Christmas cookies for breakfast. Your father says, "You're spoiling that boy rotten." He's mad. I get the giggles. We decide he needs a Christmas cooky. You feed him one. He feels better. Being spoiled isn't so bad after all.

Motherhood was not the only theme from Paul Lozano's therapy that resonated in Margaret Bean-Bayog's life. There was the matter of his illness itself, and his overwhelming fear that it would derail his plans to become a doctor.

Dr. Margaret Bean-Bayog must have related strongly to his anxiety about having to interrupt his medical training. Hadn't she been in the same spot fifteen years earlier? In the middle of her residency in psychiatry, she needed to take time out, apparently because of her concern that her alcoholism would interfere with her ability to care for patients. She shifted to a master's degree program at the Harvard School of Public Health and then a fellowship in community psychiatry—where she focused her research on Alcoholics Anonymous—until she brought her drinking under control. She was able to return and complete her residency in 1974. Her alcoholism was "in remission" during the four years she treated Paul Lozano, she insists. But only weeks before meeting him, she was arrested in a Boston suburb for driving under the influence of alcohol and lost her driver's license for thirty days.

Paul Lozano's struggle, then, must have seemed painfully familiar and the desire to save him, as she herself had once been saved, strong.

It is not unusual for a psychiatrist to harbor rescue fantasies about a patient, but in a healthy therapeutic relationship, the doctor is careful to consider the dissenting viewpoints of other professionals.

In this case, Dr. Bean-Bayog not only ignored the warnings she was given, but she also tried to enlist her own patient as an ally against Dr. Frankenberg and the McLean staff when Paul himself began to express reservations about his dependence on her.

"He offered for me not to have to always come. Thought he'd seen too much of me. I was a crutch. Not good for him. Sometime I wouldn't be there when he needed me," she wrote, adding that she told Paul it was "not so bad for him to be dependent. He was making a big change by taking a year off. Not terrible for me to see him through it. Talked about my [interaction with] Dr. Frankenberg, his getting caught in the middle."

But Paul Lozano did not so much get caught in the middle

as he was put there by Dr. Bean-Bayog, who, in a highly questionable move, informed him of the conflict with Dr. Frankenberg as soon as it occurred. "I told him [the] staff thought I was overinvolved and wanted me to pull back," she wrote. She raised the issue again three days later even though his initial reaction had been one of alarm: "What do they know? How could they make it even worse?" he had asked her.

At other points during his hospitalization, she "told him he might be right about the staff not liking him" and that she was "annoyed at the rudeness of the McLean staff," and she asked him repeatedly, "Are you angry with Dr. Frankenberg?"

His anger, in fact, was often directed at Dr. Bean-Bayog. Because he needed her so much. Because he wanted her so much. Her notes during this hospitalization are peppered with his pleas for her to "let me go" and to "leave me alone."

When the intensity of her relationship with Paul Lozano was questioned by Dr. Frankenberg, Dr. Bean-Bayog told her that she "had had various discussions about him with consultants and was scheduled to see both Dr. [Gerald] Adler and Dr. [Dan] Buie," according to her notes. But there is no record of her seeking formal consultation in this case until McLean challenged her therapy. And, even then, there is some question as to whether she was seeking a second opinion or self-justification.

In response to Dr. Frankenberg's concerns, Dr. Bean-Bayog agreed to consult with Dr. Buie, a senior psychoanalyst in Boston. She asked Dr. Buie to review only that aspect of her therapy that had been called into question: her "overinvolvement." According to Dr. Buie, she did not tell him about the role-playing or the toys or the sexual attraction that had emerged in the therapy. Dr. Buie did not meet the patient or review his medical records. The conclusions he drew were based only on what Dr. Bean-Bayog chose to tell him.

Indeed, Dr. Bean-Bayog actually wrote the summary of their conversation about her therapy and had Dr. Buie sign it after he agreed that it accurately reflected his view.

"The patient shouldn't lose you, for goodness sake. You have a flexibility in treating him which includes the frequent visits, seeing him for deferred payment, and bringing him to the hospital yourself which is capable of being seen as overinvolved by other people but which I think is working," the letter said. "I think the work sounds very good. Not the kind of work everyone would agree on, including some people at McLean."

Her selective reporting, however, caused one discrepancy in Dr. Buie's letter. He told her he feared the McLean staff would let Paul Lozano know of the professional disagreement about his course of therapy. "If the hospital were to tell him that his work with you is bad for him that would be very countertherapeutic. He shouldn't have to lose you or the hospital. If they are at odds or incompatible it would be terribly unfortunate for him." Dr. Bean-Bayog had neglected to tell Dr. Buie that she herself had informed Paul Lozano early and often of the division of opinion.

Dr. Adler, as it happened, was not her consultant; he was her personal analyst. According to Dr. Adler, the only discussion she had with him about the Lozano case, outside the privileged setting of her own therapy, concerned nothing more than the frequency of their sessions. Dr. Adler remembers only that it "seemed to be in the ballpark of very good work with a desperate suicidal patient." Dr. Adler did not examine Paul or review his medical records. Dr. Bean-Bayog did not tell Dr. Adler about the role-playing or the baby books or the sexual attraction, at least not as a consultant. What she told him during her own therapy is confidential.

Dr. Frankenberg asked Dr. Shevert Frazier, the head of McLean Hospital at the time, to see Paul as well. Dr. Frazier met with Paul twice and told Dr. Bean-Bayog, according to her office notes, that the patient was being "manipulative and seductive" and using the therapy for "gratification" and that he would like to meet with her to discuss her approach to the case.

Dr. Bean-Bayog appears to have been mystified and a little annoyed by this interest in her therapy. "Finally reached Dr. Frazier who said that he thought the patient needed some kind of protection from the intensity/ regression in the relationship with me, but he wanted longer to talk about it. I found the consultation without discussing the patient at all with me, and Dr. Frankenberg's refusal to tell me the recommendation, puzzling. Who was the consultation for? Dr. Frankenberg?"

It apparently did not occur to Dr. Bean-Bayog that the consultation might have been for the benefit of the patient. It is similarly unclear what her purpose was in telling Paul yet again about the hospital's reservations about her treatment, especially after Dr. Buie's warning. Paul had a predictable reaction: "He got upset, afraid regarding the conflict/split. Afraid he'd lose me."

In Dr. Frankenberg's view, Paul was exhibiting symptoms of borderline personality disorder, a serious psychiatric condition that can carry a prognosis nearly as grave as that for schizophrenia. Mental disturbances thought to be "on the border" between neurosis and psychosis are classified as borderline. The severity of the illness varies from patient to patient. Some retain responsible jobs; others are permanently incapacitated.

In psychiatry, where diagnosis is as much art as science, few conditions generate more debate than borderline personality disorder, especially when the condition is detected in patients known to be suffering from a major affective disorder, such as depression. There is substantial overlap between the symptoms of BPD and depression: impulsivity, identity problems, suicidal behavior, feelings of emptiness, anger, and fear of abandonment.

The difficulty of diagnosis in borderline cases is matched only by the extreme polarization of views about treatment. According to two dominant and competing views, therapists should either set strict limits or throw out all limits in dealing with borderlines, who are often dependent, demanding, and manipulative. Complicating the issue for the patient, who might want to see some data supporting the efficacy of one or the other approach, research into so-called personality disorders has barely begun.

In addition to her other disagreements with Dr. Frankenberg, Dr. Bean-Bayog was certain Paul Lozano was not a borderline. "Borderline Personality Disorder and Character Disorder have been suggested," she wrote in her notes. "I don't think so because of his capacity for empathy and his moral character: his superego is enormous and punitive, not absent. I tend to think of him as having had a depression in infancy, and child abuse, resulting in considerable additional depression, neurotic and characterological."

From her diagnosis, she developed a startling speculative theory about the conflict between herself and Dr. Frankenberg, and she found the source of the problem not in her actions but in Paul Lozano's unconscious. "I realized he had replicated his family structure in the split he set up between her and me. She is the mother, physically and sexually abusing him. I am probably Pilar, who dotes on him, and the rest of the staff are sibs who tortured him and vice versa," she wrote.

She did not share this unconfirmed theory with the McLean staff or Dr. Frankenberg, who says she never heard from Dr. Bean-Bayog during Paul Lozano's two-month hospitalization that she was considering the possibility that he had been a childhood victim of sexual abuse. For the first time, that spring, she broached the subject of sexual abuse with Paul. "Explained the split, family replica. He was interested. I guess it does feel like that—kind of familiar," she wrote in her notes.

To encourage his thinking along this line, Dr. Bean-Bayog gave Paul an article from the previous month's issue of *Psychiatric Annals,* headlined PSYCHOLOGICAL DAMAGE ASSOCIATED WITH EXTREME EROTICISM IN YOUNG CHILDREN. His response was vague, at best. It "might explain something, how I never could get close to someone, have a woman as a friend, had to stay away," he told Dr. Bean-Bayog. "I never knew what happened, just that something awful— But I'm beginning to understand a little."

At another point, he referred to the article and asked, "I tried to forget that, didn't I?"

When he expressed confusion and guilt about his sexual attraction for her and his fear that she would leave him because of it, Dr. Bean-Bayog wrote him a note, referring him back to the article on sexual abuse.

> When you think I'll leave because of it that is probably a memory of what happened when your mother got depressed. It is not coming from me. You might go read that article. People work through problems like these in treatment.

But Paul Lozano appeared far from sure that spring that anything untoward had happened with his mother when he was a boy. It was Dr. Bean-Bayog who wrote in her notes that she "thought he was pushing himself into the next issue, abuse memories, when he couldn't tell if his mom was also his girlfriend. I wasn't mixed up. It wasn't his job to ask me out. He was scared I'd leave him, scared of his own excitement, scared I'd get excited. [I] told him I thought early on something had gone wrong with mother. Do you think? Not sure. Only data we have is our experience here. But maybe partly why you're suicidal and terrified of relationship. He went blank. Asked if I'd pushed him too far, trespassed some boundary? Maybe."

His doubts surfaced that spring whenever Dr. Bean-Bayog raised the subject of sexual abuse by his mother. "We've talked about how you were raped as a child," she said during one session.

"I can't think about it," he replied.

"No, you're feeling it," she told him.

"I can't think that about her," he said of his mother.

"These things I'm thinking aren't really real," he said on another day.

"Memories," the psychiatrist told him. "Real in your head."

On yet another occasion that spring, she told him things he had not remembered about his childhood. "Can speculate what happened with your mother. Psychotically depressed. Overstim[ulated]. Pilar taking over."

"This was done to you, sometime, this devaluing, shaming when you were too young to protect yourself," she wrote during a later session.

Finally, Paul told her, "Sometimes I think you know something I don't."

According to Dr. Frankenberg, all this pushing and prodding occurred without any consultation with the McLean staff. Dr. Bean-Bayog kept them in the dark about her sexual abuse theory even as she forced her patient to confront it daily.

After Paul called his mother from the locked psychiatric ward on Mother's Day, he told Dr. Bean-Bayog he "felt guilty about saying negative things about her to others." He did not tell his mother where he was.

Her patient's discomfort notwithstanding, Dr. Bean-Bayog was not to be dissuaded. She asked Paul "whether there was a sexual component to his experience of being hospitalized, like being molested." When his response was noncommittal—"he got silent, speechless, withdrawn, despairing, sad"—she spun out her own interpretation. "I said I pushed him about it because these might be part of the feelings that dragged him off buildings."

The lack of confirmation for an abuse diagnosis does not disturb many psychoanalysts, who hark back to Freud, in defense of speculation over fact finding.

"Careful investigation of Freud's early cases reveals that he relied heavily on reconstruction, often highly speculative and at times almost forced upon the patient, of supposed early and nonremembered sexual traumas," Bennet Simon wrote in his 1992 article "Receptivity Is the Key to Successful Treatment of Highly Traumatized Patients."

But it was also Freud who later recanted his seduction theory and who warned against an oversimplified view of the unconscious. "What a measure of self-complacency and thoughtlessness must be possessed by anyone who can, on the shortest acquaintance, inform a stranger who is entirely ignorant of the tenets of analysis that he is attached to his mother by incestuous ties, that he harbors wishes for the death of his wife, whom he appears to love, and that he conceals an intention of betraying his superior, and so on!" he wrote in 1913 in his essay "On Beginning the Treatment."

But once Dr. Bean-Bayog had made her diagnosis, all roads led to sexual abuse. When Paul became angry with her, it frightened him because it "doesn't seem consistent with feelings I have about you." She concluded in her notes that he was reliving an experience from the past. "That was problem as child: beautiful love affair and terrible betrayal."

Toward the end of May, full of shame and self-loathing, Paul Lozano decided, at the urging of the McLean staff, to let his family know where he was. He had been telephoning them each week as usual, but he still had said nothing about his illness. Finally he called Pilar and told her that he was in the hospital. Concerned and frightened, Pilar said she and their mother would come as soon as they could arrange transportation.

As soon as he hung up Paul became anxious. He was worried that he had hurt them, that they would see him as a failure, that they would not understand. Hadn't Pilar just told him, "I'll talk to them; we'll get you out"? How could he let them see him like this?

Paul "was miserable about this phone call afterward and accused himself of torturing his family," Dr. Frankenberg noted in his chart.

But by now, based on nothing more than Paul Lozano's tentative reaction to her speculative diagnosis of sexual abuse, Dr. Bean-Bayog had identified his family as the torturers. She had no interest in meeting them, even with her patient's consent. To do so, she and others in the psychoanalytic community argue, could suggest to a patient that the therapist is open to other interpretations of the past, an openness that could jeopardize the therapeutic alliance.

"Overall, the most important requirement for working with patients with real trauma histories is the analyst's receptivity to the patient's story as it unfolds," Dr. Bennet Simon wrote in *The Psychodynamic Letter* in March 1992. "Without relinquishing curiosity and objective inquiry, the analyst must not question the veracity of the patient's account. If such a history unfolds, the presumption of the patient's truthfulness is fundamental to initiating and continuing treatment."

Paul initially was ambivalent about such a meeting. Dr. Bean-Bayog's office notes record Paul telling her after his mother and sister arrived in Boston that Pilar wanted to meet her. She responded that it was "not standard practice" and according to her notes he seemed "relieved." But three days later, Paul told Dr. Bean-Bayog that he felt pressured by Pilar and his mother to check out of the hospital and get back to class. On May 25, at their urging, he even filed a formal request for his release, against medical advice. The form is known as a three-day paper, so called because the hospital must accede to the request if it is not withdrawn in seventy-two hours.

Dr. Bean-Bayog recorded Paul "pleading" with her to talk to them. She did not. Instead, Dr. Bean-Bayog wrote him a note telling him that he faced a simple choice: listen to them or listen to her.

> You are caught between two belief systems. You are, while your family is here, answerable to them. That means you have to put in the three-day paper and finish in marathon style in four and a half months.
>
> That wouldn't be good for you. It would require burying the three-year-old, and he's not so cooperative anymore, and it leads to feeling despair and exhaustion and suicidal.

Dr. Bean-Bayog ended by suggesting that they inform his parents that she and Paul would go to court if necessary to keep Paul in the hospital.

But the choice was never really that stark. While he told Dr. Bean-Bayog and others repeatedly that his family was pushing him to finish medical school, her notes indicate that the family was open to a slower pace. When Paul shared with Pilar his desire to take a leave of absence that spring he told Dr. Bean-Bayog "how positive/neutral she was[,] like, why are you asking me, it's your decision." During a conversation on another day, Paul told his sister that he was torn between research and clinical medicine. "Sister supportive. As long as happy," Dr. Bean-Bayog wrote in her notes. At the least, those reports might have suggested that the high expectations about medical school were partially self-imposed.

Far from refusing Dr. Bean-Bayog permission to meet members of his family, her notes make it clear that Paul Lozano begged her during this hospitalization to talk to his mother and sister about the seriousness of his illness.

"I don't want to go back to try to finish in a year. I've been trying to please them for twenty-four years. It's part of what makes me suicidal. . . . You'll talk to them, won't you?" he pleaded.

Dr. Bean-Bayog's dogmatic avoidance of the Lozanos precluded an alliance with the family on the two fronts where, she says, Paul Lozano was most at risk for suicide: discontinuing his antidepressants and feeling pressure to finish medical school.

"There were two situations which almost invariably caused him to discontinue medication," she would say later. "One was having a conversation with anyone in his family who disapproved of his taking medication; and he would come in in antidepressant withdrawal, and I would have to figure out what was going on. And then I would ask him whether he had had contact with his family. And the other is that he would attempt to go to his rotations. And both of them made him want desperately not to be mentally ill and would cause him to deny his illness and discontinue his treatment, his drug treatment."

The doctor's avoidance of the Lozanos was out of sync with the practices of modern psychiatry. In 1985, The National Institute of Mental Health convened a Consensus Development Conference, which endorsed the biological treatment of depression in its report a year later. The panel, made up of experts in psychiatry, psychology, psychopharmacology, and internal medicine, stressed the importance of enlisting the family's help in treating a patient's depression. The panel advised that antidepressants be used "within the context of a supportive relationship among doctor, patient and family."

Paul had no record of mental illness before Harvard Medical School and, since his family was unaware of his hospitalization the previous fall, the visit by his mother and sister to McLean was their first indication of how ill Paul had become. Dr. Bean-Bayog might have helped both Paul and his family overcome their denial by explaining the biological nature of his depression and how crucial medication was to his recovery.

But instead of speaking with the Lozano family, she pulled "the three-year-old" in closer, urging him to see her as his sole source of protection and support. One note to him during that hospitalization read: "You have a disease. Give it a name for your family. You are in here because we're keeping you here. They can't take you out. Tell them it's Harvard. When you are with your family imagine that I am with you. They are only three, too, and I am bigger than all of you. You will be safe."

At every turn, the psychiatrist seems to have reinforced the image of Paul Lozano as a dependent child and of herself as an omniscient protector. When he became angry at Dr. Frankenberg and the staff, Dr. Bean-Bayog recorded her interpretation in her notes. "The boy is standing, feet planted, hands on hips, chin out. Terrified but he won't admit it." To soothe him, she urged Paul to imagine himself as her baby, riding above the scene in a pack on her back. "I told him the boy was much happier in the backpack." Paul warmed to the image. In her notes the psychiatrist wrote that the baby "likes the backpack. He can see everything, has some control, uses my hair to try to get me to go where he wants to go."

With his psychiatrist apparently intent on seeing the ties that bound the Lozanos as pathological, Paul's attempts to explain the dynamics of a close-knit Chicano family fell on deaf ears. Paul did not see himself as an independent agent the way most of his Anglo classmates did. He was part of a family; he had responsibilities to his family as well as to himself. He knew how his parents struggled financially to send him checks for rent and food and gas for his battered brown Honda Civic. He felt a responsibility to justify their sacrifice with his success. To Dr. Bean-Bayog, Paul "described cultural differences: more important to please parents, do what they want. I can't understand Anglo culture very well."

And yet, there is no indication anywhere in 986 pages of office notes that issues of class, race, and culture were ever explored in four years of therapy. Psychotherapists once argued that any well-trained therapist could counsel any patient, regardless of ethnic or cultural differences. But in 1991, the American Psychological Association urged therapists to avoid clinical misjudgments by educating themselves about other cultures. The fourth edition of the *Diagnostic and Statistical Manual of Mental Disorders,* the bible of psychiatric diagnosis, also includes notes on "cultural considerations."

An alliance, or at least a meeting, with someone in his family might have helped Dr. Bean-Bayog understand some of the tensions between Paul Lozano's working-class Chicano background and the atmosphere of privilege he had encountered at Harvard.

Certainly these were not tensions Dr. Bean-Bayog could understand from her own experience. Whatever unhappiness Margaret Bean had felt at Radcliffe College, it was not born of the clash of cultures that Paul Lozano was experiencing at Harvard. Indeed, Radcliffe must have seemed comfortably familiar when she arrived at the women's undergraduate division of Harvard University in 1961. Fresh from St. Katherine's boarding school on a bluff above the Mississippi River in Bettencourt, Iowa, she had grown up in an atmosphere suffused with intellectual stimulation and academic achievement.

One of three children of Abigail Jane Shepard and William Bennett Bean, Margaret was their only daughter. Her father, a physician and writer, was revered as a teacher at the University of Iowa. After his death in 1989, his portrait was hung in the Department of Medicine. Her mother, a poet and painter, is remembered in Iowa City as a gracious hostess who spoke flawless French and oversaw her daughter's studies and lessons in piano and ballet.

The Bean family's contact with other races was limited largely to research interactions. Dr. Margaret Bean-Bayog's paternal grandfather spent much of his medical career in the Philippines, researching his theories of racial development.

Robert Bennett Bean was chairman of the Department of Anatomy at the University of Virginia in 1932 when he wrote *The Races of Man,* which was published by the scholarly University Society in New York and is now preserved in the Rare Book Room of the Alderman Library at the University of Virginia. The book contains ideas that Paul Lozano would have found horrifying. In the chapter titled "Mental Characteristics of the Three Races," Robert Bean wrote:

> In general the brain of the White Race is large, the convolutions are rich, with deep fissures. The mental characteristics are activity, nervous and physical vivacity, strong ambitions and passions, and highly developed idealism. There is love of amusement, sport, exploration, and adventure. Art and music are highly developed in appreciation and skill. Poetry is also cultivated to a great extent. Egoism and individuality are strong but worries and cares are excessive, and psychoses and other brain affections are not only frequent but are on the increase. The religious life of the Whites is varied and highly developed. Their industry is incessant and elaborate. They are more or less immune to certain diseases that affect the other races, but are subject to others.
>
> The brain of the Yellow-Brown Race is about medium in size, with medium to good convolutions, which are sometimes varied and deep. The mental characteristics of the Yellow-Browns need further study, but they seem to be less vivacious, with emotions and passions less evident when

strong than in the other two races. They possess moderate idealism and some love of sport, but have less spirit for exploration and adventure than the White Race. They are artistic, but their musical sense is subdued and they have little ability in poetical composition. They are less subject to cares and worries and are less varied and intense in religious feeling than is the White Race and have few psychoses and brain affections. They are industrious, endure fatigue, and are less likely to succumb to many of the infectious diseases than is either the White or the Black Race.

The size of the brain in the Black Race is below the medium of both the White and the Yellow-Browns, frequently and relatively more simple convolutions. The frontal lobes are often low and narrow, the parietal lobes voluminous, the occipital protruding. The psychic activities of the Black Race are a careless jolly vivacity, emotions and passions of short duration, and a strong and somewhat irrational egoism. Idealism, ambition, and the cooperative faculties are weak. They love amusement and sport, but have little initiative and adventurous spirit. Within limits, the Blacks are rather artistic in music, but not intellectually so. They show some ability in pictorial decorations and industrial art, but generally lack steady application. They have poetry of a low order, are rather free from lasting worries, are cursed with superstitious fears, and have much emotionalism in religion. They are only moderately affected by psychoses. Their worst diseases come from sexual promiscuity, contact with the White Race, and lack of acclimatization.

There is no evidence that her grandfather's views influenced Margaret Harvey Bean, but certainly her exposure to racial minorities was limited as a child in Iowa, one of the nation's most racially homogeneous states. But in an ironic twist worthy of Freud, the granddaughter of the author of *The Racial Anatomy of the Philippine Islanders* grew up to marry a Filipino.

After receiving Paul's telephone call, his mother and sister set out for Boston. They stayed with his roommate, Victor Gonzalez, cleaning and restocking the pantry for Paul's presumed swift return.

Watching a monster movie on television one night, Victor told Pilar, "That's how those doctors see you." Pilar did not understand the comment; she kept insisting that Paul was not sick enough to be hospitalized. "Maybe it's really frightening for family members to accept," but Paul had been terribly depressed before being hospitalized, Victor told her.

Indeed, the Lozanos' first visit to McLean was frightening. "Ominous" was how Pilar would describe it later. The grounds, bursting into spring bloom, had the surface appearance of a college campus. But the few young people they saw outside did not move with the careless gait of students with spring fever. Instead, they marched with stooped shoulders, from recreational therapy to milieu therapy, from individual psychotherapy to group, under the watchful eyes of the hospital staff.

Inside Bowditch Hall, any illusion that McLean was like a private boarding school vanished. Epifania stayed close to her daughter as they made their way through the cheerless halls on the way to the locked ward Paul Lozano now called home. The clinking of the metal keys on the nurse's chain, the sound of the tumblers as the steel doors were unbolted, made them shudder.

The sight of Paul was a relief to both his mother and sister. He looked well, even though his demeanor was a confusing mix of anger and shame and he could hardly make eye contact with his mother. He had been playing basketball in the gym to stay in shape.

Looking around the locked ward, Pilar wondered aloud what Paul was doing in a place like this. He could tell her only that he had been depressed and that Margaret thought it best that he be hospitalized for his own safety.

"Safety? Margaret?" Pilar asked. Just when would she get to meet this Margaret? she wanted to know. It was Dr. Bean-Bayog's decision whether to meet with them or not, Pilar was told both by Paul and the McLean staff.

Although Dr. Bean-Bayog refused to meet Epifania Lozano and Pilar Williams, Dr. Frankenberg did, and something immediately did not square. If Paul's family was as unsupportive as Dr. Bean-Bayog said, why had they pooled scarce financial resources to fly his mother and sister to Boston? Why was Pilar offering to move to Boston for a year if it would help Paul?

There were introductions and polite greetings all around when the meeting began, but Paul was edgy, refusing to take a seat and watchful as Dr. Frankenberg and a hospital social worker asked Pilar and Mrs. Lozano to talk about the family and Paul's childhood.

He was the youngest, pampered and spoiled, Pilar began, but driven from a very young age to achieve. The questions came fast after that, she recalled. Were the Lozanos putting pressure on Paul to be a doctor? Was it important for them that he be at Harvard? Was he the golden child? Had Mrs. Lozano pushed, pushed, pushed him to be a doctor? The staff seemed to think that the entire family had pinned all its hopes on Paul to be the successful one of the Lozanos.

Pilar said, "We kept explaining to them over and over again, you know, he's not our only accomplished family member. He may be the only one at Harvard but that doesn't make him the only accomplished, successful member of this family. We all have a little brain matter. We are not just vocationally trained. I'm sure that never registered. 'Yes, yes, yes, but you're not at Harvard,' they'd say. We never got beyond that. That was it; that was what was wrong with my brother. We pushed him."

Dr. Frankenberg did hear them, though. She would later recall that:

> Mr. Lozano's sister and mother said, over and over again, how much they loved him and how they

only wanted him to be happy, and that it didn't
matter to them whether he was at Harvard Medical
School or not; that it really didn't matter what he
did, they loved him unconditionally, they always
had, they always would.

Mr. Lozano was sarcastic and horrible. At one
point his mother started to cry and he said to me,
with extreme anger, that he hoped I was happy now
that I had made his mother cry. And, after the
meeting, he told us all that this was exactly why he
had not wanted these meetings, because the family
would say one thing in front of other people and
none of this was true; that they only said this
in front of others; that what they really wanted
was for him to graduate from Harvard Medical
School and would accept nothing less. And now
that his family had come up and said all of this
to us, we would now think that he lied about
everything.

We said that we didn't think anyone was lying
and that obviously this was a case where people
perceived things differently, and that this was
something that would have to be worked out over
time, but from our point of view, we saw no one
lying.

After the family meeting, I thought that Mr.
Lozano's family wanted us to think that they loved
him unconditionally; that Mr. Lozano wanted us
to think that that was not the case, and I had no
idea what was really going on. Probably, the truth
was somewhere in the middle, but that after one
family meeting, none of us could make any conclusions whatsoever.

Paul found the session humiliating. He felt naked, exposed, as if he and his family were on display and Dr.
Frankenberg was nothing more than a voyeur. After that
meeting, he became confrontational when she came through

the ward on daily rounds. That Pilar liked her only angered him further.

"Dr. Frankenberg tried to tell me in her own way that Margaret was overinvolved and she was uncomfortable with the relationship between my brother and his therapist," Pilar recalled. "I had the same feelings. I told Paul, 'You're getting worse. For the first time in your life, you're on drugs for emotional problems. And you're in a psychiatric hospital. So tell me, what is she doing for you?' But no one told us anything specific. The only problem they identified at that time was that we were pushing him to be a doctor. I thought, Well, that can be fixed. I'm sure they see we don't care about that.'"

When she heard accounts of the session from her patient and her colleague, Dr. Bean-Bayog was relieved she had stayed away; participating might have muddied the therapeutic waters. Unlike Dr. Frankenberg, who knew it would take more than one meeting to understand the dynamics of the Lozano family, Dr. Bean-Bayog seems to have felt she needed no contact with Pilar and Mrs. Lozano to know what was going on. She smelled a cover-up, she wrote in her notes.

"I love them and my sister dearly, but we see things differently," Paul told Dr. Bean-Bayog after the meeting. One of the things that had made him furious at Pilar was that she denied any memory of his attempting suicide at age six by swallowing a bottle of aspirin.

"You predicted if I met with them I'd think you were crazy," Dr. Bean-Bayog wrote.

"I know what I remember and they tell me things I don't remember and didn't want to," Paul complained.

But Dr. Bean-Bayog's notes from the summer before indicate that he was uncertain himself about his memories of a childhood suicide attempt. The words "don't remember" are repeated three times in her notes on July 31 as he related the incident. When he told Dr. Bean-Bayog that maybe Pilar had been right at the meeting, maybe he had been "just acting out," her notes reflect her conclusion: "Who are you kidding, that was a suicide attempt."

When he told her that he felt Pilar betrayed him by not supporting his view, Bean-Bayog concluded that he was right. "She did. She turned on you," the doctor wrote. "I have a hunch she'll have grounds to feel guilty later."

After a conversation with Dr. Frankenberg about the family session, Dr. Bean-Bayog still said nothing to Dr. Frankenberg or the hospital staff about her molestation theory.

At that point the troublesome memories Paul Lozano had shared with the hospital staff had no sexual component. Being locked in a closet, being taunted by siblings, being hit by his mother with a belt—these were memories that could signal either that he was physically and emotionally abused as a boy or that his depression was distorting common childhood experiences of parental discipline and sibling rivalry.

The rivalry that most preoccupied him that spring was the one between Margaret Bean-Bayog and Frances Frankenberg. He told Dr. Bean-Bayog about an interrogation team routine he had learned at West Point. Based on the good cop–bad cop model often used in law enforcement, the team was known at the military academy as Mutt and Jeff. "You're the nice one. Dr. Frankenberg's the mean one," he told her the day after the family meeting.

The final rupture with McLean came a few weeks later when Dr. Bean-Bayog went on vacation and, either angry or despondent, Paul talked a nurse into allowing him to go off the grounds "for ice cream." Instead, he said he drove to Boston, drank a few beers, and headed to the thirteenth floor of the Harvard School of Public Health where, he told Dr. Bean-Bayog days later, he again contemplated suicide. There were those at McLean who suspected that the incident never happened, that the story was yet another play for Margaret Bean-Bayog's attention.

No matter. The incident merely confirmed Dr. Bean-Bayog's belief that McLean could not handle her patient. It must have been a relief to both Paul and his psychiatrist when he exhausted his insurance coverage for a private psychiatric hospital and had to be transferred on June 22 to

Faulkner, a general hospital in Boston with a psychiatric wing.

When he was discharged, Dr. Frankenberg underscored her concern about Dr. Bean-Bayog in her final entry on Paul Lozano's chart. "During the hospitalization, there was some question from the Bowditch treatment team as to the usefulness of his ongoing psychotherapy. Questions were raised as to the possibility of an overinvolvement on the part of the therapist and of the intensity of the therapy and the complete dependence Mr. Lozano felt on the therapy," she wrote.

"There is an ongoing question about how much his present therapy is supporting him or rather stirring up almost inconsolable yearnings and conflictual feelings. However, he and Dr. Bean-Bayog are absolutely committed to continuing this relationship."

His dependence on his psychotherapist was noted immediately upon Paul's admission to Faulkner Hospital. But because Dr. Bean-Bayog had once again failed to disclose the regressive nature of her therapy with Paul Lozano, his dependence was taken as a symptom of an inherent character disorder rather than a possible reaction to her role-playing techniques.

In her five-page note to the Faulkner staff on Paul's admission, Dr. Bean-Bayog did not mention the mom-and-boy playacting; she did not mention the use of baby toys and books or the sexual attraction that had emerged in therapy. Without that crucial information, Dr. Robert Gregory, Paul's therapist at Faulkner, understandably interpreted Paul's reliance on his psychiatrist as a natural expression of his illness, not as a consequence of the dependency fostered by the regressive therapy. "For him she has been the dependable, nurturing female that he has always desired. When she took two weekend vacations, he felt abandoned. Paul's call to her from the thirteenth floor was a cry for attention from the woman he loved and necessitated his admission to McLean," Dr. Gregory wrote.

During the four weeks he remained at Faulkner, Paul's case was presented by Dr. Bean-Bayog and the hospital staff to Dr. Thomas G. Gutheil, a Harvard psychiatrist who conducts regular case conferences at the hospital. Again, according to Dr. Gutheil, she did not disclose any of her unorthodox psychotherapy techniques.

Paul Lozano was happier at Faulkner, where he was assigned to an unlocked ward. He remained plagued by suicidal thoughts, but they were usually restricted to the evening hours.

On June 26, he spent the entire day in bed after talking by telephone with Pilar, who had returned to Texas. His sister "expressed concern for his depression but then said it was 'exasperating' that he withdraws and she doesn't understand it," a nurse wrote in his chart.

Exasperated or not, Pilar stood by Paul. She returned to Boston to see her brother during the July Fourth weekend. Their sister Martha came as well.

Pilar was upset by the deterioration she saw in Paul in just a month. Martha was near tears when they saw him in Adams House, the psychiatric unit. He was smoking. There were cigarette butts everywhere. He was unshaven and unkempt. He would ramble on like a child and, a moment later, announce plans to wrap up medical school and launch his career.

"I never saw him smoke before. And this [medical] resident keeps coming up to the door every fifteen minutes, saying, 'Are you all right, Paul?'" Martha recalled. And I think, "Of course he is not all right. What is he doing in here with these people who are drooling and shuffling?"

Pilar was even more distraught. "I thought, Oh, my God, he is supposed to be one of these residents coming in in their lab coats looking at these people like they're bugs, you know? But he's not. He's one of the bugs now."

Paul seemed more like himself when Martha and Pilar took him out for a day pass on the Fourth of July. They piled into his old Honda Civic with Pilar behind the wheel and all of them laughing uproariously as the broken driver's-side door flew open every time they took a turn. They ate Chinese and Italian food and fresh seafood at the food stalls in Quincy Marketplace. Paul walked them through Faneuil

Hall, dropping bits of Boston history as they strolled the waterfront, the three of them arm in arm.

Disappointed that he had to be back at the hospital before the fireworks began, the trip ended on a more somber note. "For a while we forgot he was a psych patient," Martha said.

"He felt sad, but then there were reassurances from him—'I'm going to make it. I'm going to get better. Don't worry. And I'm going to go home and I'm going to do something exciting. I'm going to work with Hispanics in a hospital. This is great training that I'm getting here.' Then he would become sad again and tell us he thought he should remove himself from the medical school, maybe do research, get a Ph.D.," said Pilar.

Two days later, the three Lozano siblings met briefly with a hospital social worker. In Paul's chart, the social worker noted the warmth between brother and sisters. Paul, she wrote, "appeared to interact in a healthy way with sibs, laughing with them at jokes."

But the session was unsatisfying for Pilar and Martha. "Again no one said anything to us about what was really going on," said Martha. Pilar recounted one frustrating exchange with staff members:

"What is the matter? Why isn't anybody doing anything? What is wrong with my brother?" Martha asked.

"He's very depressed," a staff member replied.

"But why is he depressed?" Pilar persisted.

"We don't know. Do *you* know why he is depressed?" the staff member asked in turn.

"No, I don't know why he is depressed," Pilar cried. "That's why he is in here!"

The conversations with the staff were frustratingly circular, but those with Paul were increasingly accusatory. "Margaret says you're always pushing me around. Margaret says you're pushing me too hard. Margaret says that I don't have to please you," he told his sisters.

"How are you going to get better if you're locked up for five or six weeks? How are you going to get stronger?" Pilar asked him.

"I'm not strong enough to cope. Margaret says I'm not

strong enough. I have to stay here. I have to stay here until she makes me better," he said.

"Well, can we speak to Margaret?" Martha asked.

"Margaret says no," he told them. "No one believes in me. Only Margaret believes in me."

"Can I please speak to Margaret?" Pilar pleaded.

"No, you can't, and if you do that I'm going to be very hurt and very angry with you, because Margaret does not want that. If you cause her to leave me because you made her angry, then it's going to be your fault."

The sisters left the ward, feeling defeated. Downstairs in the lobby, Martha's eye caught sight of a pretty picture frame in the gift shop window. As the sisters admired it, a voice behind them addressed someone as "Dr. Bean." Martha and Pilar whipped around fast enough to see a middle-aged blond woman striding past them through the lobby.

Pilar called out, "Dr. Bean?"

Dr. Bean-Bayog turned briefly, long enough to make eye contact with the two sisters, but she kept walking. Martha ran after her. "Dr. Bean, please wait, wait!" Martha shouted across the lobby.

In response, Margaret Bean-Bayog picked up her pace and strode straight through the doors without looking back.

Other Buildings

Chapter

4

Paul Lozano was furious with the McLean staff when he was transferred to Faulkner in late June. As he saw it, tying him to his bed was abusive, and efforts to separate him from his psychiatrist cruel. He was certain the staff thought he was a monster, a liar, a deviant personality. Hadn't Dr. Bean-Bayog told him, "I think you may be right about the staff not liking you"?

His greatest fury was reserved for Dr. Frances Frankenberg. He wished he could exact some retribution for what he perceived as her abusive treatment of him and for her interference in his relationship with Dr. Bean-Bayog and her diagnosis of him as a borderline personality.

During passes from the hospital, he had read articles in psychiatric journals about borderlines and railed against Dr. Frankenberg's suggestion that he fit the diagnostic description. "They really hated me," he complained to Dr. Bean-Bayog after his transfer to Faulkner. "Someone should tie them down for a day and see how they react to it. I don't understand why they treated me that way." He was angry enough to sue Dr. Frankenberg, to rape her, to kill her, he told Dr. Bean-Bayog.

Dr. Bean-Bayog designed an extraordinary visual tool to help her patient still the voices of those who would interfere with their relationship. On a three-by-five-inch index card, she drew a cork with some hand-lettered instructions: "Use to stopper F.F.'s mouth (or anyone else who needs it)."

Encouraging Paul to vent his anger at Dr. Frankenberg and the McLean staff had the effect of pulling the circle tighter than ever around Margaret Bean-Bayog and her patient. With her critics symbolically silenced, the relationship between Margaret and Paul intensified. For weeks he had alluded to his sexual attraction to her. In the summer of 1987, he began to be more direct. "I'm having those feelings now. Can't help noticing you physically . . . thinking of your husband. Guess jealousy describes it. Do your other patients do this? They must," he told her before launching into a description of "wanting to undress and touch and caress and then make love," according to her office notes.

"Do you mind if I tell you this?" he asked during a session that summer. "I don't care what other people think. You know what I'm going to tell you."

"Tell me," she said.

"I love you," he declared.

While Paul was in McLean, Dr. Bean-Bayog had moved her private practice to a new office a half mile from her original suite in Cambridge. This one she furnished with a couch for her patients undergoing psychoanalysis.

"Anyone ever use the couch?" he asked coyly during a visit there while on a pass from Faulkner, where Dr. Bean-Bayog regularly visited Paul as well.

"How do you mean use?" she asked.

"I've had this thought before but never said out loud or allowed myself to realize. I want to pull you over there," he told her, noting that the soundproof double doors would ensure privacy.

"I see the Boy's face if I ever touched him," she replied.

"I know if that ever happened it would destroy everything that has gone on before, but I'm ignoring that. . . . You're neat," he said.

In her notes, Margaret Bean-Bayog scribbled a parenthetical comment on Paul Lozano's proposal. "Not that don't want to," she wrote.

"If we slept together all the work we've done together would go all to smash," she told him.

"I guess it would," he said.

Declining sex but signaling that the desire was mutual, the psychiatrist wrote, "You can want to, you can make me want to, but we can stay in our chairs and keep Baby safe."

Even as the therapy sessions were becoming more erotic, Dr. Bean-Bayog continued to reinforce the notion that she was Paul Lozano's mother and he was her baby, her boy. When his anxiety increased as his release date from Faulkner approached, she brought more children's books and other transitional objects into the hospital to soothe him. She left notes, addressing each aspect of his personality:

"Baby can have blanket and *Goodnight Moon.*"

"Toddler can have *Owl at Home.*"

"Boy can have *Alexander and the Terrible Day* and *Where the Wild Things Are.*"

"Med student can have NEJM [*New England Journal of Medicine*] articles and Dr. Yates's article about sexually abused children being treatable."

While on a pass from Faulkner, Paul told her, he had gone to a topless bar in the Combat Zone, Boston's adult entertainment district. "Don't worry," he teased, "they can't hold a candle."

"What about the Boy?" she asked, causing an abrupt shift in Paul's demeanor.

How do you feel right now? Dr. Bean-Bayog wanted to know. "Sad?" she asked. "A little deflated?"

Paul Lozano smiled at the sexual double entendre. His flirtatiousness was a family trait, he told her. "My sister in her office gets the women up in arms," he said of Pilar. "She gets more attention from men than just her looks would account for."

Their dad was a flirt, too, Paul continued. "My mother used to be horribly jealous," he recalled. "I get it from Pilar, I guess. I think I've always had it."

Instead of seeing benign cultural differences, Dr. Bean-

Bayog again saw pathology. "It sounds like there was a *lot* of heterosexual overstimulation going on all over your family," she told him.

"I wondered about Pilar, my father," Paul said.

"You think he may have sexually abused her?" she asked.

"I can't . . . maybe someone . . . I want to change the subject," he said.

"You already did. We were talking about how you're seductive in here and then you talked about it with other women and then Pilar and then your father," she pushed.

"Guess I don't want to talk about it," he said.

"Okay for now," she said, "but something very intense and stimulating is happening in here and we've got to understand it or it will hurt the Boy."

Dr. Bean-Bayog's notes of the next session refer to their conversation about seductiveness. A comment in her notes reads, "told about my fantasy of being a child, molested by him. Usually those fantasies reflect something going on with both of us. . . ." Although she would later deny ever sharing her sexual fantasies with Paul, the language used suggests that she may have done so on at least this occasion.

Dr. Bean-Bayog seems to have been alluding to the process of transference and countertransference. Transference occurs when a patient unconsciously projects onto his therapist feelings and attitudes that were originally associated with important figures from childhood, such as parents or siblings. Countertransference is the psychiatrist's emotional reaction to the patient.

It was during this period that Dr. Bean-Bayog began to write down explicit sexual and sadomasochistic fantasies about Paul Lozano. These were not her personal feelings, she would later insist, only an expression of her countertransference. Many are based on her theory that Paul was abused by his family as a child.

> You are in a cold rage. You have me in restraints.
> This time, metal on a wooden floor. There is no
> sexual feeling. You tear open my shirt and pull one
> breast out of its bra cup and pinch my nipple as

hard as you can. I get pale and my pupils dilate and shortly I begin to scream.

You get furious: "You said you wanted to know." You whack me across the face and yell at me to shut up. You continue to pinch me. I am crying but trying not to. Then you turn me over and clamp me back in. I do not resist. You begin to strap me across the back, behind and legs with a heavy leather strap. You continue and continue until the new blows fall on the tender old swollen welts. The pain spreads and suffuses my entire experience.

Underneath it I am calmer though, accepting, welcoming it, even. And sad, terribly sad, for the baby, the boy, the eight-year-old. It is as though you are not hurting me. This is merely information, transmitted experience. This is what they did to you. This is how it felt. I could not protect you then. But, somehow, now I have insinuated myself between you and them as the pain is blocked and flows through me, and I am unalterably serene.

After his release from Faulkner Hospital on July 27, Paul Lozano continued to see Dr. Bean-Bayog for therapy three times a week. By then, her sexual abuse theory was the motor driving her therapy.

On August 21, Paul arrived at her office elated, having secured job offers from two research laboratories. He had decided to take a year off from medical school, and the prospect of interesting work with Harvard anesthesiologists at the Boston Biomedical Research Institute eased his anxiety about interrupting his medical training.

He was "all cheered up, chatty," Dr. Bean-Bayog noted. But his mood soon plummeted when she turned the discussion to sexual abuse.

Paul told her that her questions "felt like Pilar or my mother almost goading me."

"Tormenting you," Dr. Bean-Bayog corrected.

He asked for his baby blanket and began to act like a three-year-old. He told her "the twenty-five-year-old wants to do something he shouldn't." He began to hyperventilate and she had him breathe into a paper bag.

"I explained what was going on—made sense out of my experience," she wrote in her notes. "He and I were in the middle of a perversion, like how the love between him as a baby and his mother got distorted, destroyed, twisted, poisoned by her molesting and abusing. That was what he felt was happening and I had [a] parallel experience, raw, overwhelming, him molesting me, me molesting him. Shared mother-child incest fantasy: very raw but that's what I think she did."

Paul became "agitated, aroused, furious, regressed," when she raised these theories with him. "I don't remember. I don't want to remember," he protested.

She wrote that this was "too much to deal with at once, but this is the stuff that makes you suicidal, that got you into McLean—that repeated abuse by mother."

Paul was adamant. "I don't remember. I don't remember what you said."

"Maybe that's just as well," she wrote.

It was not until September 24 that her relentless prodding finally paid off. Paul had seen a statue of a mother and infant in a courtyard at Massachusetts General Hospital. The mother's nakedness upset him.

Dr. Bean-Bayog interpreted his response as a reaction to his mother's alleged sexual abuse. "We could put a jacket on the mother, protect the baby," she said. "What might happen?"

"She might touch me, rub me," he said. "When I was little my mom, I remember seeing her do it to my nephews, changing them or bathing them she would kind of kiss and fondle."

"The little boy's penis?" she asked.

"Yes," he said, adding, "I could remember her doing it to me if I tried really hard but I think I don't want to."

Having no confirmation beyond such vague statements by her patient, Dr. Bean-Bayog proceeded as though Mrs. Lozano's sexual exploitation of Paul as a baby was an established fact. Having convinced her patient that it would undermine his therapy for her to meet his family, she closed the one door that might have helped her understand the real dynamics of his childhood.

While it is certainly true that abusive families have every incentive to deny that a child was victimized, it is a fiction that there are no "data" available to the therapist beyond what a patient tells her. If, for example, Dr. Bean-Bayog had spoken to one of Paul Lozano's siblings, perhaps one not suspected of having tormented him, she might have heard another perspective.

Convinced by what she took to be evidence that Paul Lozano was wrestling with abuse memories, Dr. Bean-Bayog intensified her role-playing as his mother. "The entire focus of the treatment was to help him discriminate between his fear that I would behave like the expected abusive parent, and the fact, which was that I did not. It was repeatedly discussed throughout the entire process that what he needed was a nonabusive figure," she would say later.

It was during late summer and fall that Dr. Bean-Bayog developed what she labeled the Handy, Multipurpose Emergency and Reference Flash Card Deck. A stack of three-inch-by-five-inch index cards, the deck included a top card with instructions for Paul Lozano: "Run over these cards every day until you know them all by heart and are starting to believe them."

The messages on the cards reinforced the mother-and-child role-playing, reassured him that she would return to him from business trips and vacations, and warned him of the dangers of too much contact with his family.

> You can too feel and act like a three-year-old when you're twenty-five.
> You can curl up with the blanket, the sweater, the pound puppy, all the notes I've written you and all the books. You can breast feed and be cozy.
> No one can take those feelings from you.

1. Do NOT drink.

2. Do not call your family. If they call you, be brief. Notice what they are doing to you. Don't let them do in our boy. Call me ASAP [as soon as possible] or PRN [as needed].

3. If you begin to believe you can't be three years old it's because you're losing contact with me. Tell those voices to shut up.

4. If you still feel depressed and self-destructive, call Donna [a nurse at Faulkner Hospital] or Faulkner.

5. Do NOT hurt yourself.

The three-year-olds are on the march.

It's fine if you hate me and are furious. You don't have to like my leaving the three-year-old stranded.

I'm your Mom. I'll always be your Mom. This won't go on forever. We'll both survive. It's okay to be scared. It's OK to hate it and me. You don't have to do anything. You don't have to know what to do. You are just a baby. Babies don't have to take care of anybody. You won't disappear. You won't get all covered and shut in. You'll be OK. This is hard work. You're getting better.

I'm still your Mom. I'm your Mom. Calm down. I'm not leaving. You have an appointment Thursday 6:00. Don't play in the street. Love Dr. B.

I love you very, very much too, even when I leave you. Remember that too, please. Love, Dr. B. and the Bean Bear. [Dr. Bean Bear was their pet name for the teddy bear dressed in surgical scrubs.]

Some of the flash cards contain a negative thought on one side with a positive message to counter it on the reverse side. Dr. Bean-Bayog says that these cards were dictated to her by Paul Lozano and that she merely transcribed his troublesome thoughts and the replies he needed to hear from his "mom" to comfort him between therapy sessions.

> Are you my Mom? Yes. Do you love me? Yes. Then why are you hurting me like this?
> [On reverse]: I don't want to hurt you and don't mean to. Therapy hurts. I think you are remembering awful things.

> Do I love you? Yes.
> [On reverse]: Absolutely. Lots. I am keeping you in my heart.

> What about when you hate me and just want to hurt me. You let them torture me at McLean. You PUT me in there. You helped them. What do you care?
> [On reverse]: I'm so sorry. I don't want anything to hurt you, ever, ever, ever. I want to hold you and protect you and keep you safe always. I'm so sorry you have been hurt so much. I'd be mad, too, but that's less important than the love.

In her notes to him, in the flash cards and in the inscriptions on the baby books, Margaret Bean-Bayog repeatedly assured Paul Lozano of her love. She says he understood that the love was coming from a symbolic role-playing mother, not from her personally, but since the messages were sometimes signed "Dr. Bean," as well as "Mom," there was plenty of room for confusion on the part of a very dependent and infatuated patient.

> I'm an ungrateful wretch and deserve everything bad that happens to me.
> [On reverse]: Actually, you're very appreciative and grateful and considerate except when you're working something through. You make me feel incredibly special and valued and loved and important. I hope you feel that way too.

You're going to suck me in and make me confused and weird. I'm staying here.

[On reverse]: OK. You have the switch. You can turn it off any time. But I do love you. I have to wait till you can get close safely. I can wait.

I disappoint everyone. You'll catch on when you smarten up.

[On reverse]: Not me. Not yet. I think you're terrific. Besides, this relationship is tough and durable and flexible and can handle anything you can dream up: despair, hate, guilt, need, sadness, childishness, whatever. Try me. I pass every test.

What if I put you in a predicament and you start to resent me?

[On reverse]: I don't resent you. I resent them (McLean's). You make me happy. Over and over, every day. I'm lucky to have you and I never forget it.

I HATE you! You are such a BITCH!

[On reverse]: I'm hate proof. You can't make me disappear THAT way. Go on. Do it some more. I don't budge. It doesn't work. I'm still here.

What about when I either hate you or feel really terrible about hating you because of all you've done for me instead of just letting you hug me?

[On reverse]: You are pretty incompetent and inexperienced as a hater. You need practice and work. Set aside ten minutes a day to hate me. At night, probably. During that time, do not allow yourself to have any positive, friendly thoughts about me. Think how you could punish me, various ways to make me feel as bad as I've made you feel. Just remember I'm holding you the whole time. Your hate doesn't hurt me. Just gives me exercise for the love.

What shall I do if it feels like forever?

[On reverse]: Sometimes it will. It's long but time is passing and I'm coming back. Get mad. Hate me very hard. Devise appropriate retribution for me. Be sad. Miss me. Remember all the close, happy times. There will be more. Lots. I miss you too. Every day.

Paul Lozano followed her instructions. He did "get mad" and he did "devise appropriate retribution" for her. In 56 of the 211 sessions or phone calls she recorded in her office notes between October 1, 1987, and December 8, 1988, he talked with Dr. Bean-Bayog in graphic detail about sex, rape, sodomy, and torture—themes that grew out of the anger and humiliation he had felt when he was tied to his bed by his hands and feet at McLean Hospital.

"You were the person in restraints, and quite angry and struggling quite a bit," he said in relaying a fantasy he had been having that fall. "You had no control over the situation. I guess I bent over and asked you how you were doing. 'Gee, I'm sorry, had to be done,' and well I guess I started touching you in a tender but rather sensuous fashion. I started undressing you. You were in my favorite dress, blue cotton. Anyway, I took it off and began kissing you and touching your breasts and pressing you. You were still struggling against the restraints but that seemed to excite me all the more."

He had not had a sexual relationship with a woman since he broke up with another medical student in 1986, the event that precipitated his depression and his return to Dr. Bean-Bayog that summer. A year later, his sexual energy was channeled into fantasies about his psychiatrist.

As part of her reparenting strategy, Dr. Bean-Bayog made herself available to Paul Lozano whenever he needed her. He called her late at night at her home in Lexington and at her summer house on Cape Cod. When she was going to be away at her beach house one weekend, she wrote Paul a note reassuring him that he could call her. "If you need to see me it's only a little over an hour by car. I will be back. It is OK to hate it. Remember when the baby has a tantrum, he needs a hug not a beating."

When she went to professional meetings in Chicago, Phoenix, or New Orleans, she left the number at her hotel. She even gave him her parents' telephone number when she went to Iowa City to visit.

He used them all. Margaret's father answered the telephone in Iowa, and Paul reported being taken aback when he identified himself as Dr. Bean. She took notes while Paul talked about his sexual desire for her. "Guess Bear [is] having thoughts of tying you up and doing things to you, but I can't tell you because you're at home," he told her. "Silly. You aren't your parents' little girl anymore."

In response to Paul Lozano's fantasies, Dr. Bean-Bayog experienced explicit fantasies of her own about him. She contends that the fifty-five pages of graphic sexual stories she wrote about Paul Lozano were a means of managing his intense transference and gaining insight into her patient's relationship with his mother.

Two of her fantasies, each of which runs on for seven handwritten pages describing oral and vaginal sex, are called "Mutt" and "Jeff," after the Mutt and Jeff interrogation team routine that Paul had learned at West Point and discussed with Dr. Bean-Bayog in therapy.

> You stand at my feet, staring at my vagina. I am embarrassed and ashamed. I pull to close my legs closed but I can't. You smile. Suddenly, you notice my vagina is shining wet. You can't believe it. You love it. You kneel down between my widely separated knees and stroke it. I writhe, aroused and humiliated.
>
> "Lubricated all right." You make some notes. "Enjoys restraints. Manipulative and seductive." To me you say, "If you think you can get away with being seductive with me, think again. I hate seductive people."
>
> Tired of waiting, you kneel down beside me and reach for my breast. I tense for the pain. You laugh

and begin stroking it gently. What you want is to give it enough of an erection so you can get a good grip on it, but I don't know that.

Despite the intensity of the sexual feelings being discussed in Paul Lozano's therapy sessions, Dr. Bean-Bayog never considered referring him to another therapist. She says she discussed her fantasies with Dr. Gutheil, but he says he has no memory of such a conversation. She says she talked to Dr. Gerald Adler, her analyst, about them. But if she did, he says, she did so in the context of her personal analysis and that is a privileged communication between doctor and patient. She says she told Dr. Susan C. Adelman and Dr. Beth Brownlow, two psychiatrist friends, about her fantasies, but neither woman billed her for such a consultation and Dr. Bean-Bayog concedes those conversations were more informal than supervisory.

Her sexual fantasies were just one of many problematic areas where Margaret Bean-Bayog decided to go it alone. At no time during the four years she treated Paul Lozano did she ever seek a professional consultation with any colleague to discuss either the propriety or the likely effectiveness of her role-playing technique for treating Paul Lozano's depression.

Indeed, the role of psychiatric "consultants" throughout this case raises serious questions about their use and abuse. If a psychiatrist tells her analyst she is having sexual fantasies about a patient, is that a consultation? If a psychiatrist tells a friend who happens also to be a psychiatrist over coffee that she is having sexual fantasies about a patient, is that a consultation? And if a psychiatrist consults a senior colleague but then withholds crucial information about the nature of the therapy, is she really seeking a second opinion in good faith?

Dr. Adler concedes that the whole area of his consultation in this case is pretty confusing, because most of his conversations with Dr. Bean-Bayog occurred during her own confidential therapy sessions. It is something of an arbitrary decision to determine which parts of those conversations were therapeutic and which parts consultative. "There's a blurred boundary somewhere, but there is a distinction," Dr. Adler said, though he was unable to articulate it.

What was certain, however, was that Paul Lozano's sexual desire for his psychiatrist preoccupied more and more of his sessions with Dr. Bean-Bayog. He asked her directly to have sex with him at least four times that she recorded: "Want to really have sex with you. I'm tired of talking about it," he told her. "It would be the same perversion with your mother and the work would all go to smash. You'd end up killing yourself," she replied. But by now, her own erotic fantasies about Paul Lozano were filling up pages and pages of lined notepaper.

In those handwritten fantasies, Paul Lozano is consistently cast as her sadistic lover. She casts herself as either a naive virgin or a compliant whore. In one fantasy, she divides her personality in much the same manner that he and she split his persona in therapy, into younger and older versions of the same self:

> There was something about what I did Thursday that left me uncomfortable. One of me was left out, and she's important. You actually ought to have met her first before her older sister found you. I want you to meet the chaste girl.
>
> When I was twenty-one I couldn't have made love to you like that. I didn't know how. But more, I still wanted to preserve my chastity. . . .
>
> Finally, one day you appeared and now I am ready. It is about to happen.
>
> I am head over heels in love with you. You are the sun and the moon and the stars, and I've seen you walk on water. I can not figure out how I could be so lucky. You are the person I want to awaken me to this whole world, to initiate me, bring me inside and show it to me, share it with me.
>
> I also know I will never regret it, that I will always be glad and grateful and the memory will always be sunlit.

But I am afraid and shy. Afraid of my own response to you, afraid I won't please you, afraid you won't find me beautiful. I am so vulnerable. My body is suddenly so sensitive. . . .

. . . my chest is heaving and I am trembling. You continue watching me struggle with it. You move your hand on my neck, fingering my hair, and then down to the base of my throat, and up, and then down again. . . . You do not touch my breasts. Can you not tell that my nipples are aching for your hand? "Please, oh, please, touch them," I beg you. "Please, please." You do not. You continue to caress my neck with one hand. I am furious with desire. "Touch me. Kiss me, damn you, please touch my breasts." . . . After I am alone, undressing slowly, I find that my whole vaginal area and down my legs is wet, slippery. I dip one fingertip into it, and wonderingly smell it, and taste it. It is sweet.

Other, sadomasochistic fantasies are preoccupied with issues of power and control. In these stories, the lovers alternately beat and caress each other after taking turns clamping each other, hand and feet, into metal restraints anchored to a bare floor in a locked room.

Victimization and humiliation—increasingly the themes of Paul Lozano's therapy sessions—are recurrent themes in all of Margaret Bean-Bayog's fantasies as well:

I can't remember how to be ashamed or afraid. I feel all the more bonded to you. I see your erection and the expression on your face of sheer sensuality, lust, enjoyment of your total power over me, and satisfaction.

"Have you learned your lesson yet? (You call me a string of things in Spanish) Or do I still have to teach you some manners?"

I am suddenly possessed by a suicidal desire to provoke you again. I want to laugh. I want you to keep on punishing and arousing and humiliating me. I would do anything to be able to keep that expression on your face. Anything.

After a long time, I hear your footfall and the key in the lock. You are tired and angry. I am so happy to see you, my eyes are shining. That makes you angrier. You slap me and pinch my nipple, call me a few names. I react to the pain, but I cannot keep from smiling again. I want to jump up and down.

I wonder if I had wanted you to hurt me. It occurs to me it would be fun to provoke it, make you punish me. We'd both love it. You wouldn't show it, but I'd know.

I am in love with you. I am not able to be angry. I feel indulgent, protective, even. I am grateful to have something to give you. If you want me powerless, helpless, and totally dependent on you, I want to be that. I'll abandon myself to you. I even want you to abuse and degrade me, do absolutely anything you want to me, no matter how forbidden.

Although the stories appear to be addressing her sexual partner directly, Dr. Bean-Bayog insists she never shared her fantasies with Paul Lozano. She says that he stole them from her office without her knowledge that fall. She claims that Lozano broke into her office and went through his file in search of evidence to sue Dr. Frankenberg and McLean Hospital for what he perceived as abusive treatment of him.

She has stated that she does not know when or how Lozano gained entrance to her office. Her written fantasies were not kept with his records in her locked file cabinet, she says, but were in a personal journal, locked in a desk in the same room. Neither the lock on her desk nor the lock on the file cabinet was ever broken, however, and she does not remember ever losing the keys, which she kept on a key chain in her purse. There was no sign of forced entry into the office itself. She was not even aware of a "break-in," she says, until Paul Lozano told her on November 2, 1987.

Her office notes for that day contain no mention of a break-in, but there is a reference to his rifling her files. "I did something else. I took the folder with the McLean summary out," he told her, referring to his hospital record. "Stole it out of the file?" she asked. "Not hard," he replied. If she asked him how or when he removed the file, Dr. Bean-Bayog did not record the question or the answer in her usually copious notes. Nor did she file a report with the police.

Her office notes do record a discussion between doctor and patient about a fantasy "which he also reread when he got the disch[arge] summary—with the alternation between torturing me and turning me on." Dr. Bean-Bayog says that the fantasy referred to is one of his own that he described during a session in October and that she recorded in her office notes. He read it during the break-in, she says.

But her office notes also indicate that he had possession of at least one written fantasy and that she told him to bring it back. She noted that "my asking him to bring fantasy back made him FURIOUS," and she quotes him telling her, presciently, as it turned out, "Your [sic] just covering your own ass. If I kill myself and my family finds it and sues, all you care about is what happens to you."

The fantasy referred to is not one of her own, she contends, but rather a separate fantasy that she and Paul wrote together about incest to help him cope with his alleged childhood experiences. When Paul returned it to Dr. Bean-Bayog a year later, she wrote: "relieved gave back fant[asy]. Wanting to get rid of this stuff. We've been working on getting you rid of it." That was a reference to the incest fantasy, she says, and she and Paul destroyed it together.

Dr. Bean-Bayog, in fact, contends she did not even realize her private fantasies had been taken until after Paul Lozano's death in 1991, four years after she claims the theft occurred. The fantasies in Paul's possession were photocopies. It is not clear how or when Paul Lozano could have slipped the originals back into her locked desk drawer. But she insists they were there when she and Paul ended their therapeutic relationship in 1990. She says she threw them away.

Whether she gave Paul Lozano copies of her fantasies, as he would say later, or whether he stole them, and whether she knew they were missing or should have known they were missing, are not really the point. What is important is that the eroticized atmosphere of the therapy sessions and the ambiguous nature of the relationship between therapist and patient went unchecked.

Highly charged emotions are the stuff of psychotherapy, but responsible therapists are sensitive to sexual feelings that threaten to overwhelm the sessions and the patient. If clear professional boundaries prove impossible to maintain, a referral is in order.

But Dr. Bean-Bayog was not operating under a psychiatrist's conventional rules of engagement. Just as she improvised her therapeutic techniques, she seems to have assumed she could handle their consequences.

On December 8, 1987, Paul Lozano gave Margaret Bean-Bayog a book entitled *Inquisition, a Bilingual Guide to the Exhibition of Torture Instruments from the Middle Ages to the Industrial Era,* which described sadomasochistic devices for use on women. He signed it "To My Favorite Inquisitor, Paul." He told her it was a Christmas gift.

Dr. Bean-Bayog went on vacation from December 16, 1987, to January 1, 1988, to Manila to visit her husband's family. The Boy would go with her on this trip, in the backpack, they decided in a therapy session a few days before her departure. But the Big Brother, Paul told her, was feeling "competitive, possessive. He wants to get rid of your family so you can't go."

In fact, the Big Brother was fantasizing about "keeping you in a room, tied up, where he can come and do whatever he wants to you and no one else can. . . . I'd be able to do anything I wanted to you: touch you, stroking your inner thighs and vagina, slowly, lightly, as long as I wanted, reminding you you couldn't move and I could do it all day, and get you aroused then mock you. Maybe put you in the stocks. Then I'd be able to do whatever I wanted. But I wouldn't even need them; I'd have you so aroused, you'd be enslaved."

The increasingly pornographic tone of their therapy sessions did not signal to Dr. Bean-Bayog that it was time to find her patient another psychiatrist. Instead, she intensified her role-playing and redoubled her efforts to convince him that she was his only source of love and support.

Paul was scheduled to have surgery on his injured knee while she was away. In order to reduce his anxiety about their first extended separation, she says, she and Paul Lozano drafted letters from the symbolic "mom" to be opened each day Dr. Bean-Bayog was in the Philippines. But, as was so often the case in the material she gave to her patient, it is unclear in these excerpts who is speaking in the letters, "the mom" or the psychiatrist herself.

[On December 17]: I miss you. Separations are the worst.

I love the boy. His knee hurts and he's groggy and feels sick. He says it's too hot in here. But he lets me hold him. He's awfully cranky but he finally sleeps.

[On December 20]: I'm beginning to feel like it's too long and it's only five days. I HATE missing out. I wish I knew everything that's happening to you and everything going on in your head. Letters are a pathetic substitute. But I'd love it if you'd write one for me when I get back. In fact, keep a journal.

Give the Pound Puppy my regards.

[On December 21]: This drives me NUTS. I miss you. I want everything to be fine, but I also want to KNOW what's happening.

I miss all of you.

I want to protect you in case your parents are

tricky. Try this: think of them as if THEY are three years old. It makes it easier to tolerate them, and they're less threatening.

[On December 22]: Families can be tricky. It may all go along smoothly, but seeing them after the hospital debacle will hurt some. It will get better as time goes along.

Pay attention if they start to trigger you off to what it is. We'll work on understanding it when you come back.

Remember, I love you. If you start to loathe yourself remember it's a reaction to something they're doing which we haven't understood yet.

[On December 26]: This is HARD. I hate just talking to YOU without knowing what's going on in your head, what you're up against at the moment. . . .

I know you're home now. I know it's just after Christmas. I hope you enjoyed yours. I miss you. One week to go. I worry about the impact your time at home is having. I worry about your getting into a spiral and hating yourself. In fact I worry alot, not because I think you will, but because I want to protect you and comfort you and keep you safe. You're probably doing fine. I'M the one who's having trouble.

[On December 30]: Sometimes toward the end of an absence it gets very hard. It's been too long and it's maddening and at the same time not important and important.

When I get back I want to wrap you up with all the loss and anger and frustration and sadness & hold you till you remember what it's like to feel happy.

In the flash cards and notes that she wrote to Paul Lozano that fall and winter to help him "soothe himself" when he felt suicidal, the identity of the speaker is often equally unclear. Dr. Bean-Bayog insists that, although one sentence might be from his "mom" and the next from his psychiatrist, Paul Lozano never had trouble discerning which sentiments were coming from whom.

Only one flash card, out of a deck of fifty-two, is a message from a third party, Dr. Bean-Bayog contends. The card with a direct reference to sex, she claims, is a message Paul Lozano wanted to hear not from her but from one of his girlfriends:

> I worry about you spending so much time with me. You're gonna resent me. . . .
>
> [On reverse]: I love spending time with you. I'm going to miss so many things about you, the closeness and the need and the phenomenal sex and being so appreciated. Maybe you're having trouble getting used to being loved.

The Lozano family did not know what to make of the changes they were seeing in Paul. He came home for Christmas in 1987 clutching a stuffed dog—Pound Puppy—and a baby blanket. He was cool toward them, especially to his mother, and he talked of nothing but his therapist.

He closeted himself in his room with his tape player but would not share what he was listening to with the family. He would later tell Dr. Bean-Bayog that he had played the tape "over and over" that she had recorded for him, of her reading children's books, as well as the stories she had written for him, "especially 'Cookies' and 'Morning.'"

One overt sign of his regressed behavior to the family was the tugging contest Paul engaged in with his baby niece, Alexis, over Pound Puppy.

"It was like a port wine stain that nobody wants to look at," Paul's brother Abel recalled:

> We didn't know what to do. We didn't feel we could raise the subject if we couldn't do something

about it. Mom and Dad were dealing with it as best they could. And Pilar was very close to Paul. We were never in a situation before where we were all up against an unknown. And he was seeing a Harvard psychiatrist, right? He couldn't be in better hands, right?

We knew there was something wrong. You wouldn't have had stronger advocates than us if she had at any time contacted us and asked us for any kind of help. But she never did. And Paul told us she would not talk to us, that it would be bad for his therapy. So, we were all like, "What's next? Who are we to question a psychiatrist from Harvard?" That is exactly what different members of the family said whenever these things were brought up.

Dr. Bean-Bayog called Paul in Texas at least once from Manila during that visit and he telephoned her there, running up $75 in long-distance charges. They also spoke when she was en route from Hong Kong. The telephone calls were arranged in advance to help him cope with the thoughts of suicide that Dr. Bean-Bayog contends were inevitably triggered by his trips home, when he would allegedly witness his mother abusing his nephews.

During this visit home he took a side trip to Albuquerque and bought Dr. Bean-Bayog an expensive Christmas present in a gift shop in Old Town. He was both embarrassed and angry for missing her so much and "disgusted about getting you something," he told her in one of their intercontinental calls. "I must be out of my mind." In the end, he gave the gift to his real mother.

Dr. Bean-Bayog contends that Paul was so disturbed on that trip that he engaged in risky and self-destructive behavior, picking up hitchhikers in the middle of the night and scaling an eight-foot wall to poke around the grounds of an abandoned psychiatric hospital. His behavior, she said, was a response to his mother's alleged molestation of her grandsons.

He observed his mother sexually abusing one of his nephews and became agitated and suicidal and called to talk about it. Actually, very seriously suicidal. I think this happened more than once. But he tended to get suicidal every time he went home. He particularly became suicidal when he watched his mother sexually abusing his baby nephews.

She was changing the diaper in the living room. He saw her kiss and fondle the little boy's penis. . . . It was a repeated activity. Oh, yes, and there were other children as well. There was an older child—this was with an infant, I think; and there was an older child who[m] she also sexually abused who used to grab his penis and run around the yard saying, "I'm going to give that little girl next door my ice cream cone." And there were—I'm not sure how many grandsons there were. I don't think she sexually abused the girls.

This account would seem to indict not just a deviant mother but a household full of coconspirators.

The speculative approach to trauma diagnosis has some ethical implications in the Lozano case. Who was going to intervene to stop the alleged ongoing abuse of Paul Lozano's nephews? Paul did not report his sixty-seven-year-old mother to Texas child welfare authorities because it would have been "disloyal" and because the athletic, five-foot, eight-inch, 170-pound man was "terrified" of his four-foot, ten-inch mother, according to Dr. Bean-Bayog.

The doctor herself said she did nothing because in her view Epifania Lozano had been getting away with it for years, with the tacit approval of her husband, her five other children, her three sons-in-law, and her two daughters-in-law. "This came up over and over so that the question of her ongoing abuse of her grandchildren—which had gone on from the time he was born, for twenty-four years, and was ongoing at that time—obviously was a question whether it could be stopped," Dr. Bean-Bayog said.

On this visit, she claims, Paul called her in the Philippines, frantic, and told her he had the barrel of his father's gun in his mouth and intended to shoot. She believed him, she says. But she did not speak to anyone else in the house. She did not call the police, an approved therapeutic response. She did not tell him to go to an emergency room, another approved therapeutic response. Alone, over the telephone from the Philippines, she said she was able to stem his suicidal impulses.

She did not think it was necessary to inform the family of what had transpired, even though she thought it was quite possible he would become suicidal again during the visit. He knew there was a psychiatrist covering her practice in Boston, two thousand miles away, and he had her telephone number in Manila if he needed her. In the meantime, he could use Pound Puppy, his blanket, and the letters from "Mom" to comfort himself.

Whether the abuse actually occurred or whether Dr. Bean-Bayog was misled by a patient telling her what he seemed to want to hear, one thing is certain. By taking the position that "the only data we have is our experience here," Dr. Bean-Bayog denied herself access to information that could have helped her patient.

Physicians are mandated by law in Massachusetts to report suspected cases of abuse to authorities. The legal requirement is less clear when the alleged abuse is occurring in another state. However, the ethical dilemma of how to protect Paul's privacy and his nephews' safety apparently gave Dr. Bean-Bayog not a moment's pause. Once she concluded that Paul was "too frightened" to report his mother regarding the alleged abuse, she says that she considered the matter closed.

Chapter

5

Paul Lozano was eager to return from Texas in January 1988 to his work at the Boston Biomedical Research Institute. His leave of absence from medical school had given him the opportunity to concentrate on pure science, and his excitement was palpable.

He talked often about his anesthesiology experiments in his thrice-weekly therapy sessions with Dr. Bean-Bayog. And more and more, he complained sheepishly that his therapy was interfering with his work.

"Couldn't let you know that I was supposed to be at work," he told her in a late-night telephone call to explain missing a session. "I have [a] conflict. Have to be both places at once."

The more sessions he missed, however, the more he feared Dr. Bean-Bayog would abandon him. Needy and dependent, he would work in the lab until late at night and then call to recapture the time he had missed with her.

He was not eating or sleeping or taking his antidepressants regularly. He was consumed with his work but also plagued with self-doubt and near-paranoid fears that his supervisors at the lab were devaluing him, mocking him, and plagiarizing his work. What if an experiment didn't work? What if it worked once and then couldn't be duplicated? It was so much pressure, he told her. No wonder researchers were tempted to doctor their results. Maybe he should doctor his own.

Dr. Bean-Bayog wrote a flash card to help Paul deal with his depression and self-destructive talk of suicide and scientific forgery:

> Don't hurt yourself. Take your pills. Let your results be the real results.

>   Mom

In March, Paul Lozano went to visit Dr. Harrison G. Pope, the psychopharmacologist who had treated him at McLean in 1986 and 1987, to discuss his research at Boston Biomedical on malignant hyperthermia, a dangerous complication of anesthetics. Dr. Pope was doing research in the related area of neuroleptic malignant syndrome, a side effect of antipsychotic drugs.

"He discussed his work with me, and he and I thought that we could collaborate on a study linking two areas of knowledge that we were exploring," Dr. Pope recalled.

While they were meeting, Dr. Pope mentioned to Paul that a new antidepressant was on the market that had fewer side effects than desipramine. Paul switched for a brief period to Prozac, but Dr. Pope recalled that "it proved to be ineffective and he experienced a recurrence of the depression. So we abandoned the Prozac and resumed the desipramine and that was the end of it."

It was only the beginning, though, of their collaboration. With his colleagues at Boston Biomedical, Paul had developed a test to examine lymphocytes, a certain type of blood cell, in victims of malignant hyperthermia. The test, he thought, could distinguish the lymphocytes drawn from malignant hyperthermia victims from those of normal individuals.

Since malignant hyperthermia is thought to be related to neuroleptic malignant syndrome, Paul and Dr. Pope decided to draw blood samples at McLean Hospital from victims of neuroleptic malignant syndrome and from patients who had received neuroleptics, tranquilizing drugs, but had never had neuroleptic malignant syndrome. Dr. Pope sent the blind blood samples to Paul to see if his test could correctly identify them.

"If this test was successful, it would become an invaluable tool for subsequent psychiatrists because it would help to determine who might be vulnerable to this dangerous and potentially fatal side effect of antipsychotic drugs," said Dr. Pope. "I confess that Paul and I had visions of patenting the test and making a million dollars from doing it."

Paul told Dr. Bean-Bayog he was sometimes confused whether Dr. Pope was his doctor or his colleague but that he valued their research collaboration because it gave him the chance to counter the impression he had made during his two hospitalizations at McLean. I "wanted to show him I was something besides a flake in the quiet room," Paul told her.

After six tries it became apparent that the test could not correctly segregate the samples, and the project was abandoned. Paul was disappointed, but Dr. Pope's recollection of Paul at that time was that "he was doing very well, as best I could determine. He apparently had been successful in the very demanding program at Harvard Medical School, and seemed to be on his way to starting a research career. If you had asked me in the spring of 1988, my optimism had again risen, to a higher level than it had been a year earlier, that he would do well."

Indeed, once Paul was freed from the pressure of clinical work in medical school, his mental health stabilized. He entered enthusiastically into new athletic pursuits. He learned to sail well enough to crew on a trip to Bermuda with friends over one vacation. When he heard that his brother Abel was parachuting out of airplanes as part of his training as a Green Beret, Paul followed his competitive instincts and joined a skydiving club. The only hint that something was awry was that he listed his next of kin on the club application as Dr. Margaret Bean-Bayog, his "mom."

In addition to his research, Paul worked as a tutor in cell biology and, not insignificantly, as a mental health aide at the Human Resources Institute, a private psychiatric hospital in suburban Brookline.

Mark Burrowes, now a psychotherapist at HRI, was a mental health aide there with Lozano in 1988 and 1989. They worked the night shift and dealt primarily with adolescents. They often went out for a few beers after a long night of negotiating privileges and bedtime rules with resistant teenagers.

"He showed no anxiety dealing with patients. He was a funny guy, kind and compassionate. We all got along very well. He often studied during breaks," Burrowes recalled. "Even in a crisis situation he did well. We often had to restrain patients, and Paul was involved in restraining several kids who were suicidal or acting out. He handled it without any problem at all. Now, I don't know what happened to Paul after eleven-thirty when he went home, but we never saw any signs of a serious mental illness."

Those signs were very much in evidence, according to Dr. Bean-Bayog, in Paul's therapy sessions, which she described during this period as "stormy and demanding." His rage at psychiatrists at McLean Hospital and his collaborators at the lab sometimes reached homicidal levels, according to Dr. Bean-Bayog, who interpreted his outbursts as displaced anger at his abusive family.

Having repeatedly reinforced the notion that he was sexually abused by his mother, Dr. Bean-Bayog in June at last helped Paul Lozano "retrieve" a "memory" of being molested by his mother while he was still in diapers. He was depressed, having discontinued his medication again, when he delivered a memory of playing sexual games under his mother's skirt.

"She would even if I tried to stop her, she'd hold me down and keep doing it, even be glad I was angry, she'd stroke me and spread my legs and kiss me and kiss me and lick me till I finally wanted her to continue. . . . I'd do anything to get her to do that. I'd get into her lap and push her legs apart, get under her skirt, and do just what she did to me, caress and kiss her. . . . I could get her to stop doing anything else, and then she'd make me stay still and do whatever she wanted, as long as she wanted, over and over and over, all the things moms just do."

Hearing this story, Dr. Bean-Bayog wrote, "You are hung over and off the pills and that makes everything worse, but you're also reliving the sexual abuse."

The concept of repressed memories, such as those Dr. Bean-Bayog maintains she helped Paul Lozano retrieve, has been debated since Sigmund Freud first proposed that painful memories of childhood abuse are buried beyond reach in the unconscious. Freud had initially believed the accounts of his hysteria patients that they had been molested in childhood but a few years later Freud decided that such stories were actually expressions of his patients' repressed incestuous desires.

By the time Paul Lozano sought therapy, the prevalence of childhood sexual abuse was a tragic and well-established fact of life. More than 200,000 cases of sexual abuse are documented every year, according to the National Committee to Prevent Child Abuse. What is less well known, however, is the reliability of memories of abuse and the specific symptoms that would signal to a therapist that such childhood trauma had occurred.

Those who research the workings of memory are concerned that the mind is being seen as a sort of video camera, as if the overlay of experience and suggestion does not alter memories. Dr. Daniel Friedman, a professor of psychiatry at UCLA, compares memory to the childhood game of "telephone," where one child whispers a message to the child next to him, who repeats it to another child in turn. By the time it reaches the end of a line of listeners, the message invariably emerges in a very different form.

Elizabeth Loftus, a psychologist at the University of Washington, has served as an expert witness on memory in many criminal cases, including the McMartin Preschool sexual abuse trial and the trial of the Hillside Strangler in

Los Angeles. Her research—which has implanted in adults false "memories" of unhappy childhood events just by having them recounted by a trusted sibling—also suggests that memory is malleable, that it is influenced by subsequent events and that it changes over time.

"Therapists have been known to tell patients, merely on the basis of a suggestive history, or 'symptom profile,' that they definitely had a traumatic experience," Loftus, whose research is funded in part by the National Institute of Mental Health, told a meeting of the American Psychological Association in 1992. "Even if there is no memory, but merely some vague symptoms, certain therapists will inform a patient after a single session that they were very likely the victim of a satanic cult. Once 'diagnosed,' the therapist urges the patient to pursue the recalcitrant memories."

To be sure, clinicians have encountered patients who seemed to have "buried" the memory of sexual abuse. But other, equally compelling, anecdotal evidence demonstrates that far from forgetting events, victims of war, rape, kidnapping, and other acts of violence are haunted by all too vivid recollections of their trauma. The psychological fallout from one such event, the kidnapping of a busload of schoolchildren in Chowchilla, California, in 1976, was studied systematically over time by Dr. Lenore Terr, a child psychiatrist in San Francisco. Not only did the children not forget their experience of being entombed in a buried truck for nineteen hours but they were also plagued for years afterward by memories of the cries, the sights, and the claustrophobia. In another study of children, aged five to ten, who saw a parent murdered, not one repressed the memory.

There have been too few such studies to make any definitive claims about traumatic memory. But the debate about repressed memories of sexual abuse is less about science than about politics. Laws were rewritten in nineteen states in the 1980s to allow adults to sue their alleged molesters for damages years after the event. Those who claim to have been wrongly accused organized the False

Memory Syndrome Foundation to fight what they describe as a sort of mass hysteria fueled by therapists enamored of an easy diagnosis.

Advocates for victims fought back, arguing that sexual abuse has been denied by the culture for so long and is so painful to face that such organizations are part of a national backlash against those who are finally standing up to demand justice.

The political polarization runs the risk of diverting attention from the scientifically neutral question, How does a well-intentioned therapist make a careful diagnosis of sexual abuse that may have occurred decades before?

Dr. Bean-Bayog diagnosed Paul Lozano as an abuse victim, she says, because "he had symptoms that were characteristic of people who had been sexually abused"—nightmares, flashbacks, and sexualized behavior. But the danger of making a diagnosis from such general symptoms is that research about sexual abuse is still in its nascent stage. What studies have been done show a broad range of psychological reactions among abused children. A 1992 review by Wellesley College researchers of forty-five studies of sexually abused children conducted in the 1980s found no evidence of any identifiable sexual abuse syndrome. On the contrary, no symptoms appeared in more than half of the abused children. In addition, symptoms often noted in sexually abused children—flashbacks and nightmares—can be produced by other experiences as well, so their presence does not necessarily mean sexual abuse has occurred, the researchers concluded.

Such scientific caution, however, runs counter to the blame-assigning strain so evident in the popular culture. Television confessionals and pop psychology books have cashed in on greater public awareness of and sensitivity to the sexual abuse of children. *The Courage to Heal,* a best-seller published in 1988, for instance, bills itself as a manual for sexual abuse survivors and carries such suspect guides to self-diagnosis as: "If you think you were abused and your life shows the symptoms, then you were."

Dr. Bean-Bayog's eagerness to believe her theory extended to a total suspension of skepticism about the details of Paul's "memories." No probative questions appear to have been asked about recollections she helped him retrieve of being fondled while still in diapers. Most scientists are skeptical of such early memories. Before the age of four, the mind is thought to hold only primitive images, not coherent memory.

"He described that his mother would tell him that she had to check his diaper; and he would say, 'No, you don't. I'm dry,'" according to Dr. Bean-Bayog. "And she would come and get him and then sexually stimulate him until he said, 'I didn't want her to stop anymore.'"

She appears similarly to have accepted uncritically his reports of having so much anger as an infant that he would scream "shit" from his crib when his parents had company. Had Dr. Bean-Bayog spoken to anyone in the Lozano family, they would have told her that before he was a year old, Paul would pull himself up in his cradle, rock it until it nearly tipped over, and squeal. His screams did sound like the word *shit*. But since his family spoke to him in Spanish when Paul was a baby, he would not have known that word. The similarity in the sounds made for a great story in later years, however, and relatives and friends remember its being told repeatedly at family gatherings when Paul was a boy.

Transforming a story one has been told into a "memory" is not an uncommon phenomenon. Perhaps the most famous such case involved Jean Piaget, the Swiss scientist whose work on memory in children is one of the foundations of the modern theory of child development. In his book *Play, Dreams, and Imitation in Childhood,* Piaget recounted his memory of a man trying to kidnap him from his pram when he was two years old.

"I was held in by the strap fastened round me while my nurse bravely tried to stand between me and the thief," he wrote. "She received various scratches, and I can still see vaguely those on her face. Then a crowd gathered, a policeman with a short cloak and a white baton came up, and the man took to his heels. I can still see the whole scene, and can even place it near the tube station on the Champs-Elysées in Paris."

But years later, Piaget's parents received a letter from the old nurse, who enclosed the watch given to her as a reward for saving their son. The nurse wrote that it was all a lie. She had made up the story of the kidnapper to impress her employers and had scratched herself to add an extra touch of realism.

"I therefore must have heard, as a child, the account of this story, which my parents believed, and projected it into the past in the form of a visual memory," Piaget concluded.

Dr. Bean-Bayog herself concedes some confusion about the workings of memory. "I don't know if he actually remembered it or whether it was experienced, you know; but yes, I've never, you know, I've not had a patient who was sexually abused while they were in diapers. . . . It was unusual; but developmentally, he learned to read in English when he was three, according to him, so he—you know, he may not have been on the same time scale.

"Many patients have had memories from that period. Normally, they're repressed; but you can sometimes retrieve them in psychotherapy, but not specifically about diapers. . . . It's hard to know whether they were repressed. They weren't retrieved by me. They were retrieved by him," she says, although she acknowledges having helped him in this task "by repeatedly pointing out to him how his behavior must come from somewhere . . . the way he found himself experiencing people as raping and abusing and humiliating him."

Paul Lozano was no more certain of what to expect from Dr. Bean-Bayog. In their sessions that spring he began to disassociate, telling her he feared he was merging with her physically, that he might be "sucked in and never come out. I'd be inside of you. I'd be you. Have to keep my distance."

She made up a flash card to help him deal with his conflictual feelings about her.

You are the devil. You'll suck me in again if I
relax my guard for a second.

[On reverse]: You have to be safe. You can be.
You're an adult. You can leave. You can just say no.
You can switch it off. I'll help keep you safe.

Such reassurances ignored both his infantilism in the relationship and the sexual attraction between them. In the summer of 1988, Dr. Bean-Bayog moved her office again, this time to her Lexington home. Sometime after that move, Paul Lozano took a roll of snapshots of his psychiatrist in her home office. In the photographs, Margaret Bean-Bayog poses coquettishly, hugging the stuffed bear they played with in therapy, licking her lips, and wiggling her fingers in her ears. She would say later that she had absolutely no memory of ever posing for those snapshots.

At the same time, supported by recommendations from his supervisors at the Boston Biomedical Research Institute, Paul extended his leave from medical school to pursue graduate studies in cell and developmental biology at Harvard with an eye toward earning a Ph.D. as well as his medical degree.

In pursuing a joint program that September, Paul was typical of his Harvard classmates. Only 50 percent of any entering class emerge four years later with a medical degree. Fully half of every class takes five or more years to graduate because students pursue the available joint degree programs, research opportunities, and travel grants that make Harvard what it is.

The result is a mobile, independent student population. The school has even stopped designating incoming students by class grouping because so few will actually graduate in four years. "The most we can say is someone began with the class of ninety-seven," said Dr. Edward M. Hundert, Associate Dean for Student Affairs.

Paul Lozano did not go far when he left the medical school for graduate school, whose administrative offices are just one floor apart in the Medical Education Center. For the next fifteen months, he was involved in classwork and laboratory research. "He was one of those students we'd see every few months in the office," said Dr. Thomas Fox, vice chairman of the Division of Medical Sciences and Paul's biochemistry professor. "We try to keep track of where they are when they are between programs as best we can. That is sometimes difficult, particularly when they are in the lab and not in courses. We have very little reason to see them."

Paul would come by to pick up his stipend from the graduate studies department on the third floor of the MEC. He got to know the secretaries and office personnel as well as Dr. Fox. As part of his administrative role, Dr. Fox made himself available to students to talk about matters of concern: career, classes, work in the lab, personal problems. He knew Paul Lozano and liked him. "Paul always did well in courses and he was making progress in the lab," he said. "We had reason to believe he could have done a complete job, finished and gotten a degree."

For its part, Harvard did not probe too deeply into Paul Lozano's troubles. Keeping a respectful distance from its students is both style and policy at Harvard Medical School. In an average year, one or two students request medical leaves. Most return a year later and resume their studies without further interruption. A case of a student needing multiple leaves, as Paul Lozano did, occurs every five years or so.

"One of the major efforts that we make at Harvard Medical School, and I think most medical schools, is to really be careful to separate a student's clinical situation from their academic. You really want to convey to students that when they are being patients, they have the same kind of confidentiality that you hope they will extend to their patients," said Dr. Hundert.

To ensure that separation, the head of the medical school's health service reports to the director of the University Health Service, who reports directly to the president of Harvard. "The head of the medical area health service has no reporting chain that intersects the dean of the medical school. And the students are told that when they arrive so they understand that their medical record is quite separate from their educational record," said Dr. Hundert.

"Students wouldn't go to therapists if they thought we'd

be told," added Dr. Alvin F. Poussaint, also a psychiatrist and an associate dean.

Dr. Fox was aware of the nature, if not all the details, of Paul's problems. "He was candid about some of it. So I was aware he had taken a medical leave, that he was in therapy," he said. Far from seeing him as a psychologically disabled loner, Dr. Fox remembered that "by comparison with some of our students, Paul was gregarious. That's an exaggeration, of course, but he was not one of our more isolated students." He recalls seeing Paul, for instance, in good spirits, sporting a new parka for a ski trip he was about to take with friends.

Dr. Bean-Bayog saw something else entirely. In response to the pressures of work and school, Paul Lozano was often panicky and suicidal, spinning out elaborate sexual fantasies about his psychiatrist or retreating to their role-playing for comfort. "I'll just get worse and worse until you pick me up," he told her after doing poorly on a test. "I want to be a baby. I'm too little to do all this."

Paul Lozano's confusion about maternal and sexual love was evident when he began dating a young woman that fall. He told Dr. Bean-Bayog he felt ashamed about "wanting Cathy to be crazy about me and be mother."

Even as he was struggling in therapy, Paul Lozano's outward appearance was one of hard work and achievement. As part of his graduate studies, in 1989 Paul was assigned to a research project at the Tropical Disease Laboratory at the Harvard School of Public Health. He worked under the supervision of Dyann F. Wirth, a molecular biologist who headed the lab. She remembers a quiet but competent student.

"He was a rotation graduate student and worked on a project on the mechanism of drug resistance in protozoan parasites. He was in a training program which involved a small research project related to the work going on in my laboratory," she recalled.

"He was an average to good student, and he was interested in research. He was working in the lab while going to classes, as is standard for students at this level of training.

He successfully isolated two cloned DNA fragments containing the genes of interest in his project.

"He was quiet and he got along well with his fellow lab mates. He socialized with them outside the laboratory and went to parties with them, baseball games, et cetera."

Martha Lundgren met Paul in the lab. She was four years younger than he and was working part-time washing beakers and ordering supplies for the lab while attending the Massachusetts College of Pharmacy across Longwood Avenue.

He was serious at his work but formed friendships with his colleagues, especially a graduate student from Puerto Rico, Martha recalled. "I did not have the impression of Paul as isolated and withdrawn," she said. "He was one of the gang."

He continued to return home regularly to El Paso to visit his family. He made a special trip in July 1989 to see Pilar, who had just undergone a hysterectomy.

During that visit he met Candy Stone, Pilar's supervisor in the intensive care unit of Providence Memorial Hospital. Candy was visiting Pilar when Paul arrived.

The couple began an intense whirlwind relationship, which was characteristic of Paul Lozano's romantic involvements. He spent every day of his weeklong visit with Candy. He sent her roses. Pilar told him of her boss's reputation as a party girl and warned him not to drink while he was taking antidepressants.

Paul perceived her warnings as interference, reminiscent of her objections to his marriage to Susan, and, out of a mix of defiance and desire, he invited Candy to visit him in Boston.

Candy went. He took her shopping in Harvard Square. They went sightseeing. They read the Sunday newspaper in the park across the street from his apartment. They had sex, when he could. Impotence was a side effect of his antidepressant medication. In response, he stopped taking it.

Candy spent most of her vacation in the Tropical Disease Laboratory. "There were three or four different nights that we were up in the lab at two and three in the morning. We'd be in his apartment and he'd say, 'Oh, there's something I've got to do—I just remembered.' And we'd run to the lab at Harvard," she recalled.

"He loved his research work. Loved it. One time when I was up in Boston, we were sitting and talking and he said he was really worried about what to do. He was confused because he wanted to stay a research doctor. That's all he wanted to do. His family wanted him to be a doctor-doctor. But Paul was not very much of a people person, I guess. He was real shy. And I think he felt real comfortable in the laboratory. He got along with the people there."

He talked a lot about Margaret—he always called her by her first name, Candy said. He was grateful to her; he owed her a lot of money, he said. However, he was expecting to receive money from an insurance company as settlement of the accident he was in three years before, and he was going to use some of that money to begin paying her.

Candy spoke to Margaret once when the doctor called for Paul after he had missed an appointment, but Candy declined when Paul asked if she would like to come along sometime to meet his psychiatrist. She wondered if there was something more to their relationship. "I came right out and asked him," she said. "And he told me no. But of course he told me no."

After Candy returned to El Paso, she and Paul kept in daily touch by telephone. "There were times he'd call me from Boston and he was crying. A lot of stress or pressure, and he just wanted to talk to someone," she recalled. "I mean, he called all hours of the night and day. Two o'clock in the morning and he'd be in the lab."

He was invited to present a paper on his hyperthermia research at a professional conference in New Orleans. It was a big honor for a student. He was excited, but jittery, too. He asked her to join him there. He also asked her, somewhat nervously, if she could get some cocaine for the trip. It was Candy's impression that Paul had never used the drug before.

"We were getting ready to go to New Orleans. And he asked me if I could get some cocaine. And I said, 'Well, I guess I can. It's probably easier for me than for you.' He said, 'Yeah, it's kind of hard for a medical student to stand out on a corner.' So I did," she recalled. "It was all over Providence; it was just all over the place," she said of the hospital where she and Pilar worked, one of the first in El Paso to start testing its employees for drugs because of the proliferation of cocaine.

She asked a friend, who dropped the cocaine on her desk the next day. No money exchanged hands. She and Paul sniffed the cocaine, once, in New Orleans, Candy said. But she and Paul never used cocaine together again after that trip.

Paul told Pilar what they had done. He also told Margaret. On the subject of his relationship with Candy Stone, both women were in agreement, warning Paul that this could be a dangerous romance for someone with his problems.

Their warnings were just more evidence to Paul that no one—not his family or his psychiatrist—would ever let him grow up. "He liked me because he told me I was the only one who made him feel like a grown-up," said Candy. That Christmas, he bought her a one-carat marquise diamond.

He arrived at her house one evening, acting shy but buoyant. He led her into the living room and asked her to sit down. He handed her a small porcelain statue of a little boy and a little girl. The boy was holding out a ring box that bore the words "Marry Me."

Paul dropped to one knee, took Candy's hand, and asked, "Will you?" as he slipped the diamond on her finger.

They took their parents to dinner at the Great American Land and Cattle Company, El Paso's best steak house, to celebrate. They gave red roses to their mothers and took snapshots of everyone toasting their future with champagne.

As it turned out, their future lasted about a week. They had an argument "about something so small I don't even remember the details," Candy recalled. Paul went back to Boston earlier than he had planned. He called a few days later to ask for the ring back. Candy sent it and never heard from Paul again.

Candy Stone looks back on that period with something

approaching mystification. "He was very immature. But I think a lot of us fostered that in him, at times. I think he was starved for affection," she said. Candy saw Pilar's hand in their breakup. Paul's sister had been furious about the cocaine, and Candy knew how protective Pilar could be of her brother. "I really didn't want to go to Boston, anyway," she would say years later in an El Paso restaurant. "I mean, I had lived here all my life. He wanted me to just quit my job and move up there. He didn't understand finances and how was I going to live. I had a house down here. And he just wanted me to pack up and leave."

In her office notes, which dwindled to brief summaries in the last two years of treatment, Dr. Bean-Bayog recorded the demise of this romance. Curiously, the notes about his brief engagement are dated summer 1989, months before it actually occurred.

After his return to Boston following the Christmas holidays, Paul Lozano was determined to put aside his graduate work and resume medical school in 1990. Dr. Bean-Bayog reminded him that it had been his clinical work in medical school that had precipitated so many of his psychiatric episodes. He knew the danger himself and, before their breakup, said as much to Candy Stone.

"Nothing scares me more than that," Paul told her, "and that's why I put it off for so long."

"Do what you want to do," Candy replied.

"You don't want me to be a doctor in an office, do you?" he asked.

"I want you to do whatever you want to do. I don't care what you do," Candy said. "I'd rather you be happy than miserable."

Looking back on her time with Paul, Candy said, "He was trying very hard to make everybody happy, and he wasn't making himself happy. He tried and tried and tried and tried to make everybody happy but himself. And there were a lot of times he would stop his medication and try to do it on his own. And I would tell him, 'Please don't do that, it's just that much worse.' But he would be embarrassed to take it around me, so he just wouldn't take it."

He took his antidepressants even more erratically when he returned to Boston that January. Medical school clerkships were beginning, and he needed to be alert, he rationalized.

His own family was unsure he was ready and uncertain about why he was allowed to return to medical school. But Paul insisted that Dr. Bean-Bayog assure Harvard that he was capable of resuming clinical work, and she did.

All that Harvard required was a brief letter. "It is not expected that they'll give the diagnosis, treatment plan, or anything else. It's usually a very short one- or two-sentence letter," said Dr. Hundert.

Paul was thrilled to be back in medical school in 1990. But pressured for time, he reduced his visits to Dr. Bean-Bayog from four to one a week. She warned him that he was not devoting enough time to his therapy during a period when he was vulnerable to a relapse. She noted that he was already showing signs of depression, having stopped his medication. She suggested that if he was going to resume responsibilities for the care of patients, the Impaired Physicians Committee of the Massachusetts Medical Society monitor his compliance with his antidepressants.

Paul would hear nothing of such supervision, fearing it would jeopardize his career. He began to suspect that his psychiatrist was looking for an excuse to dump him. She had dropped a bomb just after vacation, telling him she planned to adopt a baby soon and take a maternity leave, which would necessitate a break in his therapy, anyway. Maybe she no longer wanted to be his "mom."

Dr. Bean-Bayog insists that Paul Lozano always understood that she was not really his mother and so felt no displacement by the prospect of a new baby. She says it never occurred to her not to tell him of her adoption plans. Yet her office notes are full of references to his confusion about her role and his dependence on her for maternal nurturing—a dependence that she fostered as central to her therapeutic technique. At different times he told her:

"I wanted you for a Mom; I never had a Mom."

"Feel like you're my Mom, think you are my Mom, then [I

get] angry and don't want to see you. [I] end up really confused."

"I really hate needing you this much."

"I want to marry someone like you. I think about wanting to marry you."

"You never expect me to grow up too fast."

"Want to be your baby. Realize I can't. Just a patient. Mad."

"I love you. Want to leave. Want to stay. Want to be a baby. Afraid if I do I'll never come out of it, get fused, disappear. Terror. Just stop being. I'm just a baby. Take care of me."

"I really need you. I like feeling like you're the boy's mom."

Paul paid Dr. Bean-Bayog $9,000 from the settlement for the accident that had injured his knee, but she told him she wanted a regular payment schedule established as well. It was not an unreasonable request, he knew. He appreciated that she had been seeing him for free all these years, but it had led to some confusion in his mind about their relationship.

"Lots of things about you I don't understand. You have helped me a lot. Most patients pay their doctor. Confusing. Don't know what to make of it," he told her during a session.

For the first several weeks, Paul Lozano's confidence in his ability to resume medical school seemed well founded. He excelled in his parasitology course and finished his clinical work in obstetrics without difficulty.

He did fine until late February when he began his clinical work in psychiatry at Massachusetts General Hospital under the supervision of Dr. Gerald Adler, who, coincidentally, was Dr. Bean-Bayog's personal analyst. Paul began flirting with suicide. On one occasion he injected himself with a potentially fatal combination of lidocaine and ketamine and then—perhaps panicking at what he had done—added Narcan, a reversal agent.

He told Dr. Bean-Bayog that under the influence of ketamine, an anesthetic which can produce hallucinations, he had heard her voice telling him to kill himself. She was adopting a real baby; she did not need him anymore.

Dr. Bean-Bayog arranged to see Paul Lozano every day. One night in March, according to Dr. Bean-Bayog, he came to her home when she and her husband were out. He began shouting her name and banging on the windows, frightening her stepchildren.

A few days later, Dr. Adler led a group of medical students including Paul Lozano into the hospital room of a psychiatric patient with a history of incest. Dr. Adler was demonstrating how a clinician takes a patient's medical history. He focused his attention on his patient.

Across the room, as Paul Lozano listened, he became more and more distraught. As the group left the room, he took Dr. Adler aside. "Can I speak with you?" he asked. "I really have to talk to you because that patient upset me very much because I had a relationship like that, an incestuous relationship, with a member of my family and I am really, really upset."

Paul then told Dr. Adler that he was working on this issue in therapy. Dr. Adler urged him to call his therapist. That was the last day Paul Lozano appeared for his psychiatry rotation. The next Dr. Adler heard from Paul was a message on his answering machine, telling his professor that he had been admitted to Faulkner Hospital with a "gastrointestinal disturbance."

In fact, Paul Lozano had attempted suicide. The Brookline police had driven him to the emergency room after receiving a call from Dr. Margaret Bean-Bayog. Paul had failed to appear for a therapy session, and when neighbors could not rouse him, she sent the police. He had injected himself with ketamine, fentanyl, and lidocaine after having auditory hallucinations of Dr. Bean-Bayog instructing him to kill himself.

According to the hospital admission note, Paul Lozano had had an acute psychotic reaction to the drugs. He became so psychotic, in fact, that he heard disembodied voices, had paranoid delusions, and felt his body merging with that of one of his attending physicians.

When Dr. Bean-Bayog saw Paul in Faulkner, he told her that she was free to do what he most feared: "You can terminate with me now if you want. Your responsibility is ended." By the end of their session, she wrote in his chart, "He was talking about believing deep down that I hate him and want to get rid of him and that, while one part of him wants to live and go to school, the baby part of him thinks only one of us, not both, can survive the relationship."

Paul Lozano was probably not off the mark when he suggested to the staff at Faulkner that by then Dr. Bean-Bayog was "burnt out." She had boxed herself in; she had created a therapy that made her patient as dependent on her as a small child is on his mother, and she was near collapse under the weight of his demands.

But instead of recognizing that her therapy had backfired —she had "reparented" Paul Lozano, but rather than growing up healthy, he was hearing hallucinations of "Mom" ordering him to kill himself—she fell back on the same failed technique. She made new flash cards to chase away his demons and continued to hold herself out as his savior:

Dear Badoctor Bean, you aren't real. I made you up. Dr. Bean says shut up and go away. She'll give you a talking to and make you leave me alone.

[On reverse]: I have to stay self (and safe). I can't hurt myself no matter WHO says to do it. If you say so, you have to talk to her. So there.

Dr. Bean hates me. She wants me to kill myself. She wants to get rid of me.

[On reverse]: That's a paranoid reaction when your feelings get hurt. I love you. If you are going to hurt yourself, CALL ME. Don't hurt yourself.

This time, he had not called "Mom" to rescue him. By the time he wound up at Faulkner Hospital's emergency room, a "tearful, childlike Latin American man sitting quite anxious, embracing himself," Paul Lozano was too sick to escape the notice and intervention of others. Faulkner interceded, as McLean had tried to do three years before. This time, exhausted, Margaret Bean-Bayog had to listen.

The Faulkner staff saw immediately that she was too involved and drew up a plan for her to get supervision and to ease out of the case. "We tried to broker the termination. It started out as our idea; she came around to it," said Dr. Jerome Rogoff, chief psychiatrist at Faulkner. "He had to pay something. She had to see that she was overinvolved, that she was blurring the boundaries. We felt she should pull out or get organized supervision."

The Faulkner Hospital staff's suggestions were reflected in the new notes and flash cards that Dr. Bean-Bayog prepared for Paul Lozano.

> I want to be able to see you. There is a safe place for the baby here. But there also needs to be a safe place for me. I generally need an alliance with you. I should get paid something for my time.

> We need ongoing consultation. My practice and family should generally not be disrupted. If you are hearing voices, hurting yourself or unable to keep the therapy protected it means you need more. You may need to be hospitalized.
> [On reverse]: That doesn't mean you can never call me or see me extra. We can discuss it.

Paul Lozano was devastated. He was losing medical school as well as "Mom." Dr. Fox visited Paul at Faulkner to reassure him that his place in the graduate program was secure, that Harvard would stand by him.

It was a gesture of support from an institution that eschews the in loco parentis role. While most students arrive fresh from college, many are older, having come to medical studies after years in the work force or other academic pursuits. "We think of students as our colleagues in medicine from the time they come," said Dr. Hundert. "If they've gotten here, the school is making a huge investment in them and commitment to them."

The collegial atmosphere explains why no one ever flunks out of Harvard Medical School. If a student is having academic difficulties, tutors are provided. If he or she is experiencing psychological troubles, referrals are made. Dropouts are rare; the psychic investment is too great, not to mention the financial one. (In 1992–93 Harvard Medical School tuition alone was $20,250 a year, and annual increases of 5 percent are standard.)

But the emphasis on collegiality can sometimes obscure the reality that these are students, not doctors, and the desire to cut them some slack can rebound later.

Paul Lozano, for instance, had barely begun his psychiatry clerkship when he was hospitalized for a suicide attempt. Even so, his professors bent over backward to rationalize giving him a passing grade. "People saw him as a very odd-looking guy. He looked frightened. He looked anxious. Some people used the word 'spooky,' that he had a spooky feeling to him," Dr. Adler said, in describing Paul Lozano during the few weeks he spent on his psychiatry rotation.

" 'Should we pass this guy? We hardly know him,' " Dr. Adler said they asked themselves. "My sense of the conversation was, here's a guy who's so scared and he's not going to become a psychiatrist, why torture the guy? Why fail him and say you didn't complete the rotation? He's clearly not going to go into psychiatry; it's so upsetting to him. Let's do sort of the compassionate act and let him get credit.

"He tried hard. I mean, the usual platitudes of wanting to pass a guy you don't know. He tried hard. He had an interest in biological psychiatry and talked about that interest, and convinced people he was a bright guy. The feeling was, in spite of the fact that he missed two weeks, we should pass him."

Paul was quite a sight in Faulkner's psychiatric unit—a patient with his nose buried in his psychiatry text. He obtained a pass to visit his professors to demonstrate that he had mastered psychiatry. Learning he had passed, he arranged to do his next clinical rotation during the day and return to Faulkner's psychiatric ward at night.

When he called Pilar to say that he was hospitalized but continuing his medical clerkships, she was astounded. "How can they let you see patients or work in a lab when you are on so many drugs?" she asked him.

But so much of Paul Lozano's self-esteem depended on completing his education that those who treated him were reluctant to pull the rug out. They all feared how much sicker he might become without the reassurance he received from being a Harvard Medical School student.

The willingness of Harvard and Paul Lozano's psychiatrists to accommodate his need to continue in medical school did not always serve Paul well. On the first day of his pathology rotation, he became distraught at having to assist at the autopsy of a stillborn baby.

Abruptly he excused himself and called the psychiatric unit at Faulkner, anxious for support and reassurance. The baby "looked abused," he told the nurse on duty. He was frantic, too panicked to rejoin his classmates. Instead, Paul rushed back to the safety of Faulkner, where his scheduled release was immediately delayed. He remained hospitalized for two more weeks.

Chapter

6

For two weeks after Paul Lozano was released from Faulkner in the spring of 1990, his family telephoned his apartment every day and got no response. When the backed-up messages finally disabled his answering machine, his sister began dialing the office of Dr. Margaret Bean-Bayog.

Pilar Williams placed three calls in three hours, and when the doctor did not respond she enlisted the aid of an operator, who left an urgent message that Dr. Bean-Bayog return the call immediately.

Several hours later, the telephone rang in Pilar Williams's two-bedroom ranch house in El Paso.

"What can I do for you?" Dr. Bean-Bayog asked.

"Well, I would like to know where my brother is," Pilar said.

"I cannot talk to you about him," the psychiatrist replied, citing her patient's right to confidentiality.

"Let me put it to you this way," Pilar Williams said in her first and last conversation with Margaret Bean-Bayog. "You either tell me where my brother is or I promise you I'll hang up this phone, I'll call the Boston police, and I will tell them that I think my brother is dead and that you know where the body is. And I guarantee you that within a very short time they're going to be knocking at your door."

"Give me five minutes," the doctor said. "I'll get right back to you."

A few minutes later, Pilar's telephone rang again and she heard a small, exhausted voice.

"Pil, Pil, it's me, Paul. I'm in the hospital," he said. "I'm very, very sick."

By then, Paul Lozano was very, very sick indeed. He was calling from the locked ward of the Human Resources Institute, the private psychiatric hospital where he himself had worked as an aide. He landed there as a patient only days after his release from Faulkner, plagued once again with thoughts of suicide at the loss of medical school and Margaret Bean-Bayog. He remained there only a few days, until a bed on a locked ward became available at Faulkner.

"In the seventeen years I've been at this hospital there are only four patients of whom I've said to my staff, 'this person will kill himself'—that you get the sense that they really mean it. Paul was one of them," said Dr. Jerome Rogoff, the chief psychiatrist at Faulkner who saw Paul Lozano during his two 1990 admissions. "There was an emptiness in him that was profound. It was ultimately the determination to do it. He was utterly convincing about it. There wasn't much ambivalence about it. He meant it."

Marcos Lozano flew to see his son immediately. "His father's presence gives him strength and perspective on his problems," a nurse noted in Paul's chart when Mr. Lozano arrived. In fact, the hospitalizations that spring provided an opportunity for Paul Lozano to reconnect with the family Dr. Bean-Bayog had urged him to avoid. From the notations in his chart, it is clear the staff did not detect the same toxic effect of contact with his family that Dr. Bean-Bayog had seen.

"Sister called from Texas . . . to discuss her desire to come to visit," another nurse noted. "He agreed she was a positive support."

During Marcos Lozano's visit in May, Paul's father finally met Dr. Bean-Bayog.

During the four years Paul Lozano had been her patient, he was hospitalized four times, attempted suicide at least once, and threatened it countless other times, yet Dr. Bean-Bayog had met no one in his family until she was ready to cut Paul loose.

There were only three people in that hospital room on the afternoon of May 18, 1990. One is dead, and the other two do not agree about what was said. Dr. Bean-Bayog concedes she did not ask Marcos Lozano if he could corroborate Paul's memories of sexual and physical abuse because it seemed unnecessary to her. "The patient had told me that the father knew about the sexual abuse and had, in fact, made comments on it all through his childhood, including things that humiliated the patient terribly, such as saying to the patient—I don't know what the Spanish word for this is, but it was a term for a woman's genitals; that the father would say to Paul, 'You really like your mother's breadbasket, don't you?' And the patient would be tremendously humiliated by this, so I don't think it was news to anyone. The sexual abuse was open in the family. Paul would see it when he went home. The father saw it when Paul was a child."

In her note in the hospital chart, Dr. Bean-Bayog wrote that she told Mr. Lozano that his son was seriously ill, that his mental illness had a "chemical component," and that "there may have been childhood trauma including a [question] of physical abuse, and a [question] of sexual abuse."

She noted that Mr. Lozano "denied any knowledge that PL had ever been suicidal till yesterday," but made no reference to his reaction to her questions of abuse. She would say later that she was surprised he did not have any. But, in speaking with Paul after his father left that day, Dr. Bean-Bayog heard another explanation for the silence of Mr. Lozano, who still has trouble with English. "He didn't understand," Paul told her.

Marcos Lozano insists he was never told by Dr. Bean-Bayog, or anyone else, that Paul's experiences in childhood contributed to his depression. It was a brief meeting with Dr. Bean-Bayog, he said tearfully, and the doctor spoke too fast. "I say, 'Dr. Bean, what is the problem with Paul?' Dr. Bean, she says, 'Paul have no problems; it's a chemical in the blood.' She tells me Paul has an eighty percent chance of dying by suicide. I don't understand, why this change in him? 'It's in the blood,' she says. 'He's got depression, too much, that's all.'

"I tell her I come here in nineteen forty-six. I work twenty-five years, become an American citizen. I work hard. I have good reputation. I raise six kids, Dr. Bean, and never on welfare, never take food stamps. My kids, they go to college. She never asks me: 'Did you hurt Paul? Did his mother hurt Paul?'"

Burdened by the cost of airline tickets and the difficulty of taking time from their jobs, Paul's parents called upon their children to stagger visits to Paul that spring so that he would not be alone.

Abel's immediate reaction to their request was annoyance. He was busy at work in Fayetteville, North Carolina, and he did not have the time or the money to drive to Boston. Besides, he suspected Paul's chief malady was malingering. The two had not kept in close touch in recent years, and Pilar and his parents had not kept Abel abreast of the seriousness of Paul's condition.

"I have a real sharp memory of being here at home late in the afternoon when my mother calls. She is crying. Not crying hysterically. But she is upset," he said.

"Paul tried to kill himself," she told Abel. "You know he's been sick."

"No, I don't know. You guys haven't told me anything," Abel protested. "Why do you wait until he's tried to kill himself to call me? Where is he? What do you need?"

"We can't afford to go and see him again. We're spent," she told him.

Abel began making his own mental calculations. He and Sandy had no savings; they did not have any discretionary money for a trip like this. What he did have was a Rolex watch, a sort of trophy from his high-energy days as a salesman in Albuquerque. Those were heady times. He would routinely put in twelve-hour days and never feel exhausted. Only later would he crash, unable to make good on all his commitments when his energy leveled off. The pattern eventually cost him his job, but he still had the Rolex as a reminder. He pawned it.

"I had worn it all through the army, and I was really proud of it," Abel remembered. "And I resented the shit out of Paul making me go through these sacrifices to go up there and hold his hand. The approach I was taking is really confusing. But part of me knew that something was wrong and I just didn't know what. Out of frustration, I was angry."

He and Sandy packed the car and drove north with three-year-old Alexis. They reached Boston, tired and frazzled by the traffic. The house in which Paul was renting a room was dark. There was a light on in a basement apartment, however, and the young man living there directed them up the stairs to Paul's attic room.

"There is nobody else in this huge house. All the rooms are dark. We go up this spiral staircase to his room, and I'm thinking, 'Why is he living here?' The apartment smelled like a cat box," Abel remembered. "He could be living opulently in Texas and going to medical school there. Why is he putting up with this?"

Abel telephoned the hospital for directions, and the three weary travelers set off for Faulkner. "When I first saw him, he gave me the biggest hug I had ever gotten from him. I thought, 'Good, at least he wants me here.'"

It was not until the next day that the brothers could get past the pleasantries to talk about Paul's situation. Abel told him he had pawned his watch to make the trip and was feeling a little angry about it.

"If you really want to kill yourself, just tell me, I'm not going to get mad. Just tell me what's going on," Abel said.

The two were sitting on the lawn outside the hospital while Sandy played with Alexis. Abel remembers Paul's half of the conversation as "sort of stream of consciousness." One minute he was talking about his research, the next about the games they had played as children.

"What did they teach you in that army medical course

you took about medical records?" Paul suddenly asked his brother.

"That they're the property of the federal government. If I make a medical record I'm responsible for it for the duration of its existence. The only person I could pass it to is a physician," Abel answered.

"Did you know that in the civilian world medical records are personal property of the physician?" Paul asked.

"Well, yeah," said Abel, wondering where this conversation was leading.

"That's my problem," Paul said.

"What do you mean?" Abel asked.

"There are things in my record, they're horrible, and I can't change them," Paul told him.

"Paul was as coherent as I've seen him," Abel insisted later, but at the time he had no idea what his kid brother was talking about, and Paul grew reticent when Abel pushed for more of an explanation.

Abel got no additional information from the hospital staff. He told them what Paul was like as a child, sometimes "spacey," he said, always smart. While Paul was having a meeting with a staff member, Abel found a bag of prescription drugs in the bedroom closet of Paul's apartment. He drove to Faulkner and interrupted the meeting.

"I'm supposed to have those," Paul told him.

"Nobody has that much of anything unless they are hoarding it," Abel said.

At that point Abel looked at the staff member for support. It seemed obvious to him that if Paul was suicidal, he shouldn't be hoarding drugs.

"That's really not an issue right now," the staff member responded.

Chastened and still confused when he left Boston, Abel was no more certain of what Paul's problems were than when he had arrived. But Abel's visit did have a positive effect on his brother's spirits. "Paul states he had not appreciated how much he missed a sense of family around him," a nurse wrote during Abel's stay.

The nursing notes also reflect the trouble Paul Lozano was

having with the idea of never seeing Margaret Bean-Bayog again. More than once, he reported to nurses that he felt as though he was "losing his mother."

Christi Clark, Paul's primary nurse, remembered him clutching Pound Puppy to his chest, telling her "that he supposed he had been abused as a child," and speaking "in a little boy's voice." He often wore a T-shirt with Asian writing on the front, a gift from Dr. Bean-Bayog. "He said she gave it to him after a vacation that she took, which made him feel cared about. That's why he wore it," according to Clark.

Paul Lozano tried desperately to hold on to Margaret Bean-Bayog: asking Harvard Medical School that spring about loans to fund his psychotherapy; soliciting support from Dr. Thomas G. Gutheil, the Harvard psychiatrist whom she had brought in as a consultant when her management of the case began to fall apart that spring. He made inquiries about selling the new Honda Accord he had bought with his insurance settlement to raise money to pay her. His parents, by now skeptical that this psychiatrist could help their son but eager to calm him, offered to dig further into their retirement account, which was already nearly depleted by their cross-country trips to visit Paul during his hospitalizations.

"We tell him, 'Paul, if this Dr. Bean is what you need, we'll find the money,'" Marcos recalled. "What else could we do? No one told us what does a family who loves their son do."

But Paul would not take their hard-earned savings. In the end, he thought he should let go. He might be "better off without her," he said.

When he was especially distraught at the idea of losing Dr. Bean-Bayog he would pull out his Handy, Multipurpose Emergency and Reference Flash Card Deck and thumb through all her messages about a mother who would always love him and who would never leave him. "He said he used them when he was upset to soothe himself," Clark said of the flash cards she often saw him fingering. But, amazingly, Clark says neither she nor anyone else at Faulkner ever reviewed the cards for content. If they had, Dr. Bean-Bayog's unorthodox techniques would have been discovered and, perhaps, challenged.

Dr. Bean-Bayog had prepared flash cards to address Paul's intense separation anxiety:

> I want to get close because this makes me so sad. You betrayed all my love and trust, ALL of it. I hate you so much. I hate myself and I'm dying of sorrow and I want to die. I have to leave and start over and not trust anyone.
>
> [On reverse]: We've got to figure out how you can get comforted safely. If getting hugged will get crazy, you'll have to stay safe. I think you'll figure out some ways to get comfort safely.

> Sure. Fine. So if you love me and care for me, how can you possibly leave me when it makes me hurt so much?
>
> [On reverse]: Sometimes people leave each other even when they love them so much, as much as we love each other. Even though it hurts terribly. Just remember the love is bigger. LOTS bigger. And stronger. And lasts. Outlasts the pain and hate. I hate your pain. I want to hold you till it's all gone.

When Dr. Bean-Bayog did disengage at last, she seemed to blame her patient, not her therapy, for the bad ending. "Discussed how he put me into a bind where if he got what he needed, I was exploited and abused, or else I set a limit and he was abandoned and deprived," she wrote in his chart, ignoring the fact that it had been the doctor, not the patient, who had established the limitless terms of the therapy at the outset, on that November day in 1986 when "we invented a baby version of him who might have something on his mind."

Whether from the natural progression of his mental illness or as a consequence of her therapy, there was no disputing that the patient Dr. Bean-Bayog left behind in

1990 was a far more disturbed young man than the one she had met four years before. Paul accepted her departure with a mixture of pain and terror. In a final note, handed to her during their last meeting at Faulkner on June 17, 1990, he wrote:

> Thank you for all you have done for me. I have many memories, good and some bad, which I keep forever. Missing you is a difficult thing, but I must keep in mind what I receive from you lasts forever. In that sense the relationship never ends. I'm having difficulty with my thoughts right now. They seem intolerable. The thought of never seeing you again disturbs me deeply. I only wish I could express how much I will miss you. Sometimes I wonder what I will do without you, but maybe I need this experience to grow up a little bit. I'll miss the books we shared, the small gifts, like the shirt, the phone calls which helped me through difficult times. I am trying to understand why we need to terminate for financial and other reasons.

Margaret Bean-Bayog's last notes to her patient were no less personal, reflecting the ambiguous mix of love and need that had marked their relationship from the very beginning:

> We've done an incredible piece of work. I want you to get well. I want you to take good care of yourself and not hurt yourself. I still love you and always will care what happens to you. You've been stuck feeling either you would get rejected or get too close. The choice I had was either to let you in close or inflict pain. It will be easier in a new therapy to understand what happened, and to have more life besides therapy. I will miss you, too. Dr. Bean-Bayog.

> I love you. I loved working with you. I want you to stay alive and get well. I'll miss you too. Some-

times we had a wonderful time. Sometimes it hurt.
We both got angry, too. You know how to use help
to get well. I want you to get all the way well so you
can take what I gave you and fly. Things you wish
you hadn't done or said weren't your fault or mine.
Take care of yourself. Let me know from time to
time what has become of you. Love, Dr. B.

The Lozano family had no ambivalence about Dr. Bean-
Bayog's departure. They were hopeful that a fresh start with
a new therapist could turn things around. And from here on
in, the family was determined not to be shut out. It was a
family decision to send Coral Grossman, Paul's sister
Norma's daughter, to look after her uncle when he was
released from Faulkner Hospital in July. No longer would
the family piece together what was happening to Paul in
long-distance telephone calls to nursing stations in faraway
hospitals. They now had their own emissary on the scene.

No one was more enthusiastic about the idea than Coral
and Paul themselves. Four years apart in age, they were
more like cousins than uncle and niece. They had played
together as children and, as adults, they shared the same
perspective on the world, aligning with Martha to form the
most liberal wing of the centrist Lozano clan. Abel, who had
appalled them all when he registered as a Republican at
eighteen, had the right-of-center position all to himself.

Coral was twenty-two in 1990, active in her church, and
searching for a way to apply the principles of social justice
that she had learned there. Keeping house for Paul during
this difficult time promised to be that opportunity.

Paul looked terrible when Coral arrived on July 22. His
acne, always an annoyance to him, was out of control. He
was pale and thin but less fragile than she had expected.
They spent the first two weeks playing tourist. He took her
whale watching and to all the museums. They went canoeing
and to a lobster bake on Cape Cod with Paul's friends from
the Tropical Disease Laboratory at the Harvard School of
Public Health, where he had resumed work as soon as he
was released from the hospital.

His cheeks soon regained their color, he put some weight back on—his niece's marginal cooking skills notwithstanding—and he looked after Coral as much as she did him. The night before she was to begin a part-time data-processing job to help with expenses, Paul took her out on the highway for a dry run to the office so she would not get lost during the morning rush hour. He once choked down what she described as an indigestible dinner of bean sprouts and tofu rather than hurt her feelings.

Outwardly, he appeared to be holding himself together, but he confided to several people the strain he was feeling. He often called the Faulkner ward where he had spent almost four months, to talk to the nurses. He kept in touch with patients he had met there who had resumed their lives. One of them remembers him as sensitive and kind and terribly vulnerable. Paul would call, needing to speak with someone who understood; he said it was not easy to talk to his medical school classmates or his lab partners about his mental illness. "Sometimes when we talked it was like when an old person is recalling a childhood experience—and there is that shift on their face, you can see the child in them again," his friend from Faulkner said of their long talks and pizza dinners that summer. "That happened with him sometimes. He was a child. He didn't present like the competent Harvard student he was."

He often would hold back the details of what he was feeling, but his friend could tell that he was troubled. The subject of his old therapist was a recurring theme. "I knew he cared very much about this person. He was very angry at her. I saw both aspects of him. He struck me as a very intelligent person. He also expressed an intense willfulness, like a four-year-old who gets that look on their face—they want what they want *now*. He couldn't get her to do what he wanted and he was very upset."

With the help of the Faulkner staff and the knowledge of Dr. Bean-Bayog, Paul had hooked up with a new therapist while he was still hospitalized. Twice a week, he was to see Dr. Leonard Lai, a psychiatrist-in-training at the Massachusetts Mental Health Center. He was assigned to a resident, rather than an experienced psychiatrist, for financial reasons: he could see Dr. Lai for reduced fees.

From the first, it was clear that the loss of Dr. Bean-Bayog would preoccupy much of their work. That relationship was ending when Dr. Lai first began seeing Paul in the hospital. His problems making the break with Dr. Bean-Bayog had, in fact, prolonged his stay at Faulkner. At his initial meeting with Paul, Dr. Lai could see the challenge facing him. Paul was anxious, distant. He wanted Dr. Bean-Bayog, not a substitute.

Ending a long-term therapeutic relationship, what psychiatry refers to as "termination," is a difficult process under the best of circumstances. And these circumstances were far from the best. Paul felt abandoned, dumped, replaced by the son Dr. Bean-Bayog was about to adopt.

From Dr. John Vara, Paul's new psychopharmacologist and Dr. Lai's supervisor, Dr. Lai learned that the termination was prompted by her pending adoption and Paul's lack of funds to pay for therapy. From the Faulkner treatment team, he learned that the patient's suicide attempt followed auditory hallucinations of Dr. Bean-Bayog urging him to kill himself. From Dr. Bean-Bayog herself, Dr. Lai says he learned absolutely nothing. Throughout the transition, and after, they never spoke.

The shadow of Margaret Bean-Bayog hung over every session, however. Paul Lozano still talked about the pressure to succeed in medical school, but mostly he talked about his yearning for his old psychiatrist. Because Dr. Bean-Bayog and Dr. Lai never spoke, Dr. Lai was left to learn what details he could about her therapy piecemeal and incomplete, from the patient himself.

Even before he was discharged from the hospital, Paul told Dr. Lai he both was sexually attracted to Dr. Bean-Bayog and felt that she was his mother. "He said that she proposed that he may have been sexually abused, but he's unclear," Dr. Lai also recalled. "He felt that he had become dependent on Dr. Bean, that he needed to see her."

He pressed Dr. Lai for the same limitless access he had had with Dr. Bean-Bayog. Could he call him at home whenever he wanted? Would Dr. Lai see him on weekends? At night? On demand? Dr. Lai told Paul there was a crisis intervention team at the Massachusetts Mental Health Center for emergencies, that he needed to rely on a support network, not just his primary therapist. That was not Paul Lozano's experience of therapy, and Dr. Lai's resistance to the role of rescuer angered him. As a result, the two never formed a working alliance.

Dr. Lai was not the real source of Paul Lozano's fury, however. At the end of July, he cycled the two miles from his apartment in Brookline to Dr. Lai's office for his regular session. Dr. Lai remembered that he was alert, oriented, and coherent. With some difficulty Paul told his therapist that he was wrestling with his anger at Dr. Bean-Bayog. It was not just that she had left him. "He felt used," Dr. Lai said, recalling their conversation that day.

"She gave me some manuscripts, explicit—these manuscripts were explicit about her sexual fantasies about me," Paul said.

"When was this?" Dr. Lai asked.

"Several years ago," Paul told him. "Therapists are not supposed to do that. It is strange, don't you think?"

"It's unusual," Dr. Lai conceded. "Did you talk about the manuscripts with Dr. Bean?"

"Yes, for a few sessions. I've never told anyone this," he said. "Do you want to see them?"

"Yes, if you want me to," Dr. Lai replied. Then he inquired delicately, "Did you have any physical contact with Dr. Bean?"

"Yes, but it was just a hug," Paul answered. "It felt strange, but there was nothing sexual about it. She shouldn't have shown me the manuscripts."

Dr. Lai said when Paul Lozano finished talking there was a moment of silence and his patient closed his eyes. "It's not easy talking about this," Paul said. He had considered reporting Dr. Bean-Bayog to the state medical board, Paul told Dr. Lai, "but he felt they probably wouldn't do anything about it because he cared for her."

Dr. Lai never did review Paul's copies of Margaret

Bean-Bayog's fantasies. Nor did he contact Dr. Bean-Bayog herself or alert the Board of Registration in Medicine to possible improprieties. He said he felt he did not have enough information and did not want to push a patient with whom he had a tenuous alliance at best.

The session was difficult for Paul. Soon afterward, he stopped taking his antidepressants and his Haldol, a drug added to his daily regimen at Faulkner to control the psychotic features of his illness. "He was very upset that he had this illness, and he wanted to control it. But there was a certain kind of irresponsibility," his friend from Faulkner recalled of Paul's failure to take his pills regularly. When he did not take his medication, however, the hallucinations returned and that was even more upsetting to him. "He wanted to change it, to not be ill, but he couldn't change it."

Dr. Lai saw in Paul the same refusal to acknowledge the seriousness of his illness. His patient talked "about not wanting to disappoint me and wanting to show how well he was doing, but not wanting to be dependent on me. He said that he was too dependent on Dr. Bean. He thought that she was not very professional about it; that he wanted to stand on his own.

"Then he talked about going back to medical school and wanting to be a normal medical student, and mentioned that Dr. Bean used to give him gifts, that she treated him like a son and suddenly it all changed. That Dr. Bean didn't help him when all he wanted to be was a normal medical student."

Without his medication, his condition worsened. His middle-of-the-night calls to Pilar increased. He became paranoid, telling her that people were staring at him, discriminating against him because he was a Mexican-American. He slept all day and worked all night. Coral had trouble keeping track of him. When he was home he spent most of his time alone in his room, staring blankly into space. He sometimes asked her to sleep on the sofa in his room so he would not be alone.

Pilar began to suspect that something in her brother simply had "snapped." "By then I'm almost beginning to believe that it's genetic. That he has, in fact, gone mad. That he is losing his mind. Because I don't see evidence of street drugs; I don't see any evidence of alcohol abuse. I'm just seeing him in and out of this madness. Mostly in. And all I hear is Margaret, Margaret, Margaret."

Paul began skipping his appointments with Dr. Lai. By the last week of August, he was barely going at all. "He told me that he had called Dr. Bean sometime during that week and that she was angry and said that he was splitting his treatment [i.e., pitting his old therapist against the new one]," Dr. Lai said, adding that Dr. Bean-Bayog never called him. She did call Paul, however.

"He took the phone over to his desk. I could hear him say, 'What do you mean it's over?'" Coral recalled. "He hung up and came over to my room. He said, 'That was Margaret, a woman I was really in love with. She says she won't see me anymore.' I said, 'Who's Margaret? Your girlfriend?' 'No,' he said, 'she's my therapist.' He showed me two of the baby books and said, 'Look, she gave me these.' I didn't know what to make of them. Maybe I should have paid more attention. But he was in a big uproar after her call, so we went out for ice cream, and he was fine. I could tell he was still thinking about her, though."

Paul Lozano was on Dr. Bean-Bayog's mind as well. That summer she discussed her sexual feelings toward a patient she described as a "Mexican-American medical student" with a small group of more-junior therapists who met every Wednesday afternoon in her Lexington home. The women paid Dr. Bean-Bayog $50 an hour for her help with their most difficult cases, and she often discussed some of her own.

It was a professional group, but it also had its personal, informal moments. Participants swapped gardening catalogs, and Dr. Bean-Bayog shared with them the bureaucratic delays she and her husband were experiencing in their quest to adopt a son.

Only two of the five women who attended those sessions later recalled Dr. Bean-Bayog's mention of the patient they would later learn was Paul Lozano. Kathryn Kogan, a clinical psychologist, remembered that Dr. Bean-Bayog briefly "mentioned that she was having sexual feelings and fantasies as part of her ongoing work with this patient" and that she was writing down her fantasies "as a way of staying on top of the situation, a way of keeping it within a scientific framework." Dr. Bean-Bayog did not share the explicit and sadomasochistic nature of her fantasies with the group.

Amy Stromsten, the social worker who first met Paul in 1986 during his hospitalization at McLean, objected when Dr. Bean-Bayog began to discuss her sexual feelings for a suicidal Mexican-American medical student.

"Don't you remember? I was his therapist at McLean. I know the patient you are talking about. I feel there is a little boundary conflict here," Stromsten recalled interjecting. "She brushed me off and went right on. It wasn't in the context of 'this is how you manage countertransference.' It was just that she was oozing all over the place," she said of Dr. Bean-Bayog's comments about Paul Lozano.

By the time he became the topic of Dr. Bean-Bayog's supervision group, Paul Lozano was in search of yet another therapist. He did not want to continue with Dr. Lai, so he called Massachusetts General Hospital for help in locating a new therapist. When he was assigned to a young psychiatrist-in-training for evaluation, he was delighted. With her straight, shoulder-length hair, Dr. Carol S. Birnbaum even looked a little like Margaret, he thought, although at twenty-eight she was twenty years Dr. Bean-Bayog's junior.

On the afternoon Paul Lozano met with Dr. Birnbaum he was agitated, having gone without sleep for days. He was sweating; he tapped his foot nervously as they talked in the small office. He told her he had been drinking and taking fentanyl, a barbiturate used by anesthesiologists. He needed a new therapist, he said, because his psychiatrist could no longer afford to subsidize his care. It was as though he had never been in therapy with Dr. Lai, as though the interlude had never happened. He reverted to his years with Margaret Bean-Bayog.

"He described her in idealized terms," Birnbaum recalled. "Extremely empathetic, kind, always there for him. Basically, irreplaceable. It specifically sounded like she could do no wrong whatsoever, which is humanly impossible. I was afraid of his idealizing me in the same way, even though I had only spent a total of forty-five minutes with him."

His description of Dr. Bean-Bayog and the end of their therapeutic relationship made Dr. Birnbaum "wonder whether boundaries were an issue in the therapy," she said. "It's important to recognize what the patient's sense of boundaries are and it's important to help the patient see where boundaries are between yourself and them in the treatment."

He shared with her his feelings of loneliness, worthlessness, and both his indebtedness to his family and resentment for the pressure he felt from them to finish medical school. All the self-blaming emotions that had characterized his illness from the outset were on display before yet another psychiatrist.

Paul told her that he had been hospitalized after injecting potentially fatal substances but that if he were really trying to kill himself, he would use potassium chloride. He was showing signs of psychosis; he seemed to be responding to an internal voice, Dr. Birnbaum recalled. It was difficult for her to focus his attention.

"The pervasive memory I have was one of being very frightened. I was very frightened," she said. "I had the feeling that he was an extremely high suicide risk. He was very reluctant to accompany me down to the emergency room. I was seeing him up in the general psychiatry practice. I cut the session a few minutes short because I felt that it wasn't a case of evaluating someone for long-term therapy, but that I wanted to commit him to a locked unit."

Paul went along reluctantly, protesting that he was fine. The emergency room staff immediately put Paul Lozano in restraints and transferred him to the Massachusetts Mental Health Center. From there, he was sent to a locked ward at Malden Hospital, just north of Boston. "He was hospitalized three times and I never saw it coming," Coral remembered. The telephone would ring and only then would she notice that the Pound Puppy was gone from its usual resting place on the bed. "It would be the hospital on the phone. The Pound Puppy went with him to the hospital every time."

Paul protested that this was all a "misunderstanding"; he just needed a new therapist. He tried frequently to reach Dr. Birnbaum by phone from Malden Hospital, but her supervisors, concerned about his instant and intense attachment, deflected his calls. He knew he was upset by the loss of Dr. Bean-Bayog. His description of the reason for termination —that he had become a burden for his psychiatrist—struck Douglas F. Watt, the psychologist who evaluated Paul at Malden Hospital, as "a rather damaging and very unfortunate note on which to end."

Paul insisted he would get over the loss of Margaret Bean-Bayog. He told the staff that he had a new girlfriend and that his life was looking up. He signed out against medical advice.

He did have a new girlfriend, but Paul Lozano's behavior was beginning to alarm her as well. Martha Lundgren had worked with Paul in the lab at the Harvard School of Public Health for some time before he gathered the courage to approach her. "The way he asked me out was real childlike," she recalled. "He came up and took a deep breath and sighed, 'Will you go out with me?'" They went out to lunch on their first date. They were scheduled to meet at the Museum of Fine Arts for their second, but "he never showed. He gave me a dozen roses he was so apologetic. He said he got really busy at work." In fact, while Martha was waiting at the museum, Paul was in the hospital.

Other dates followed—to a Thai restaurant for dinner, to the movies. He never drank on their dates. They talked mostly about their families and their plans for the future. He told her that he would like to make enough money as an anesthesiologist to buy his parents a house. Martha told him about a family member who had had psychiatric problems and about her desire to learn dance therapy and one day work with emotionally disturbed children.

"We talked a lot about what we could do to help people through our work. He wanted to make money, to buy his family a house, but he also wanted to make a contribution to the world," she said. "Paul was a nice man, a kind man."

Martha liked Paul, she said, but "I was getting very confused. He was calling me every day. My roommate would say, 'He's called three times this afternoon.' He wanted to be with me all the time. When I entered the lab, he'd follow me around. I was self-conscious. I mean, we were at work.

"He gave me five separate phone numbers where I could reach him at all times because he was sometimes hard to get in touch with. He worked a lot, at night too. They were mostly Harvard-related numbers, but it seemed strange. I didn't need them all."

Paul got upset when Martha said she would be visiting her family in Pittsburgh for three days. "I'll worry about you," he told her. She offered to call from the road during the drive, but he was unappeased. "I could tell he was angry," she said.

He never told her the details of his psychiatric history, but he did not need to. Martha knew he was preoccupied and depressed. "He was blanking out sometimes. We'd be talking and then he'd just look off into space. I'd wait—it would last maybe a minute—and then I'd ask what he was thinking about and he'd pick up the conversation from before as if he'd never blanked out. He looked like he was walking on air," she remembered. "He was depressed, but he could be a normal person, too."

He was not a normal person for most of the autumn of 1990.

Bouncing between therapists and refusing to take his medication, Paul "just disappeared from the lab," Martha recalled. "No one told me where he went and I was afraid to ask. In fact, when I was dating him I wanted to say to them in the lab that he didn't look well. What should we do? But they just didn't seem to be paying attention. When he died, it was really strange. No one ever talked about it. I just figured maybe this is the Harvard way: pretend it isn't there and it will go away. And if you can't pretend, then keep a tight lock on it."

In the week following his release from Malden Hospital, Paul turned up several times in crisis at the Massachusetts Mental Health Center, preoccupied with thoughts of suicide. On the eighth day, he was admitted to the psychiatric unit of Carney Hospital in Boston.

He had not seen Dr. Lai for weeks; he had discontinued all his medications; and, despite his obvious distress, he talked about his need to resume medical school. "He was trying to pretend that there wasn't anything seriously wrong, when it seemed clear to me that there was something very seriously wrong, and that his not taking the Haldol was kind of a way of saying, 'I'm okay. I'm really okay,'" Dr. Dean Solomon, the psychiatrist in charge of his care at Carney, recalled.

"He had signed out AMA [against medical advice] just a week before. He was insisting that he had to go keep up a pretense at his work, and it seemed to me it wasn't clear to him that that was really not going to work, that he was sicker than that, but he wasn't willing to hear it when I said that to him.

"I remember at the time thinking what he needed was some older, maternal kind of social worker who might be able to see him once a week and kind of be sensible and help him to focus on the real challenges that he faced in his life. He was not going forward in his life."

The leaves were falling in Boston, but Paul Lozano was stuck in time, locked in the previous spring when he still felt some hope of saving his relationship with Dr. Margaret Bean-Bayog.

"He obviously still had thoughts of her regularly," Dr. Solomon said. "I thought that he was deeply involved. I felt that the involvement was, in fact, problematic for him, that he probably was experiencing more strong feelings than he knew what to do with and that he probably didn't expect that."

When Paul left Carney, again against medical advice, Dr. Solomon recalled that Paul was so regressed in his behavior that he was "essentially helpless, not having a capacity or a force directed at trying to get his life back.

"The patient wanted to deny the seriousness of his difficulties, wanted to pretend that things were going to be fine and not allow any of this stuff to interfere with his plans, with, you know, going ahead with his work and his schooling."

Paul Lozano "had a long road ahead of him," in Dr. Solomon's view. "I did not think that he would be able to go back to finish medical school in the first year or two. I thought he would probably lose at least a year or two. I felt that he would probably have more hospitalizations, even with a good therapist."

In his discharge note in the hospital chart, Dr. Solomon wrote: "It seemed possible that the patient was continuing some kind of attachment to his longstanding therapist, Dr. Margaret Bean, by continuing to be unable to progress in his life, staying attached to her in a regressive fashion."

Paul Lozano's attachment was so strong that, even as he told Dr. Solomon that he would ask Dr. Gerald Adler, his supervisor during his aborted psychiatry clerkship the previous winter, for help finding a new therapist, he actually was plotting how to win Dr. Bean-Bayog back.

He asked Dr. Adler to intervene with Margaret. "He was upset about the termination, feeling he didn't know why they terminated and whether they really had terminated and he was upset," Dr. Adler recalled. "So, as a professional thing to do, you want to straighten out a mess."

He offered to call Dr. Bean-Bayog. Their conversation was brief, as Dr. Adler recalled it. "She told me she had told him clearly why [they had terminated] and that he was confused and distorting and was in treatment with other people. I think I said something like, 'Would it help him in any way, do you think, if you were to tell him that personally? Would it then help him to go into another therapy?' She said she would be willing to talk with him and that was the end of the discussion with her."

Dr. Bean-Bayog did talk to Paul Lozano, telling him their relationship was over and that she would not take him back into therapy. At Massachusetts General Hospital, he was assigned as an outpatient to a young Hispanic doctor doing his fellowship in psychiatry. When Dr. José Saporta first met Paul, it was his sense "that I should not get too invested in whether he gets through medical school. I was having my doubts whether he could do it."

Dr. Saporta could see from the moment they met that Paul Lozano was in no shape for outpatient psychotherapy. Just as he had bounced for months from evaluators to therapists to crisis intervention teams to emergency rooms to psychiatric wards, Paul landed next on the doorstep of Harvard University's Stillman Infirmary.

Assessed there as psychotically depressed, he was transferred on October 19 to Newton-Wellesley Hospital in a suburb west of Boston for a course of electroconvulsive, or shock, therapy—a treatment option that, ironically, was first recommended for Paul Lozano at McLean Hospital three years earlier, in the event a serious trial of medication failed to reverse his depression.

Chapter

7

It was well after midnight when Pilar Williams's plane began to circle Logan International Airport, waiting for clearance to land. The lights of the city below were invisible, shrouded from view by heavy rainclouds.

"No wonder Paul got depressed living here," Pilar murmured and allowed herself an indulgent moment of wishful thinking. If only her brother's problems were as simple as longing for sunnier climes.

But there was no pretending any longer that her brother's depression bore any similarity to rainy-day blues. How many times had she or her parents or one of her siblings made this trip to Boston in the last six months? How many psychiatric wards had Paul been in since her last visit? So often and so many that she found herself actually relieved that her brother was now starting electroshock treatments.

As her plane broke through the cloud cover, the beacon atop the old John Hancock Building cast a crimson glow. The beacon is programmed to shine red in rain and blue when skies over Boston are fair. Pilar Williams was sure she had never seen it blue.

For someone else Boston might be the City on the Hill, an

educational and medical mecca, hugging the shoreline that had once welcomed the nation's first immigrants. For Pilar Williams, it was the end of the earth, a place so elitist and tradition-bound that it could extend no welcoming embrace to the outsiders she and her family felt themselves to be.

At least this new psychiatrist had called her to discuss his treatment plans, she thought. That was certainly a change from Margaret Bean-Bayog. And this Dr. William Barry Gault had sounded sincere when he said he was looking forward to meeting her.

After getting his call, Pilar had never been more grateful to be a nurse. Her parents' notion of shock treatment was formed by Hollywood; they shuddered at the *One Flew Over the Cuckoo's Nest* image of their son strapped, helpless, to a metal table, his body convulsing in spastic reaction to bolts of electric current zapping through his brain.

She had explained that these freakish images belonged to the past, but still, she understood their fear. ECT does, after all, entail electric current running through the brain. But the fact is, she told her parents, it is a tiny amount of electric current and what happens is actually very undramatic.

Through an intravenous drip, the anesthesiologist gives the patient a fast-acting hypnotic, which puts him or her to sleep in five or ten seconds. The patient is then given medication that prevents all of the body's muscles, except the heart, from contracting. Because the breathing muscles are paralyzed, the anesthesiologist uses a rubber bag attached to a face mask to pump oxygen in and out of the patient's lungs.

Through wires attached either at both temples or from the apex of the head to one temple, the electric current passes for a fraction of a second into the brain. For approximately thirty seconds, all of the cells of the brain become active. Each cell discharges in its normal manner. What is abnormal is that all of the brain's cells are discharging at the same time.

If the patient were not put to sleep and the muscles not controlled, he would experience the grand mal seizures of which horror movies are made. Instead, the atmosphere is decidedly calm. The machine through which the electric current passes emits a low-level electronic tone. The patient's toes might wiggle a bit, but basically, there is nothing to see.

The patient awakens after three or four minutes, feeling confused. It takes another ten minutes for him or her to become alert and oriented. Short-term memory can be disrupted for a few days, but long-term memory suffers no adverse effects.

Although the procedure appears benign, the results are often dramatic. While the precise cause of incapacitating depression is not known, antidepressant medication and electroconvulsive therapy can bring the system back into balance by acting on the neurotransmitters that carry messages between brain cells. The result can be a full remission of the depression.

Far from being disturbed by Dr. Gault's recommendation of ECT, Pilar Williams saw it as cause for hope. Her telephone conversation with Paul from the hospital had given her some reason for optimism as well. His speech was slow, his tone weepy, and he talked incessantly about Margaret. But his lamentations about missing her, needing her, and loving her made Pilar wonder if her brother's depression this time was triggered by a broken heart. Maybe he had simply fallen in love with his therapist. That certainly was not unprecedented.

If Dr. Gault could reverse his depression, it would not be too difficult a matter for a supportive therapist to help him understand that, as strong as the bond might be between a patient and a therapist, it is not love.

She was curious what Paul had meant when he told her there was material in his apartment that would explain everything. It had been a long day and she had worked her regular shift in the recovery room before catching her plane. Pilar Williams hoped she would not be too tired to read whatever it was that Paul was talking about.

Coral met her at the departure gate and led her out into the rain to catch the shuttle bus to the subway for the trip back to Paul's apartment, where Pilar's mother was waiting. Epifania Lozano had flown to Boston as soon as she heard Paul was hospitalized. She did not want to wait until Pilar arranged coverage for her shift at work.

She was sitting in the rocking chair when the sodden pair of subway riders arrived. She made tea while Pilar searched for the materials that Paul had said she should read. It did not take her long to locate them.

In a box near his desk, Pilar found neatly stacked hand-written notebook pages, greeting cards, and index cards. There were books and an audiocassette, stuffed animals, a T-shirt, a baby blanket, a woman's shawl from the Philippines.

The rain dripped from her hair onto the title pages of the fifteen books she pulled from the box. What are these children's books doing here? What are they for? she wondered as she read the inscriptions inside:

The Velveteen Rabbit by Margery Williams. "For all of you, when someone loves you for a long, long time, not just to play with, but really loves you, then you become real. Sometimes it hurts, though. Love, Dr. B."

Alexander and the Terrible, Horrible, No Good, Very Bad Day by Judith Viorst. "For any of you who are having a day like this. Dr. Bean."

Where the Wild Things Are by Maurice Sendak. "This one is for the boy, but I think his older brother will like it, too. Dr. B."

Goodnight Moon by Margaret Wise Brown. "This one is for the baby. Love, Dr. Bean."

Owl at Home by Arnold Lobel. "This one is for the boy, Dr. Bean."

The Adventures of Tin-Tin. Tin-Tin in America. "I didn't forget their Cynical Protector and Older Brother. Love to him, too. Dr. Bean."

Sarah, Plain and Tall by Patricia MacLachlan. "With love to the boy. Dr. B."

I Am Not Going to Get Up Today by Dr. Seuss. "Love, Dr. B."

The Cat in the Hat by Dr. Seuss. "Love Dr. B."

Miss Rumphius by Barbara Cooney. "Love, Dr. B."

A House Is a House for Me by Mary Ann Hoberman. "For the boy with love."

"Good God," Pilar whispered to Coral, afraid of alarming her mother. "Maybe my brother has multiple personality disorder. Perhaps he has written these things because he imagined them. He is writing these things because he is just so very sick."

Then she noticed the signatures. She ran across the room to Paul's desk and furiously searched through lab sheets and computer printouts, until she found some notations in his own hand. She compared them with the book inscriptions. The handwriting on the books clearly was not Paul's. "Could his psychiatrist have written this stuff?" she asked Coral.

As she dug deeper into the box the answer became both more obvious and less clear.

There was a postcard from the Manila Hotel: "This is where the Bean Bear stayed for five days. He liked it. The lobby never looked like this. It was always jammed. I miss the boy. I miss you. I hope you're doing fine. I think of you a lot every day." It was signed "Love, Dr. B."

There was a Christmas card from "Santa Bear," and another of flying geese signed "This is how I see you. Love, Dr. Bean," and yet another wishing him "a restful Christmastime and a wonderful one." It was signed "Mom."

There was a Valentine's Day card, featuring a cartoon of a blue elephant holding a balloon that said "With Love, Son: This elephant brings lots of love because it's plain to see that you are loved as much as any son could be!" It was signed "Dr. B."

Maybe it was the predawn hour or the chill from the rain, but Pilar Williams began to feel that, like Alice, she had stepped through the looking glass.

What was this Handy, Multipurpose Emergency and Reference Flash Card Deck? And who was pretending to be her brother's mother? Who was the woman in all these photographs, posing with her thumbs in her ears, holding a teddy bear in surgical scrubs, licking her lips? Was this a picture of the same woman, in a canoe somewhere, stapled to some handwritten story called "Fishing"?

Pilar had Coral bring out the tape player and she inserted the audiocassette from the box. It was a woman's voice. She appeared to be reading: "Do I love you? Absolutely. Lots. I am keeping you in my heart." Wait, Pilar thought, I just read that! It was in the flash card deck. This woman was reading the cards.

As she and Coral continued to listen, they heard the same voice read *Goodnight Moon* and some Kipling stories. The woman seemed to be addressing a child, telling him to sit up or cuddle up with his blanket, as she moved seamlessly from one book to the next.

The sun was almost up by the time Pilar Williams reached the bottom of the box. She pulled out a thick sheaf of photocopied notebook papers. They were from Dr. Bean-Bayog, she knew, because of her distinctive script. In stunned silence she read the papers, now and then looking over at her mother, who nervously rocked back and forth in her chair.

You kneel between my legs and begin to lick and nibble my inner thighs. Softly, systematically, you work your way up to my labia and vagina. I am lubricated again, and horrified at myself and my own stupidity, aroused beyond telling and drowning in shame. I would give anything to be able to close my legs. You begin to lick my clitoris. I am ecstatic with the pleasure of it, and adore you. You keep licking and sucking me, taking pleasure and aroused, but watching me. Finally you see me fully relaxed, pressing myself into your mouth, moaning with pleasure.

I start begging you to make love to me, fuck me. You refuse at first, keep on stimulating me. I am desperately struggling, begging you. Finally, you relent, at first touching my vaginia and clitoris with your penis, then entering me. I begin to climax immediately. In a minute you continue moving in and out, stronger and stronger and finally you climax and I come again.

Pilar read enough to determine that the contents of all fifty-five pages were numbingly similar, and then she slipped the papers back into the box and excused herself to go and take a shower. She scrubbed herself so hard her skin turned raw.

Her brother would be awake soon, and he was expecting her. Pilar pulled herself together, put her mother to bed, and, with Coral acting as navigator, set out, sleepless and upset, for the western suburbs to see Paul.

Pilar Williams was a critical-care nurse; few sights left her weak. But she was unprepared for the sight that greeted her on the third-floor psych unit of Newton-Wellesley Hospital. The man she saw bore little resemblance to the dark and handsome athletic brother she knew. Paul already had had several electroshock treatments. He was shuffling in paper slippers around the lounge, chain-smoking. His face was a pasty shade of white. The pants he wore were wrinkled and dirty, and his T-shirt was even filthier. His arms were thin, and his normally taut stomach muscles had gone slack from lack of exercise.

Pilar watched him for a long time from a spot in the hall where he could not see her. She choked back tears. I can't let him see me horrified, she thought. I don't want him to feel ashamed. She put on her broadest smile and strode with a confidence she did not feel into the smoky lounge.

As he came toward her to embrace her, Pilar could see the glue from the ECT cap on his temples. She knew that ECT disrupted short-term memory, but she was stunned by how disoriented her brother was. He could not remember his room number or how he got to the lounge. He had a headache, he kept saying.

A nurse directed them back to the room that Paul shared with an elderly patient. His roommate had vomited while he was gone and the stench was overwhelming. Sleepless and

Paul Lozano as a baby. *Courtesy of the Lozano family*

Paul Lozano, number 23, with his schoolboy football team in Upper Sandusky, Ohio. *Courtesy of the Lozano family*

Paul Lozano's college yearbook picture from the University of Texas in El Paso. *Courtesy of the Lozano family*

Paul Lozano, as a high school track team member, in Upper Sandusky, Ohio. *Courtesy of the Lozano family*

Margaret Harvey Bean as she appeared in her Radcliffe College yearbook in 1965. *Courtesy of Harvard Yearbook Company*

Paul Lozano (front row, fourth from the left) with his plebe class at West Point in 1981. *Courtesy of the Lozano family*

Paul Lozano in a research laboratory at Harvard University. *Courtesy of the Lozano family*

Paul Lozano and Candy Stone, toasting their engagement with her mother, Jean Stone, in El Paso, December 1989. They broke up a week later. *Candy Stone*

Paul Lozano, posing with his parents, Marcos and Epifania Lozano, in 1989. *Candy Stone*

Paul Lozano looking out over the Franklin Mountains in El Paso. *Courtesy of the Lozano family*

Dr. Margaret Bean-Bayog's office in her Lexington home. The photo was taken by Paul Lozano during a visit there. *Courtesy of the Lozano family*

Dr. Margaret Bean-Bayog cuddling with "Dr. Bean Bear," a teddy bear she used as a therapy aid with Paul Lozano. *Courtesy of the Lozano family*

Dr. Margaret Bean-Bayog in her home office, as photographed by Paul Lozano during a therapy session. *Courtesy of the Lozano family*

Dr. Margaret Bean-Bayog in October 1991, with two colleagues from McLean Hospital, addressing high school students during Mental Health Awareness Week. © *Keith E. Jacobson, 1993/TAB Newspapers*

Paul Lozano being greeted at El Paso International Airport by his sister, Martha (holding balloons), his niece, Nicole, and nephew, Erick, two months before his death. *Courtesy of the Lozano family*

Dr. Margaret Bean-Bayog arriving for a closed-door session with the Massachusetts medical board in March 1992 to defend her treatment of Paul Lozano. One of her lawyers clears a path through the press.
Justine Ellement, The Boston Globe

The Lozano family at the grave of Paul Lozano on April 2, 1992, marking the first anniversary of his death. His mother bends to place a kiss on his grave.
F. Carter Smith, NYT Pictures

heartbroken by her brother's condition, at once baffled and angered by her overnight discoveries, Pilar Williams was near collapse. But Paul needed her, and she knew she had to get him out of there.

"We need to get your jacket. We need to get your wallet and we need to leave here for a little bit," she told him. "Dr. Gault has left a pass for you and I'm going to take you to the apartment for a little while."

Paul was eager to leave but impeded by his memory loss. Where is my jacket? Where are my medications? What time do I take this pill?

On the drive from Newton to Brookline, Paul sat in the front passenger seat while Coral drove. Pilar tried to close her eyes in the rear seat, but Paul had turned completely around in his seat to stare at his sister. "I'm so happy to be here with you," he said, over and over again.

At the apartment, however, his smile faded. He walked around his mother instead of hugging her and would not look at her while he ate the food she had prepared for him. He relaxed only when she went into his bedroom to put away the clothes she had been washing and ironing for him all morning.

When his mother did speak, Paul began to panic, wringing his hands and pacing. "Please make her stop talking," he begged Pilar and Coral. "I can't bear hearing her voice."

"I'll just sit here and be very quiet. I won't say a word so he doesn't get upset," Epifania Lozano said, hurt and confused.

"Honey, why would Mother's voice disturb you so much?" Pilar asked him.

"Please don't make me talk about it," Paul replied. "I need to take my medication. I need to be asleep."

Pilar gave him his pills, turned down his covers, and settled him into bed.

When she was sure that her brother was asleep, Pilar stuffed the contents of the box into plastic shopping bags and headed back out alone into the rain to Newton-Wellesley Hospital to find Dr. Gault.

* * *

Everything about the office of Dr. William Barry Gault, Jr., said medicine, from the location on the third floor of the medical building adjacent to Newton-Wellesley Hospital to the waiting room, where the radio was tuned to Boston's all-news station and the tables were stacked with month-old copies of *People* and *Time* magazines.

Analytically oriented psychiatrists, like Dr. Margaret Bean-Bayog, are more likely to have their offices at home, where patients arrive through side entrances and listen to one of the city's two classical music stations while they flip through back issues of *Smithsonian* or *The New Yorker* that invariably fill the magazine racks.

There was nothing homey about Dr. Gault's Swedish modern furniture or the two armchairs upholstered in the same shade of gray tweed as the wall-to-wall commercial carpeting. A floor-to-ceiling wall of bookcases faced a row of windows overlooking the Woodland Country Club, a golf preserve favored by Boston Irishmen whose grandfathers had been excluded from the private clubs of the city's Protestant moneyed class.

The view was apt. Dr. Gault was something of an outsider in lineage-conscious Boston. He was a Jesuit-educated Catholic schoolboy who had come east from Milwaukee to attend Holy Cross College in Worcester, fifty miles west of Boston, and then Yale Medical School. He had been a psychiatrist for twenty years when he met Paul Lozano in 1990. That made him a newcomer by Boston standards. "I have sort of felt like a fish out of water in some ways," he conceded.

But the lack of local roots had not adversely affected his practice. If anything, he was too busy. With thirty to forty-five patients a week, he could not handle all the referrals he received. Because he specialized in acute psychiatry, Dr. Gault was likely to have from four to nine patients hospitalized at any given time. Many came from working-class neighborhoods in and around Boston. General practitioners sent their patients who were in psychological distress to Dr. Gault because, he said, "they tell me I am not a totally egregious dork."

A psychiatrist anchored in reality was just what Paul Lozano needed when he arrived at Three Usen, the psych unit of Newton-Wellesley Hospital. He was in psychotic turmoil when Dr. Gault first encountered him on the ward. He was agitated, his eyes darting from side to side in search of menacing forces. His speech was slow, and he spoke so softly he could barely be heard. He was reluctant to sit down but would stand only with his back to the wall, as if he were expecting an attack. He had the "look of a person who is acutely crazy," Dr. Gault recalled. "He was obviously stark, raving mad."

Paul Lozano was suffering from a psychotic depression, not surprisingly, since he had stopped taking his medication and spent the last several months "like a pinball," in Dr. Gault's words, bouncing around in the mental health system but never really connecting with it. Once Dr. Gault established that Haldol had not worked, whether from lack of compliance or lack of effective monitoring, he had decided that a course of ECT would be the best treatment option.

As sick as he was, Paul Lozano retained his self-deprecating sense of humor. As a nurse prepped him for the electric shock, he joked about his new status as Dr. Diehard, just as he had once told Dr. Bean-Bayog that, unless he brought his moods under control, his M.D. would stand for Monster Doc.

"There was about him, for a fellow who was twenty-eight years old, a quality of boyishness that was really excessive. It was appealing in a way. There was an unaffected, spontaneous, innocent quality which I've often seen in kind of brainy math and science types, a kind of worldly innocence," Dr. Gault recalled. "I always thought of him as a kid. Often in speaking of Paul, I'd think, 'What a nice kid' or 'Gee, the poor kid.' I remember giving him the ECT—and he is older than my son—but I felt like I was giving it to a kid."

Before proceeding with the ECT, Dr. Gault had observed Paul for several days and, with his patient's ready approval, consulted his family in Texas. "Contacting the family is important with a suicidal patient; when you're treating a patient who has an incapacitating, potentially deadly psychiatric disorder, as an acute psychiatrist in my field, you have to establish some kind of an alliance with the family," he explained. "You can't treat the patient in a vaccuum."

Learning that Paul had a sister who was a nurse was a gift to Dr. Gault. Pilar Williams understood the medical lingo and was eager to help. At that juncture in her brother's illness, they were facing a medical decision, in Dr. Gault's view. All the theoretical debates about the psychological versus biological causes of depression had always struck him as just that—theoretical. Given that the definitive cause of depression is not known, Dr. Gault's interest as a clinician was to provide the necessary medical interventions that had been proven to alleviate or even eliminate depression. He was, foremost, a psychiatrist who believed in evidence and results.

Despite the ascendancy of biopsychiatry, his is by no means the universal view. Psychoanalysis retains a firm grip on the nation's cultural imagination. It has influenced not only mental health practices but also child rearing, the criminal justice system, and society's basic assumptions about human behavior.

That individuals are driven by unconscious motives with their roots in childhood is accepted as true in our culture. That such ideas are no more or less than unproven theories of a brilliant but human nineteenth-century Viennese physician does not dilute their power. America's children are reared on the assumption that they are driven by aggressive and sexual impulses as they proceed through oral, anal, and Oedipal stages; our criminals are often judged less responsible for their actions if they suffered abuse and neglect in infancy; and our interpersonal relationships are shaped by shared beliefs about the repression of sexual desire.

The subtle weaving of Sigmund Freud's ideas into the fabric of American life has had a far more profound impact than the practice of analysis itself, which, for reasons of cost and time, has always been sought by the privileged few. Strict Freudian analysis involves a patient lying on a couch five days a week at a prearranged hour for an average of seven years. At a minimum cost of $90 an hour—$120 is closer to the going rate—that's at least $450 a week.

With the analyst sitting out of the patient's line of vision, the patient is encouraged to free-associate—to say whatever comes to mind—with the expectation that his thoughts, dreams, and slips of the tongue will reveal unconscious conflicts. The interpretations of those unconscious signals are designed to provide insight and bring relief of mental distress.

By 1990, when Paul Lozano arrived at Dr. Gault's doorstep, Freudian analysis had waned in popularity even among those able to afford the high fees. But therapy itself had never been more popular. An estimated 10 million Americans sought help from the nation's 200,000 psychiatrists, psychologists, and social workers that year, and millions more saw marriage counselors and family therapists. The desire for a quicker fix and the proliferation of trendy therapies in the 1970s and 1980s gave those in search of greater self-awareness broader options, if not deeper insights.

The need for mental health services in the United States was documented in a 1993 report by the National Institute of Mental Health. The study found that 52 million Americans suffer from psychiatric problems severe enough to interfere with their daily lives. An estimated 20 million suffer from incapacitating phobias that keep them from performing simple tasks such as crossing bridges or riding elevators; about 15 million Americans suffer from depression; half of those are severe cases. More alarming than the prevalence of mental illness was the study's finding that only 8 percent of those 52 million Americans received any treatment. That conclusion suggests that many mental health professionals are spending time counseling people with relatively mild problems while individuals who are more in need go untreated.

The development of psychotropic drugs in the treatment of mental disorders has gradually diverted medical attention from psychoanalysis. Since Henri Laborit, a French surgeon, first demonstrated the tranquilizing effect of chlorpromazine in 1952, research laboratories have been producing a steady stream of so-called psychiatric wonder drugs. Chlorpromazine, under the brand name Thorazine, altered hospital psychiatric care forever by freeing formerly abusive and destructive patients of symptoms that had made them unmanageable and unresponsive to therapy. Thorazine was followed in the next decade by a host of antipsychotic drugs, developed from different chemical families and marketed under such brand names as Mellaril, Haldol, and Navane. Elavil and Tofranil were developed to fight depression, and lithium carbonate, a simple metal ion, was discovered in Australia in 1948 to be effective in the treatment of mania. Once it was made commercially available in the United States in 1970, lithium became central to the treatment of manic-depressive illness.

Medicine, intrigued by Freud's theories but unable to confirm their validity by methodological means, shifted its focus to the laboratory, where biopsychiatrists were concentrating not on the contemplation of childhood conflict but on the study of the central nervous system. Research results contained good news for both schools: antidepressants combined with psychotherapy produced better outcomes than drug therapy alone; family therapy combined with antipsychotic medication for the treatment of schizophrenia resulted in fewer relapses; medication and behavioral therapy both affected brain function in patients suffering from obsessive-compulsive disorders.

Drugs alone were no simple miracle cure. Medication did not work in many cases, and when it did, relief often came at a cost. Such benzodiazepines as Valium and Xanax are addictive, and the withdrawal symptoms can ape the original illness. Such tranquilizers as Miltown and Librium were overprescribed for years to women, who became dependent instead of well. Haldol, the antipsychotic prescribed for Paul Lozano, can cause tardive dyskinesia, an involuntary facial tic that often lingers after the medication is stopped. Fear of developing that side effect was one reason Paul gave for not taking his medication.

But even with those caveats, the development of psychotropic medications has reshaped the psychiatric scene from the heyday of psychoanalysis in the 1950s, when Freud was the dominant influence in American psychiatry. Then, most psychiatric departments in hospitals and at medical schools were headed by analysts, especially in Boston, where the Boston Psychoanalytic Society and Institute exerted a powerful influence.

One of the first psychiatric units in a general hospital opened in 1934 in Boston at Massachusetts General Hospital, under the direction of Dr. Stanley Cobb, a member of the Institute. Members then established other psychiatric wards at Beth Israel Hospital, Boston University Hospital, the Peter Bent Brigham Hospital, and Tufts–New England Medical Center.

Medical students were trained in analytic methods at the old Boston Psychopathic Hospital, now the Massachusetts Mental Health Center, as were would-be social workers at Smith College. By the end of World War II, Boston's medical institutions that taught or provided psychiatric care were dominated by analysts, many of whom had been trained in Vienna or Berlin and came to Boston to flee the Nazi threat. By 1949, as many as 90 percent of the Boston Psychoanalytic Society and Institute's members held academic appointments at the city's top hospitals, medical schools, and universities.

While the New York Psychoanalytic Society is the oldest, the largest, and the most renowned in the United States, the Boston Psychoanalytic Society and Institute was the fourth, behind those of New York, Chicago, and Baltimore-Washington, to be recognized by the American Psychoanalytic Association as a training center for analysts.

The American Psychoanalytic Association had been founded in 1911, three years after Freud established the International Psycho-Analytical Association in Europe. The American branch has always been more Freudian than Freud, setting stricter standards than the international society. In 1923, for example, it ruled that only physicians could be analysts. The American attempt to give the fledgling profession respectability in this country ignored the fact that such esteemed European-trained practitioners as Erik Erikson and Anna Freud were laymen. Freud himself opposed a medical requirement, arguing that analysts treated the mind, not the body.

The infatuation of Massachusetts with Freud dated to 1909 when he gave four seminal lectures elucidating his theories of human nature at Clark University in Worcester. Led by Harvard neurologist James Jackson Putnam, Freud's admirers began to meet informally in one another's homes. The group went through a few reorganizations and a number of re-formations before emerging in its present form in 1935.

Boston was fertile soil for the growth of psychoanalysis. The lucid brilliance of Freud's prose and his theories about dreams and early life experiences having determining effects on adult personality traits caught hold in the intellectual environment of a university town. "All important intellectual movements in America have originated in Boston," Freud once told Putnam. European analysts who brought their Viennese perspective to Boston found eager ears in the city's Back Bay salons.

"In the eyes of early American analysts, the Europeans brought a richer, more elegant cultural patina to the professional life of Cambridge and Boston," Sanford Gifford told a symposium on psychoanalysis in Boston in 1973. "Many of us were internal refugees ourselves, from the small towns of rural New England, the Midwest, and the South, part of the reverse migration to the cities and universities of the East. The European analysts belonged to a much larger intellectual diaspora from the Nazi occupation, of whom analysts, nuclear physicists, and architects from the Bauhaus seemed the most prominent locally. As the American country mouse became accustomed to Vanillakipferln, multiple handshaking, and Austrian ski techniques, he was also assimilating other, deeper cultural values, in an intellectual atmosphere where analysis occupied an increasingly respected position."

By 1952, the Institute had grown large enough to be in search of a permanent home. It found one in a Back Bay brownstone, on Commonwealth Avenue, one block from the Boston Public Gardens. The building had once been home to Oliver Ames, a Massachusetts governor. The current owner had intended to use it for a school of embalming. The basement floors had been tiled in preparation, but the zoning permits were not forthcoming. So the elegant old brownstone was sold instead for $85,000 to the Boston Psychoanalytic Society and Institute. The high-ceilinged rooms were readied for night classes and the social affairs that provide the collegiality missing from a profession that is isolating, by definition.

Although the brownstone is the center of academic pursuits, the real work of a would-be member, or candidate, is conducted in his or her own personal analysis. Every candidate for admission to the Institute is required to undergo analysis with a senior member of the Institute. It is not an easy or a speedy process, often lasting a decade or more. In addition, each candidate is required to analyze three patients under the supervision of a senior colleague, known as a training analyst.

Dr. Margaret Bean-Bayog had completed her classwork and two of her three supervised cases when Paul Lozano began treatment. She was still in analysis herself when they met.

Being accepted as a candidate for the Boston Psychoanalytic Society and Institute was something of a coup for Dr. Bean-Bayog. A cautious and conservative organization, the Institute is selective and more than a little reluctant to admit candidates with histories of mental illness or substance abuse. Margaret Bean-Bayog was determined to convince the analytic establishment that, her alcoholism notwithstanding, she was a good risk.

Acceptance meant as much to Margaret Bean-Bayog as it had meant little to her father. William Bennett Bean and Boston had been a bad match. The town was too stuffy and Harvard too self-important for Bill Bean. He had come to

Boston after graduating at the top of his Johns Hopkins medical school class and completing his internship in Baltimore. He joined the Harvard Service at Boston City Hospital and the research team at Harvard's Thorndike Laboratory. But he lasted only one year.

"The environment was too formal; the chiefs were too high and the Indians too low," James A. Clifton, the dean of the University of Iowa Medical School, recalled in Dr. William Bean's eulogy in 1989. "Much to the dismay of his superiors, he often took his tutorial group of four Harvard medical students to watch the Red Sox rather than patrol the wards."

Approval was far more important to Bill Bean's daughter. "I knew she was working very hard on her career, and I think the whole issue with the Psychoanalytic Institute was a major victory, because, you know, they are very traditional and old-fashioned in a lot of their views. And they were very reluctant to accept someone with a history of alcoholism. Extremely reluctant," said Dr. Carol C. Nadelson, a Boston psychiatrist and the former president of the American Psychiatric Association.

"They know more than a lot of others because the process is so extensive. They interview people more extensively. You have to write a biography. And eventually most things come out. But they knew. And she was up front about it. She never tried to hide that from them. So it was really important to her to do a good job and to do the right thing, and be accepted by the leaders. She really wanted acceptance, in some ways maybe more than those of us who don't have that baggage."

Margaret Bean-Bayog was seeking admission to an ever-shrinking club. There are approximately three thousand practicing analysts in the United States. The extensive training required has dissuaded many prospective candidates, and the lack of patients willing to commit the time and money to analysis has steered would-be analysts to other types of therapy.

In part to increase the pool of future analysts, the

American Psychoanalytic Association in 1986 dropped its requirement that only physicians could train as analysts. With the appropriate waivers, training institutes were thereafter free to admit social workers, clinical psychologists, and scholars from other academic fields to the mysteries of psychoanalysis if they were willing to submit to the rigorous training.

Since 1975, the Boston Psychoanalytic Society and Institute too has had to deal with competition. That year one of the splinter groups that psychoanalytic institutes are notorious for spawning broke away to form the Psychoanalytic Institute of New England, or PINE.

In recent years, BPSI has circulated discreet advertisements to entice new patients for their candidates in training. Being accepted as a patient is almost as much work as becoming an analyst. A prospective patient must submit a detailed application, write an autobiographical essay, submit a medical history, and undergo a physical examination. If a would-be analysand has been in therapy before, the screening committee will request permission to speak to his previous therapists. If the applicant survives this initial screening, he must still be interviewed by a member of the Committee on Institute Psychoanalysis. Accepted or rejected, the $30 application fee is nonrefundable.

There are philosophical as well as practical reasons for the decline in psychoanalysis. No school of thought, except perhaps Marxism, has come so regularly and so passionately under assault as Freudianism—by feminists for the theory that women suffer from penis envy; from child abuse victims for the suggestion that memories of abuse are really unconscious wishes; from the political left for the diversion of energy from social change to personal insight.

The Patients' Rights Movement in the 1970s contributed as well. Even more than such revered specialists as obstetricians or surgeons, psychiatrists had long enjoyed a sort of cultural deification. By dint of training or special insight, they were thought to know the secrets of the human mind. The waning notion of doctor as God prompted more patients to begin asking more questions, and psychiatry had to concede that it had few definitive answers about the causes of mental illness.

That admission hit psychoanalysts particularly hard, because claims for the efficacy of analysis are based on clinical experience, not empirical data. Every analyst's files contain cases of patients whose lives have been indisputably changed for the better, but there is no body of evidence to suggest that the expensive and time-consuming approach is any more successful at relieving mental distress than a less intense, and less costly, relationship with a well-trained, compassionate social worker.

Pilar Williams walked into the office of Dr. William Barry Gault on November 10, 1990, bearing both a gift and a burden.

In one hand she held a small clay sculpture from the Southwest of an American Indian storyteller. In the other, she held a story itself. Before Paul Lozano's sister dumped the contents of her satchels onto the table in Dr. Gault's office she warned him that the material that he was about to see was disturbing and could put him in an awkward position vis-à-vis Paul's former psychiatrist, Dr. Margaret Bean-Bayog.

Dr. Gault did not know Dr. Bean-Bayog. If the information in Pilar Williams's shopping bags could help his patient, he thought he should see it. So he nodded and watched, fascinated and confused, as greeting cards, baby books, and reams of paper spilled onto the table. Pilar handed him a sheet of loose-leaf paper. The handwriting was legible, but there were crossovers and margin notes where the writer had revised her work. Dr. Gault began to read:

> My head is between your legs kissing and nibbling you. I start kissing one of your balls, taking it into my mouth, playing with it, and then the other. I lick the crack between your leg and your body. I

come to the base of your penis, which is erect by now. I begin to trace over it with my fingers and mouth. I kiss the shaft, starting at the base up to the tip, working my way around it. I kiss the tip of it, working over it with my whole mouth, nibbling it, sucking lightly . . .

Suddenly, I stop. "Hey, what the fuck? Come back here," you say. "I'd love to," I say, but I don't move. You get furious and start swearing at me. I move off, picking up a magazine. "That's no way to talk to a lady." "Oh, for Christsake, a lady, yet."

Dr. Gault's Celtic complexion turned crimson as he read. Pilar Williams asked if she could get him a glass of water.

"How do we know she wrote this?" he asked.

Pilar handed him the Handy, Multipurpose Emergency and Reference Flash Card Deck and the books that bore the doctor's signature. "Is that not the same handwriting?" she asked.

"My God, what else is in here?" Dr. Gault asked.

They stood at the table by the window, which was streaked with rain, and methodically picked their way through photographs of the psychiatrist posing with the teddy bear, children's books, notes, flash cards, and page after page of sexual stories.

I want you like an ache. I close my legs and breathe in and out. You remain standing above me. I begin wondering if you can die from desire. You walk away.

"Please don't leave. Oh please don't go away."

"Why shouldn't I? I can't think of a reason."

"I need you. I'm dying for you. Please don't leave me."

"Oh, spare me," you say. You think a minute. "OK," you say. "I'll tell you what. If you want me to, I'll touch you, turn you on, play with you and THEN leave. Or I'll leave now. Which will it be?"

"NEITHER, dammit. That's not a choice.
DON'T leave me. I'm dying for you."

It was five o'clock on Saturday afternoon. The administrators of the hospital were not in their offices. Thomas F. O'Hare, an attorney who served as a consultant to the Psychiatry Department, was at home, in bed with the flu. Dr. Gault insisted he come to the telephone just the same.

With some difficulty, Dr. Gault explained what appeared to be "bizarre and noxious elements" in his patient's relationship with his former psychiatrist. They arranged to meet on Monday.

As Pilar Williams rose to leave, she was unsteady on her feet. In the last thirty-two hours, she had worked her regular shift as a critical-care nurse, then flown two thousand miles across the United States to see her brilliant younger brother shuffling down the corridor of a psychiatric ward, obsessed with the psychiatrist whose sexual and maternal fantasies Pilar Williams had spent the night and next day either reading or puzzling over with Dr. Gault. She still had not been to bed.

Dr. Gault assured her that they would get to the bottom of what had happened between her brother and Dr. Margaret Bean-Bayog. "You know I've made it a practice never to raise my eyebrows upon hearing any story in this business," he told her. "Today was the exception to that rule."

The truth was, he had never seen anything like this before. The material was not just odd or inappropriate; it was shocking. He read the flash cards over and over again.

I think you're my Mom.
[On reverse]: Right you are. I'm your Mom and I love you and you love me very, very much. Say that 10 times: you're my Mom and I love you very, very much.

I love you.
I'm coming back.
You can be mad. Just don't hurt yourself.

You can try and try and try to hate me and be furious and fire me and I'm STILL coming back. I'm not mad. Love, Mom.

It still might not work.
You might not be a star.
I'm STILL your mom then.
                              Mom

I'm not leaving.
I am your Mom.
Even if you win 500 Nobel Prizes and fly to the moon and back, you're still my boy. You don't have to destroy it. You can stand it, becoming a star. I'm still your mom.

"I know that in treatment, patients will have feelings as if their therapist were a parent, but in general—especially if the patient is quite ill—it's important for the doctor to help the patient see clearly that that's just a feeling and that the doctor, in fact, is not the parent," he said later. "So, it was quite shocking to see the doctor saying the opposite, saying, 'Yes, I, in fact, am your mother.'"

That, of course, was only half of it. The cards urging Paul Lozano to avoid his family had a sort of "global quality" that disturbed Dr. Gault. "It seemed like not only unwise but impractical advice. How could he not communicate," since his family was so large and he was, at that point, living with a niece?

"The most hair-raising documents," said Dr. Gault, were the sexual fantasies. Having erotic feelings toward one's patients is certainly not uncommon in the practice of psychiatry, but these stories were "an expression of sexual wishes" written in the "language of 'you' and 'I'" and "then a narrative account of doing these things: you're doing this to me; I'm doing this to you." It did not resemble any attempt by any psychiatrist Dr. Gault ever knew to manage erotic countertransference.

Dr. Gault, attorney O'Hare, and Pilar Williams arranged

to meet at 3 P.M. on Monday to talk to Paul about the material they had seen. Paul's primary nurse, Betty Spargo, was there as well. She said she had heard from Paul himself that his former therapist had read her sexual fantasies to him. She accompanied him to and from the meeting but, at the suggestion of Dr. Gault and Dr. José A. Saporta, his psychotherapist, from that point forward she discussed Dr. Bean-Bayog with Paul only at Paul's initiation.

Her nursing notes in his chart reflect the difficulties Paul Lozano was having with the subject. "He acknowledged feeling self-conscious in disclosing information about his relationship with former therapist," said one. At another point she quoted Paul telling her, "All this is really hard. I feel like I'm exposing what she told me in confidence."

At the meeting in Dr. Gault's office, Paul was anxious. He confirmed that the writing was Dr. Bean-Bayog's, and he answered the lawyer's questions briefly but directly before Betty Spargo led him back to his room. Pilar found him there soon after, pacing anxiously.

"Now they know about Margaret. Margaret is going to hate me. I betrayed her. She made me promise that I wouldn't tell and now I've told. Now they are going to do something to her,'" he said to Pilar.

She grabbed her brother firmly by the shoulders. "I will not live through another session of you being tied up like an animal," she said. "If you don't calm down they are going to drug you and they are going to put you in restraints. I don't want that to happen. I am here. I will help you."

He stopped pacing. He sat down, calmer but still worried.

"You're hurting me when you're doing this, because you are so worried about her," Pilar said. "Where is she? She is not here. She doesn't care. I'm the one who cares. I've always been there; so has your family. You need to think about me now. I'm the only one who has been here loyally all the time no matter what you did, no matter what happened. Where is Margaret, who supposedly loves you so much?"

During Paul's brief pass to his apartment two days before, Pilar had told Paul that Dr. Gault might be obligated by law to report Dr. Bean-Bayog's conduct to the Massachusetts Board of Registration in Medicine, known more commonly as the state medical board, and he became overwrought. He slipped a prescription bottle of Ativan, a tranquilizer, from his medicine chest into his pocket and took it back onto the ward with him.

It was not the first time Paul had used Ativan without strict supervision to control his anxiety. Dr. Bean-Bayog had encouraged him to use tranquilizers at his discretion. "Take Ativan when you need it," she instructed him in one note.

In the past four years, self-medication had become a pattern. Martha Lundgren, his girlfriend that fall, said Paul told her he often wrote himself prescriptions for nortriptyline, an antidepressant, when he felt his prescribed dosage was too low. He told Dr. Gault he worried about being a substance abuser.

"He told Dr. Gault that he had some Ativan in his room," Betty Spargo recalled. "He did turn it in. He reported it and he turned it in."

As Dr. Gault saw it, "this was less about substance abuse than self-medication. He knew he shouldn't be doing it and he told me about it."

Paul Lozano was in the midst of a series of nine shock treatments during the period when his relationship with Dr. Bean-Bayog was discussed. After one such conversation, Dr. Gault wrote a note in the chart that Paul "recounts aspects of her behavior in treatment that are so startlingly bizarre that it is hard to believe it happened." But Dr. Gault noted that his patient was lucid and not delusional whenever the subject was raised over the next week before his release from the hospital on November 21.

A patient who became friendly with Paul Lozano during their hospitalization remembered Paul alluding to his troubles with a prior therapist. "We were going into a group therapy session and I mentioned something about my therapist, and he said that his was weird," his friend recalled. "There had been this sexual thing he was trying to deal with. He didn't tell me much about it, but he said, 'My therapy was weird.' It was clear it was a problem for him, so I didn't pry."

Paul struck him as more confused than angry about what had happened. "He wasn't hostile. At first he was very quiet, stayed in his room all the time. His personality came out more after the ECT cleared up his depression. He was a really nice guy," said his friend, who saw Paul socially after they were both discharged.

The details of his relationship with Dr. Bean-Bayog were slow in coming, Dr. Gault recalled.

> He told me that at some point in the treatment—I don't remember when—her behavior seemed to change. He told me that, rather abruptly at some point, it seemed that she was dressing more seductively. At about that time, she somehow conveyed to him that she felt sexual desire for him and that at about that time, she read to him from her sexual fantasies.
>
> For instance, he told me that at some point in their therapy, he would try to explain to her that he knew that there was a method of police interrogation that I think of as "good cop–bad cop" but that he apparently referred to as "Mutt and Jeff" in which apparently one interrogator is unkind and the other is kind. He reported that she, shortly thereafter, brought to him two sexual stories called "Mutt" and "Jeff," and told him, "These are the thoughts that I had about what you told me about Mutt and Jeff."

"Mutt" begins:

> Today, remembering yesterday, I am very scared, still a little sad, but very determined. I look radiant, not at all like someone who had the daylights beaten out of them and is expecting more of the same.
>
> You come in, grimly excited, thinking of what

you are going to do to me. You have an idea, a cynical, furious idea. First, you are going to reduce me a bit. You can't stand how well and secure I look.

You tell me to take off all my clothes. I am startled, then ashamed, but I start to undress. You watch, restless, sitting on the arm of the chair.

I carefully fold my clothes. That makes you angry. You grab them, throw them in a corner, and strip off what is left of what I am wearing. You grab my arm roughly, staring at me naked. Then you reach over and grab a nipple and pinch. I gasp and pull back, trying unsuccessfully to shield myself. You wanted me in the restraints anyway to be sure of my helplessness and your power.

Paul Lozano initially told Dr. Gault that Dr. Bean-Bayog had masturbated during their sessions but denied that they had had sex. In a subsequent conversation, he told Dr. Gault that they had had sexual relations "a couple of times" in her office.

"Neither of us spelled out what we meant by sexual relations," Dr. Gault said. "Paul himself didn't suggest to me that very much of that went on. And if they did have sexual contact, I wouldn't think of that as having been one of the most harmful things that happened." According to Dr. Gault, the harm was in the therapy itself.

I had seen the writings, so I was virtually certain that the doctor had written and the patient had read these sexual stories, plus the "I'm the mother, you're my baby" stuff. So, I felt pretty sure that that alone had unsettled him, had made him more emotionally stirred up than he ought to have been, had not helped him to be securely grounded in reality and, you know, had not been at all conducive to his avoiding relapses and staying on a secure footing. But I assumed that if, in addition to the reading and the writing, which I could be sure had occurred, the doctor had been masturbating and reading her fantasies to him and doing the things that he said she did, then surely that must have worsened the course of his disorder during the time that he was her patient.

Common sense. I mean, if you imagine yourself or a relative of yours having a depression this severe, I think human intuition would tell you if the doctor to whom you entrusted yourself for care sat there masturbating and reading her sexual fantasies to you, it would not help you to become less depressed.

Throughout their conversations about his former therapist, Dr. Gault said Paul never made a hostile comment about Dr. Bean-Bayog. He was confused by what had happened between them and thought his treatment was inappropriate, but his primary worry was that she would lose her medical license and feel that he had betrayed her. He still longed to resume their relationship.

"It seemed to me that it was his impression that she had tried to help him . . . that something had gone wrong with the therapy. It seemed to me that he was fond of her, that he had a strong feeling of attachment to her. It seemed to me that he was frightened by the idea of harm coming to her," Dr. Gault recalled.

"In my experience with Paul he did not speak harshly or critically of her ever. Ever. He was reluctant to speak about her at all. He disliked it when I asked him. He realized that it was going to have to be recorded. He felt terrible about what happened."

Dr. Gault did not probe too deeply. Having been advised by O'Hare, the attorney, that he was obligated under the state's disclosure laws to report Dr. Bean-Bayog, Dr. Gault assumed that a thorough investigation would be conducted soon by the appropriate authorities. His concern was for his patient.

Dr. Gault called Dr. José A. Saporta, Jr., Paul Lozano's psychotherapist, to alert him to developments. During his visits with Paul at Newton-Wellesley and after his discharge, Dr. Saporta also approached his patient cautiously on the subject of Margaret Bean-Bayog.

"I wanted Paul to know that I was not going to be involved in the report to the Board of Medicine, or in any of the legal proceedings, so that he could have a place to talk about his feelings and know they would be private," he said.

"It was clear that that relationship had, in his experience, caused him to be very confused. He was also mourning her loss and felt very bad about it, and I at the time had formulated the goal of treatment to help him work through what had apparently been a very confusing relationship to him."

Much of the confusion had to do with her maternal role-playing, Dr. Saporta recalled. "He told me that she would tell him that he was her little boy and that she was his mom, that he was very confused about that. I remember asking him at this session or another, 'You mean you *felt* as if you were her little boy?' And he said, 'No, I thought I *was* her little boy.'

"I recall him feeling extremely anxious about what had come to light; very very frightened, very anxious about having betrayed Dr. Bean-Bayog, very worried about what would happen to her, very sad about losing her and wondering if this would mean that he had lost her forever.

"Most sessions were about: I miss her. She was my mom. Why would she leave me? I'm angry at her. Why would a mom do this to a kid?"

The sexual interplay had heightened his confusion. "One of the things that was confusing for him was that she had a bear, he said, that was dressed as a doctor, and she would say, 'This is my doctor bear. You're my little doctor bear. You're my little boy.' And then he told me she would put it down and then begin to masturbate and to tell him fantasies, sexual fantasies.

"He would say quite angrily, 'How could she be my mom and then leave me? How could she dump me?' Other times he expressed the fantasy that he would go through residency and earn enough money to start treatment again with Dr.

Bayog. He was quite terrified of Dr. Bayog getting in trouble because of Dr. Gault's report to the board and that Dr. Bayog would never want to see him again. That was a source of great anxiety for him. So, there was both anger and longing, missing her, a whole range of feelings."

Paul told Dr. Saporta, just as he had told Dr. Gault, that it was her interpretation of his symptoms that he was molested by his mother. "He told me once, 'Dr. Bayog told me that my mom abused me sexually. My mom never abused me sexually,'" Dr. Saporta said.

Paul's depression remitted after the electroshock treatments, and he was able to discuss what Dr. Saporta thought could be the real root of Paul Lozano's vulnerability to depression. "He has a fear of failing which approaches terror," Dr. Saporta wrote in his notes. "This panic of not excelling academically and fear of failure is what has driven him to excel since his teens, and may represent part of the dynamic that explains his vulnerability to debilitating and suicidal depressions; i.e., rigid ego ideal and harsh retaliatory superego."

In other words, Paul Lozano had a fixed image of himself as a physician, and anything that cast doubt on his ability to achieve that goal he interpreted as evidence of his worthlessness. His habit of stopping his medication was a form of denial: he simply could not accept simultaneously the image of himself as a doctor and as an individual with a mental illness.

It was Dr. Saporta's habit to call his new patients' former therapists. He told Dr. Gault he intended to do the same in this case but would not mention the revelations Paul had made. He left a message on Dr. Bean-Bayog's answering machine, and she returned his call a few hours later.

She told Dr. Saporta that Paul Lozano had been a difficult patient, that he suffered not only from recurrent depressions but also from borderline personality disorder, a diagnosis she had once ruled out and about which she would vacillate later. Almost as an afterthought she told him that the McLean staff had worried that she was overinvolved with her patient. But she reassured Dr. Saporta that Dr. Dan Buie supported her therapy.

"I, at that time, was surprised and said, 'Did Dr. Buie see the patient?' and she said no, that Doctor Buie had not seen the patient but had reviewed the case with her. She said Paul was demanding, that he even started to have memories of funny things that his mother had done when he was in diapers. She said it had been a very abusive family."

Her omissions were glaring. According to Dr. Saporta, Dr. Bean-Bayog told him nothing about the mom-boy role-playing, nothing about the flash cards, the baby blanket, the children's books, the audiocassette; she said nothing about her later assertion about the patient having a substance abuse problem, nothing about his having broken into her office and stolen files, nothing about his allegedly being homicidal, nothing about his refusal to take his medication or to be supervised by the Impaired Physicians Committee —all information she would later cite as evidence of how untreatable Paul Lozano was but that she apparently did not think relevant to impart to his new therapist.

"I asked her why she terminated with the patient," Dr. Saporta recalled, "and she told me that he was very taxing in terms of time, money, and energy, and that she and her husband had been planning to adopt a son for some time, and she told me that that had come through, and that she decided that if she was going to have a son, she would not have the energy to continue to devote to the care of this patient."

Dr. Saporta reported the substance of his conversation with Dr. Bean-Bayog to Dr. Gault, who was astounded. "I think if she had said something like, 'Gee, I really need to talk to you a lot more about this case. It is quite extraordinary, and my kind of treatment is quite unusual, so if you are going to be picking up, there is a lot you should know,' if she had done anything like that, it might have made me put the brakes on about reporting her to the board. But, in fact, she just said, 'Oh, this is a difficult borderline patient. I may have gotten a little overinvolved.'

"I probably felt pretty much the way Paul felt. This stuff is not good for the patients; it's not good for the profession. It's upsetting to me. Why does there have to be so much silly stuff in psychiatry? And this, this went way beyond silly."

On December 10, Dr. Alvin Becker, the chief of psychiatry at Newton-Wellesley Hospital and a clinical professor of psychiatry at Tufts University School of Medicine, wrote to the Board of Registration in Medicine regarding Dr. Margaret Bean-Bayog:

> Dear Sir/Madam:
> According to Massachusetts General Laws, Chapter 112, Section 5F, it is my responsibility to report to you an alleged instance of inappropriate psychiatric treatment. A 28-year-old patient on our inpatient unit revealed to the unit nursing staff as well as to W. Barry Gault, Jr. M.D., his attending physician, that Dr. Bean-Bayog's treatment was unusual, upsetting, and according to the patient, harmful. Although I have no way of ascertaining the veracity of his allegations, I am obliged to report them to you for your evaluation. Dr. Gault, I understand, is the primary reporter and is aware of many more details than I.

Two days later, Dr. Gault wrote to the board as well:

> Dear Sir/Madam:
> A 28-year-old man who has been under my care since October 19, 1990, has reported to me that between approximately 1986 and 1990, Dr. Bean-Bayog conducted his psychiatric treatment in an irregular manner. It appears that her treatment of this patient calls into question her competence as a psychotherapist and may have caused damage to the patient.
> The patient reports that during a number of therapy sessions Dr. Bean-Bayog read to him at length from detailed accounts of her own sexual

fantasies about him. He further reports that Dr. Bean-Bayog consistently counseled him not to communicate with his family, and told and wrote him over and over that she was his mother, and that he was an infant. She sent him many children's books as gifts, as well as numerous cards and letters on which she said she was his "mom" and he was her little boy. He says she openly masturbated during some of the therapy sessions.

During this period of time, Dr. Bean-Bayog hospitalized the patient on several occasions, sometimes involuntarily. He has spent many months in psychiatric inpatient units, and has been treated with antipsychotic medications and electroconvulsive therapy.

The patient has consulted with Attorney Thomas F. O'Hare, of Wellesley, and has provided Mr. O'Hare with copies of a large volume of material, allegedly handwritten by Dr. Bean-Bayog, and given by her to the patient during his therapy. Included are 40–50 pages of detailed sexual fantasies involving Dr. Bean-Bayog and the patient. There are also a number of children's books and stories inscribed (variously) "to the boy" or "for the baby." There are also a number of letters and notes which affirm that the doctor is the patient's mother, and that he is her baby or infant.

The patient also has an audiocassette, allegedly given by Dr. Bean-Bayog. It is a recording of a woman's voice reading several of the children's books given to the patient, as well as several children's stories allegedly composed by Dr. Bean-Bayog. Both the patient and the family aver that the voice is that of the doctor.

If this patient's allegations are true, his course of treatment with Dr. Bean-Bayog between 1986 and 1990 was improper. During the past five years his life and professional education have been severely disrupted. If Dr. Bean-Bayog's behavior and conduct of his treatment have been as described by the patient, it amounts to serious mismanagement of his psychiatric disorder.

I have composed and conveyed this letter in order to discharge what I understand to be my obligation under M.G.L. c. 112 s.5F.

For the moment Pilar Williams was satisfied. At last, she thought, Paul would get the help he needed, and Dr. Margaret Bean-Bayog would be held accountable for the price Paul had had to pay for trusting her and her unimpeachable Harvard credentials.

Chapter

8

There is a photograph that anchors the living room mantels of all the homes of all the members of the Lozano family of El Paso, Texas. It is a snapshot that Martha took during a party at her house during the Christmas holidays in 1990. Her brother Paul is wearing surgical scrubs and sitting on the edge of a white piano bench, smiling radiantly, his arm around Pilar's son, Erick.

The photograph captures the hopes of a few precious days when his family thought Paul Lozano was well at last. His depression had remitted after the electroconvulsive therapy. He had kept his weekly appointments with Dr. Gault and Dr. Saporta after his release from the hospital in late November. He was just as faithfully taking the lithium prescribed to prevent a relapse.

Paul was doing so well that Christmas that Pilar, who had been embarrassed and frustrated by his illness, was once again proud to introduce him to colleagues at Providence Memorial Hospital. A group of anesthesiologists invited him on rounds and, impressed, urged him to come back to El Paso to practice if anesthesiology was, indeed, his choice of specialty.

But the holidays proved to be only a respite, not a reprieve. Paul Lozano was preoccupied with thoughts of Margaret Bean-Bayog, desperate to see her and confused by his feelings of anger and desire.

As soon as he returned to Boston in January, he telephoned Amy Stromsten, the social worker he had first met when he was hospitalized at McLean in 1986. He had kept in touch with her sporadically over the years, letting her know how he was doing. He asked if he could come by her office in Harvard Square.

"It was the first week of January," she remembered. "He came in and he just poured out his heart about this thing." He told her what he had already told Dr. Gault and Dr. Saporta, that in the course of their therapy sessions Dr. Bean-Bayog had read aloud her sexual fantasies about him, masturbated, and had sex with him.

"He was really in bad shape, really depressed. He was crying a lot. He was saying, 'I want to call her. I want to see her. I miss her so much.'

"I said, 'Paul, you can't call her. You, right now, are suffering from a horrible trauma and you need to get help for that. And seeing her is not going to help you.'"

Stromsten remembered the supervision group from the summer before, when Dr. Bean-Bayog had talked about her erotic feelings for a Mexican-American medical student, and she concluded that the tearful, depressed young man in her office had been sexually abused by his psychiatrist.

Paul did not share Amy Stromsten's unambiguous indignation, however. "He felt very guilty. He said, 'What if she loses her license?' And I said, 'Paul, she should. What she did was illegal, immoral and she really hurt you. Look where you ended up. You ended up in the hospital. She's still in her big house in Lexington. You can say what you want, but this is not acceptable clinical behavior. You were sexually molested, and you are going to have a lot of problems for a lot of years, and you are going to need a lot of help.' He got that that was true. But he was so in love with her."

There were therapists who specialized in treating men who had been sexually abused, Amy told Paul. She referred him to Michael Lew, one such counselor in Cambridge. She said she then wrote a letter to the Massachusetts Board of Registration in Medicine to alert the panel to what she later called a case of "sexual abuse and gross malpractice."

Paul Lozano called Michael Lew on January 8 and went to see him seven days later. He told Lew that he had experienced four years of "sexualizing" in therapy. "This female psychiatrist had shared reams of sadomasochistic sexual fantasies about him and she had told him that she was his mother. That was what he meant by sexualizing," Lew recalled. "And Paul was blaming himself because he still thought about her."

It was Lew's impression that Paul Lozano was working on these issues with Dr. Saporta and that his visit was a quest for further reassurance that it was not abnormal to be both upset about the relationship with Dr. Bean-Bayog and to long for its resumption. Lew gave him that reassurance, but he never saw Paul again.

Not only was Dr. Saporta working on these issues with Paul but the entire focus of his psychotherapy, he said, was "to help Paul with his overwhelming anxiety, and to help him get some clarity on the meaning of his relationship to Dr. Bayog as he understood it."

Paul talked about her constantly, telling Dr. Saporta at one point, "I can't imagine living without her." He was angry at his sister Pilar, who, he told Dr. Gault, Dr. Saporta, Betty Spargo, and Amy Stromsten, had not been directed by him to the box of writings and gifts from Dr. Bean-Bayog in his apartment but had stumbled on them.

He was conflicted about disciplinary action being initiated against the psychiatrist whom he so longed to see, the woman he so loved. "He at times wished it wouldn't happen and at other times he felt that she deserved it. . . . He was very ambivalent," Dr. Saporta said.

Paul was certain enough, however, to hire Thomas F. O'Hare, the attorney for Newton-Wellesley Hospital, to represent him in a possible malpractice suit against Margaret Bean-Bayog. "He was a reluctant dragon slayer," O'Hare remembered, "but we talked about this action as a redemptive act, as a way of seeing that this was not his fault. I think he may have decided to proceed on the day I asked him, 'What do you think would have happened if you had walked into Barry Gault's office in 1986 instead of Margaret Bean-Bayog's?'"

It was certainly true that Dr. Bean-Bayog's therapy techniques had not caused his underlying depression, but had they caused or exacerbated the behaviors that subsequent psychiatrists had labeled as borderline?

From O'Hare's perspective, shaped by twenty years' experience in psychiatry and the law, Dr. Bean-Bayog had taken a depressed young man, who tended to become dependent on key figures in his life, and had so mismanaged his care that his future was precarious at best.

"It was very hard for Paul, facing that; he was still in love with her. It was easier for the family," said O'Hare, who described the Lozanos as supportive, not manipulative. "There was no undue influence exerted. Paul was my client. It was his decision to go forward. I'm not about to take on a case like this if I think the family is pulling the strings."

The emotion Paul most often evinced in the dozen private discussions attorney and client shared between November and January was shame, as O'Hare recalled it. "He was very fragile. He was in love with her, and he was embarrassed by it. He would say, 'I should have known better; I'm a medical student, but I loved her and wanted to keep seeing her.'"

"What on earth did you find to talk about four and five times a week?" O'Hare once asked him as the two sat in the lawyer's suburban Wellesley office.

Paul laughed nervously. "I'd make stuff up," he said. "I knew the kind of things she wanted to hear."

O'Hare had the children's books, the flash cards, the fantasies, the audiocassette, the baby blanket, the Pound Puppy, and Dr. Bean Bear in his office for safekeeping. Paul longed to take his only tangible links to Margaret Bean-Bayog home with him. "He felt that it was wrong that these things were taken from him, and that they wouldn't cherish them," Dr. Saporta said.

Missing Margaret and anxious about the prospect of

resuming medical school, Paul began to display psychotic symptoms. On January 3, Dr. Saporta noted, Paul "appears to be psychotic with severe identity diffusion in that he imagines himself as other people he admires. This appears to be a chronic experience/vulnerability for him, perhaps exacerbated due to experience with Dr. Bean," when he did not know whether he was a three-year-old boy or a Harvard medical student.

Paul's reaction to this identity confusion was panic and denial. He told Dr. Saporta, "That's crazy. I'm a doctor. I'm not supposed to have such crazy thoughts." It was one more attempt at controlling his illness by sheer force of will.

"He regarded various experiences he'd have, such as hearing a voice or imagining himself to be someone, as 'crazy.' So he just had to be a doctor, and anything that he would regard as crazy he had to just not admit into his mind at all. He was maintaining extremely rigid control over his thinking and feelings," Dr. Saporta said.

Even though he was in the best position to judge Paul Lozano's mental state, Dr. Saporta chose not to be involved in the decision about his resuming medical school. When Harvard called, he said, "I discussed this with Paul, and we decided it would be against the best interests of his psychotherapy for me to be the arbiter of whether or not he goes back to school, and we decided that I would remain neutral."

It fell, then, to Dr. Gault to tell Harvard whether Paul was ready to return. Since Paul Lozano's prognosis depended on his taking his medications and seeking help if he needed it, both problematic areas in the past, there was no way to predict the future with complete confidence. Dr. Gault relied on Paul, and his current assessment of his patient, to be his guide.

Paul vacillated about returning home, telling his nurse at Newton-Wellesley Hospital that he had "mixed feelings. He thinks he will always feel he was 'defeated' if he leaves this program," Betty Spargo wrote in his chart.

Dr. Gault said, "There had been some phone calls from people at Harvard wanting me to tell them whether it was okay for him to come back to school. My conversations with Paul were about 'What is it you're trying to do, Paul? What's the schedule? What should I tell them?' There were no psychiatric contraindications for his resuming his clinical rotations, that was my opinion."

Once he was readmitted to Harvard, in fact, his mental state improved immediately. "He had resumed the identity of a medical student, and that gave him a sense of self and identity and security, and so he was feeling better," Dr. Saporta noted.

Even if he was ready to resume responsibility for patient care, why, given his fragility, did Harvard administrators allow Paul Lozano to do his clinical work in Texas, two thousand miles from their supervision, with only a telephone link to his treating psychiatrists?

There was nothing extraordinary about a student's request to do two clinical rotations so far from Boston, said Dr. Hundert, the Associate Dean for Student Affairs and psychiatrist who received Dr. Gault's assurance that Paul Lozano was ready to resume his studies that January. The request was approved because Paul would be going home to Texas, where he felt he had a lot of support. "His going home to be near family was very much part of his request and part of the reason the request was approved," Dr. Hundert said.

Because of Paul Lozano's right to confidentiality, Harvard Medical School told no one at Texas Tech University Health Sciences Center about his psychiatric problems when he resumed his studies in cardiology and obstetrics at Thomason Hospital in El Paso in February 1991.

The family was eager but anxious about Paul's return home, Pilar remembered. "We wanted him home but we knew it was at great risk because we were worried about pulling him away from Dr. Gault, the people who were his lifeline. I was not necessarily convinced he was ready. It was a very tentative situation. And we had no psychiatric setup here."

Dr. Gault was under the misimpression that Paul's sister had made arrangements for him to be seen by a psychiatrist in El Paso. But Dr. Gault's records noted how well Paul was doing and his expectation of seeing his patient again in the spring. "He is without psychosis, is not depressed, is only mildly anxious, seems to be functioning okay. He will spend February and March in El Paso, doing clinical rotations in cardiology and obstetrics at the medical school there and living with his family. At the end of March, he will return to continue his medical studies at Harvard, and his next appointment with me is on Tuesday, April 2nd."

Dr. Saporta's office notes reflected Paul's complicated motives for returning home. "He reports his decision to go home to El Paso [for] two months for some rotations, and to use family support. Gives good reasons for this, but also acknowledges that in part it's a way of getting away from inner turmoil, and a way of getting away from Dr. Bean," he wrote.

Paul had been fighting the urge to call Dr. Bean-Bayog "and his move was, in part, an attempt to get away from that, and also to be with his family, who he hoped would be supportive."

Dr. Saporta's prognosis for Paul was tied to how well he did in his clinical work in El Paso. "I felt that he had a severe personality disturbance. And I thought that he would probably do okay if he could do well in his rotations at medical school," he said. "I did not find him to be acutely suicidal, but I thought he represented a chronic sort of long-term suicide risk; and I thought overall he was a disturbed young man who would need to continue treatment."

In his last session with Dr. Saporta on January 28, Paul Lozano confessed that he was terrified of failing in El Paso. "It's my last chance to do well," he said.

Pilar Williams drove home relieved and exhausted after dinner at her parents' apartment on the first Friday in February. Paul had arrived from Boston that morning, looking well and expressing excitement about resuming his clinical work.

Their mother was certainly thrilled to have her youngest boy at home, Pilar thought. She had already washed and ironed the pastel madras shirt he would wear on Monday to Thomason Hospital. That afternoon she had made him a banana milkshake, his favorite study snack, while he reviewed his cardiology textbook.

Paul Lozano's parents had set aside an apartment for him at Nell Gardner Pilot Homes, the retirement community they managed. At the end of a long row of single rooms facing a courtyard, the apartment they selected for Paul was the largest in the complex. They had a private telephone line and cable television installed as soon as they knew he was coming.

"Maybe it will be all right," Pilar told her husband and son before turning in that night. "Maybe coming home will be enough to make him well."

But even as Pilar was beginning to relax, her brother was flipping frantically through the El Paso Yellow Pages in search of a suicide prevention hotline.

Jane Jackson was in bed when her telephone rang at 10:30 P.M. She was the psychiatric nurse on call for Sun Valley Hospital's crisis line. With her two toddlers finally asleep, she had been hoping for a full night's rest herself before her early-morning shift began.

The anxious voice on the other end of the line identified himself as a fourth-year medical student. He had flown into El Paso earlier in the day and was due to begin a clerkship in cardiology at Thomason Hospital on Monday. He was in a panic. This was his last chance to prove himself. What if he couldn't handle it?

It sounded like an anxiety attack to Jane Jackson. But when her caller said he was feeling suicidal, she pulled herself out from beneath the covers.

"Are you likely to do that?" she asked.

"Probably not," he said.

"If you were going to kill yourself, how would you do it?" she pressed, trying to determine whether his thoughts had advanced to the planning stage.

"My father has a gun," he said. "But I probably wouldn't use it."

Jane Jackson was not convinced. She kept him talking. He

was back living with his parents. His siblings had just left after a big homecoming dinner. He had missed his family so much when he was in Boston. "Boston?" she asked. "Harvard," he clarified. "Oh, you poowah bastahd," she cried in mock horror, eliciting a laugh from Paul Lozano as her Boston accent burst through the telephone wires. "No wondah you're depressed."

For twenty-five minutes Paul Lozano and Jane Jackson swapped stories about her hometown. They talked about his education at Harvard Medical School and hers at Boston College nursing school; about his attic apartment in Brookline and her third-floor walkup in North Cambridge; about his favorite Indian restaurant and her favorite ice cream shop.

Paul was calm when their conversation ended, but Jane Jackson urged him to head for the hospital if the panic returned. Three hours later, overwhelmed by anxiety, Paul Lozano was pacing back and forth in the Sun Valley Hospital emergency room. Judged to be a suicide risk, he was admitted to a locked psychiatric ward.

Pilar was deep in sleep when her telephone rang at 2:00 A.M. It was Sun Valley. "Your brother is here. He came in and said that he was contemplating killing himself, and we want to keep him," the emergency room nurse told her.

"I'll be there in five minutes," Pilar whispered.

She tried to dress quietly, without turning on the lights, but it was no use. Hal and Erick were awake, and angry. "Not again," her husband said, sighing. There was nothing she could say. Pilar knew how tired they were of this. Their family life and their finances had been shattered by the demands of Paul's illness. For four years, she had been preoccupied with Paul, taking his predawn telephone calls, flying to Boston at a moment's notice. She understood her husband's frustration; in fact, she shared it. But what could she do? He was her baby brother.

She drove to Sun Valley Hospital.

"He looks fine to me," she told the attending physician. "What's the problem?"

"What's the problem?" he replied. "He was pacing back

and forth and he said he was going to kill himself. He tells us he has not taken his lithium for a week."

Pilar looked at Paul for an explanation. "I just had an anxiety attack. My rotation starts on Monday. I'm fine now," he said.

"Well, you look fine. You sound okay. I'll take you home with me and everything will be fine," she announced.

But Paul broke through her denial, and his own, to suggest that he at least spend the night. "If something happens to me tonight," he told his sister, "I should be in a safe place."

"Okay. All right," she said. "Stay Saturday night and you leave Sunday morning. Is that acceptable?"

"That's acceptable," Paul told her.

The next day, Dr. Francisco Marquez, a staff psychiatrist, called Dr. Saporta in Boston to learn more about his new patient. "Dr. Saporta stated that Mr. Lozano was a patient in chronic suicide risk, overconcerned about his performance in school and about his clinical expectations in the new rotation," Dr. Marquez wrote in the chart. "In his opinion, it was best to let the patient go on his rotation and explain to Mr. Lozano that I would be available and the hospital also would be available should he need help. The feeling was that the patient would be more suicidal if he missed his rotation than if he was released from the hospital."

Paul was still anxious the next morning when Jane Jackson reported to work and discovered that her late-night caller had checked himself in. He brightened when his father arrived a few hours later with his medical books, and he spent most of his stay reading or chatting with other patients on the ward.

Before he was discharged on Sunday, Dr. Marquez met with Paul and Pilar. They agreed that Paul should live with his sister to ensure supervision, that he should continue his medication, and that he should resume weekly therapy while in El Paso. The gun, Pilar told the psychiatrist, had been removed from her parents' house.

They left the hospital for an afternoon matinee. Paul spent that night at Pilar's and reported to Thomason

Hospital on time to begin his clinical work Monday morning.

His work at the hospital went smoothly for a few weeks until he stopped taking his lithium again. "It made him feel like he was in a box," Jane Jackson said he told her. The two had become friendly during Paul's follow-up visits at Sun Valley. When she visited psychiatric patients at Thomason, she would page him, and they would have lunch in the cafeteria.

Jane Jackson had been in El Paso with her U.S. Army surgeon husband long enough to move fluidly between Spanish and English, sometimes in midsentence. She had grown up in Massachusetts and had trained as a nurse at Boston College and in a graduate program in psychology and chemical dependency at Boston University and the Massachusetts Mental Health Center. She learned most about psychiatric nursing on the job on a forty-six-bed locked unit at the Veterans Administration Hospital in Northampton, Massachusetts, where some nights she was the only nurse on duty.

She took an immediate liking to Paul Lozano. He reminded her of her younger self. "I remember what it was like to be well into my twenties, at the end of my education, lonely and unsure socially. That was Paul. He was a very bright guy and a very scared, insecure guy, too. We hit it off immediately. I saw all my old vulnerabilities. His sisters are older, so I was just one more sister."

Jane Jackson had met Paul's oldest sister, Norma, the previous November at Fort Bliss when Norma's second husband, Steve, was on active duty and Jane was setting up a stress management program for the men in Desert Shield. She liked Norma and her family. "The Lozanos are not a traditional machismo-type Mexican family. It's big and close, but the women were sent to school just like the boys, and they all have strong personalities."

Paul became such a regular at Jane Jackson's dinner table or in front of her television set that three-year-old Daniel Patrick began calling him Uncle Paul and one-year-old Kelly Kathleen would fall asleep in his lap. "He was an interesting kid. He was cute and seductive in a way, but he also really brought out your maternal instincts. It was an irresistible mix," she said of Paul.

In March, they took a day trip with her children to Mesilla, a lovely old town in New Mexico. He needed to talk. "Pilar got most of it, but I think he needed an ear outside the family. I was it those last months," she said. "He never talked about Margaret, except to say that he had been in therapy back east and that it had not been a beneficial relationship, that she kept talking about his childhood, making mountains out of molehills."

That day in Mesilla, as they pushed Kelly's stroller past the pottery shops and art galleries, he talked about Boston and the loneliness he could never shake when he was there. "It was a big city, culturally very foreign, and he was away from his family. He said how much he had missed having them there for support," she recalled.

He envied Jane her marriage and her children and he told her so with a frequency and an insistence that bordered on a whine. "What kind of woman would want me in this condition?" he lamented.

"Depression is not the end of the world," she scolded him. "I know half a dozen doctors on antidepressants. Treat it like a handicap, live with it, and get over it."

"How can I put this on my residency applications?" he asked.

"How can you not?" she replied.

Paul Lozano wanted nothing more than to be well but, at home especially, there was no denying that he was not. Pilar's house was too small to accommodate everyone's need for privacy, so he had returned to his apartment at Pilot Homes. He still saw or spoke with his sister every day, so Pilar saw the disturbing signs of psychosis as soon as they reappeared.

"One moment he was gung-ho: 'I'm going to be a doctor. I'm going to be this. I'm going to do that.' He was going to conquer the world," she recalled. "The next moment he would be saying, 'I miss Margaret. I need Margaret. I love

Margaret. How could I have betrayed her? How could I have turned on her?' "

When the pacing and sleeplessness accelerated, Pilar called Dr. Marquez, who suggested that his medication be adjusted. It was not the answer Pilar wanted to hear. The use of psychotropic medications had bothered her from the outset of Paul's illness, and no one had ever adequately explained his need for them. To Pilar, they were merely tranquilizers, dulling her brother to the reality she and the rest of the family could not ignore.

His insomnia was followed by paranoia and delusions. He avoided his parents, especially his mother; he would lock his door if he heard her footsteps on the walk outside. One night when Pilar was visiting Paul in his room, he turned suddenly to her and demanded, "Are you my mother? I wish you were my mother. You know, you raised me. You do know that you raised me, don't you?"

"Me? I raised you?" she replied. "That's not true, Paul. Who told you that? That's just not true."

"You're just in denial," he told her.

"What am I in denial about?" she asked.

"You know," he said.

"No, I don't know," Pilar said. "Can you tell me what it is you're talking about?"

"Margaret says you're just protecting her because you don't want me to know what happened," he said.

"What? Protecting who? About what, Paul?"

In place of an answer, her brother curled up in a corner of his bed and broke into uncontrollable sobs. "I'm sorry," he wept. "I don't deserve your love. I'm sorry."

There was to be no explanation, and no end to Paul's expressions of grief for the loss of Dr. Margaret Bean-Bayog.

"He needed her. And he couldn't have her anymore because he had committed the ultimate sin—he had turned her in. So he could not reconcile himself with the fact that it was over. He could not live without her anymore," said Pilar.

His longing for his psychiatrist and his misery about

having betrayed her were such that his parents and sister agreed they would do anything to end his anguish, including dropping plans for a lawsuit.

"We got to the point where we said, 'Let's drop this. Let's forget about you and Margaret. What do we care about the rest of the world? Let's just put this behind us. We won't do this to Margaret,'" Pilar recalled. "But we had no control over the medical board process. It was Newton-Wellesley and Dr. Gault who had filed the complaint against her."

It was late at night when Paul Lozano stopped by Jane Jackson's house to chat after a long shift in the labor and delivery rooms at Thomason Hospital. He often showed up unannounced to unwind after a shift, but this last Wednesday in March he was especially revved up.

He talked louder and faster than usual. He would not sit down. He opened and closed the refrigerator and wore a path in the pile of the living room rug where he paced and held forth on the night's deliveries, the approach of the national medical board exams, and his plans to stay in El Paso for another month to do a clerkship in internal medicine.

The psychiatric nurse wondered as she watched his frenetic movements and listened to his accelerated speech whether Paul Lozano was manic. He had been diagnosed with depression, but as she observed him Jane Jackson wondered if Paul might be manic-depressive, or bipolar, a condition that alternates periods of despair with hyperactivity.

Paul was still going strong when she ran out of steam at 3 A.M. and turned in for the night. She told him to crash on the couch but as she drifted off to sleep she could still hear his footsteps as he roamed between rooms.

Paul Lozano was sleepless for much of the last week of his life. The lithium he had been taking to stave off a relapse of his depression made him feel claustrophobic, so he stopped taking it. The longer he went without rest, the more manic he became.

Without the stabilizing effect of lithium, Paul's disturbing symptoms returned. He called Sun Valley Hospital one Sunday complaining of hearing Dr. Bean-Bayog's voice speaking to him over the Thomason Hospital intercom. He suspected that someone had broken into his apartment. He had taken the antipsychotic drug Haldol when he had had similar psychotic symptoms in the past, he told Dr. Marquez, who urged him to come in. Dr. Marquez then spoke with Pilar, who confirmed Paul's paranoia.

In the emergency room, Paul Lozano was observed to be "clean, casually dressed, a tie on, reading a book about obstetrics." During his mental status examination, the hospital notes reveal, he said he "got anxious last week after getting a letter that an expert witness will investigate his previous [doctor], and also that board of medical examiners is getting involved. He doesn't want to give his previous [doctor] problems."

The letter, dated February 14, had come from his attorney, Tom O'Hare. He was writing to let Paul know that Dr. Larry H. Strasburger, an analyst and Harvard-affiliated psychiatrist, had reviewed the materials and was firm in his rejection of Margaret Bean-Bayog's methods. "Dr. Bean-Bayog engaged in a consistent pattern of inducing a dependent, infantile state in Paul Lozano . . . to the degree that he required her support, companionship, approval and love," Dr. Strasburger wrote in his assessment. "This deviant course of 'therapy' erased appropriate boundaries of the psychotherapist-patient relationship and violated acceptable standards of psychiatric practice."

The level of Paul's anxiety about Dr. Bean-Bayog fluctuated with his compliance with his medication, rising when he stopped taking his lithium and falling when he resumed. By the end of March, he had discontinued his medication yet again. His mother and Pilar watched with distress one afternoon as he made fifteen pointless trips between his apartment and his car within ten minutes.

The Lozanos were worried, but unsure what to do. Calling Dr. Marquez, or Dr. Gault in Boston, might prompt another hospitalization. Broaching the subject with Paul had been a disaster; it had triggered accusations that the family was trying to sabotage his career. His work was not affected, so the family decided to wait and to watch.

It did not take long for them to realize that they had made the wrong choice. "We should have called Dr. Gault. I know that now," Pilar said later, choking back tears. "But we were so afraid they would lock him up for good this time."

Paralyzed by fear and protectiveness, they watched Paul slide from insomnia into paranoia in the days before his death. For six weeks, Epifania Lozano had risen at 5 A.M. to prepare eggs and chorizo with beans for her son's breakfast. Suddenly he no longer came to the kitchen. Neither did he stop at the screen door after work as he had for weeks to tell her the weight and gender of the babies he had delivered that day. When she brought him his banana milkshake each night, he would open the door only wide enough for her to hand it through.

Pilar was appalled by what she took to be his rudeness to their mother, but soon she was frightened by something much worse. Visiting Paul one night in his room, Pilar was talking about her day at work when he raised his palm to silence her.

"Shhh, did you hear that? Did you hear it?" Paul asked.

"Hear what?" Pilar replied.

"Shhh. She's talking to me. Can't you hear her voice? She's talking. Listen. You have to lock the door quickly. They're coming, they're coming."

"Who? Who's coming, Paul?" Pilar asked, frantic now herself.

"Mom and Dad. Quick. Lock the door," he said, backing into a corner of the room.

Oh, my God, she thought, but she did as her brother asked.

"They've been searching my room. They've been trying to find out what happened. They're going to find out what happened," Paul said.

"About what? What happened?" she asked.

"You know. You know what happened," he snapped.

"No, Paul," Pilar insisted. "I really don't know what happened."

"Shhh. Margaret says you're protecting them. But I know.

I know what she did," he told his sister. Then, suddenly lowering his voice, he asked, "Is Margaret my mom?"

Pilar sank into a chair and stared at her brother. His eyes were darting from the door to the window, his words a horrible hint that he no longer saw her or her parents as they were but as monsters of some shape he would not, or could not, name.

Oh, my God, what if he kills Mom and Dad? What if he kills me? she thought as his agitation began to subside. He curled up on his bed. She sat with him until she was sure he was calm and then she slipped out to her parents' apartment.

Her mother would hear nothing of what had just transpired. "He is fine. He is overtired, that's all," she told Pilar, waving her hand in dismissal.

"Mom, please, I need to get help," Pilar pleaded. "I think he might hurt you and Dad. He doesn't see you the way you are anymore. You're somebody else—I don't know who. But he thinks we're these monsters."

"No, no, no," a stern Epifania Lozano told her daughter. "Why would he hurt us? He is just tired. Do you want to ruin his career? To be a doctor, this is the only thing he says he wants. What if you turn on him, and then they lock him up and they hurt him? What if they put him in jail? Or what if they put him in a place for the criminally insane? You would do such a thing to your brother?"

Jane Jackson was witness only to Paul Lozano's depressions and sudden spurts of hyperactivity, but she was no more sure than Pilar about the right thing to do for him that last Wednesday in March. Paul did not want to call Dr. Marquez, the psychiatrist at Sun Valley Hospital he had been seeing as an outpatient, so she arranged for him to visit a physician friend on Thursday afternoon for a tranquilizer so he could at least get some sleep. Paul kept the appointment, but he was on call Thursday night so he never filled the prescription.

Early on Friday he telephoned Jane to ask about her plans for the day. He joined her and the children on an outing to buy Easter outfits at the Cielo Vista Mall off Interstate 10, the elevated highway that slices through El Paso, bordered on both the east and west by strip malls, fast-food restaurants, and cowboy boot outlets.

With Kelly Kathleen's new spring dress and Daniel Patrick's new shoes purchased, Jane drove to the outskirts of the city in search of an open stretch of road where she might hit some tumbleweed but no traffic. A long drive down Montana Avenue might lull Paul into some needed sleep, she thought. If she was lucky the kids would doze, too.

Paul napped during the drive and when he snapped awake, he asked Jane to drive him to his sister's house.

Pilar Williams had been wrestling with her conscience all week, keeping her answering machine on to avoid another argument with her brother. One minute he would agree that he needed to drop out for a while; the next he would accuse her of not being as supportive as Margaret. It's like a marriage, she thought, like she's the other woman.

She had made her decision, knowing she would incur the wrath of both Paul and her mother. But she had no choice. She kept returning to her responsibility to all those women whose babies her brother was delivering. She was Paul's sister, but she was a nurse, too. She had taken the Hippocratic Oath to "do no harm," just as he had. She called him and said she needed to talk to him.

Paul Lozano knew what he was up against. He knew Pilar. When his sister took a stand on ethical principle, no one could be more righteous. And nothing would dissuade her. Just ask Candy Stone. When Paul told Pilar that Candy had gotten the cocaine they used in New Orleans from a dealer at Providence Memorial Hospital, hadn't Pilar marched up to hospital administrators and demanded that Candy be fired?

It was a matter of principle, she had argued. How could the nurses like Pilar who worked with Candy be certain she was not using drugs on duty? What about patient safety? Candy had insisted she was not a regular cocaine user, and she passed three random drug screens. But that was not enough for Pilar, who enlisted the hospital's doctors in support of her campaign to rid Providence Memorial of Candy Stone. "I don't give up easily. If I think something is wrong, it's wrong," she said. But was Pilar being ethical or vindictive?

"I know they thought I was purposely trying to destroy her so she couldn't take my brother away from me," Pilar said. "I did do it to her because I warned her. I told her to stay away from him because he wasn't well. And she defied me because I think sometimes these women, they see me as a source to him of strength and a protector, and they think they are vying for him. And to me I think their intentions are never good. Who turns around and does exactly what a person asked you not to?"

Candy Stone did not much care what motivated Pilar Williams, whom she described as a "good nurse with very high standards." The hospital allowed Candy to resign and then helped her find a job at a medical center across town. "I admitted it because my mother told me there are only two things she can't abide: a thief and a liar. People tell me you never admit anything. Did they want me to lie? Just misrepresent the truth? At what cost?" Candy asked two years later, having worked her way back to a supervisory post at her new hospital. "I'm happier. I was not an impaired nurse, and I wouldn't say I was. I made a mistake."

Of Pilar, she said without apparent bitterness, "I think she believed she was doing right. I also think she did it because I was a reminder. I was still in her life. She saw me every day."

Standing on Pilar's doorstep, the locked wrought-iron gate between them, Paul must have known how formidable an opponent his sister could be.

She told herself she had to do it as she invited Paul inside. He settled onto the white sofa. She felt that whatever had happened had happened, and was their problem, but it shouldn't become anyone else's problem, too.

With her son and husband standing nearby to lend support, she got straight to the point. "I'm going to be perfectly honest with you," Pilar began. "If you cannot straighten yourself out, if you cannot get better, then I must turn you in. Because no one else will do it. I can't let you treat innocent people if you are not well.

"I love you more than my life. But I cannot do this anymore. I cannot play this game with you anymore. You are not capable of finishing medical school. You are not well enough to be a doctor. I don't know what happened, but you don't have it anymore. And I'm very sorry about that."

Paul was furious. Who was she to question his competence when he was doing well at work and his supervisors had no complaints? Who was she to sit in judgment of him?

"My chief resident thinks I'm okay," he said, then accused his sister of suffering from a bad case of envy. "Margaret said you didn't want me to do well. You never wanted me to do well because then I would be better than you."

Pilar's eyes flashed, but she held her tongue. She grabbed her jacket and brushed past him on her way to work.

A few hours later flowers arrived at the nurses' station. A dozen long-stemmed red roses, surrounded by baby's breath and tied with a wide satin ribbon. You're buying me, she thought angrily. You're trying to manipulate me, so that I won't turn you in, so I won't do what I have to do. On the accompanying card, Paul promised Pilar that he would get well, that he would realize his dream, that he would become a doctor and make them all proud. He sent his mother an identical bouquet.

When he did not hear from his sister, Paul stopped by her house. "You didn't call me to thank me for the flowers," he said.

"I don't trust you anymore. I'm afraid of you," she told him. "It is as though she is speaking through you now. I don't know what it is that's happened to you. And you won't let go of her so that we can help you."

"She was right," he shot back. "You just don't want me to succeed. You're trying to destroy me."

Pilar's protests that her ethical obligations outweighed her personal loyalties fell on deaf ears. She talked ethics, but he heard betrayal.

Later that night, Paul telephoned, momentarily conciliatory. "I can't believe the responsibilities that I have. I'm pretty messed up to be a doctor," he told her. "What was I thinking? It's killing me."

Grasping at the chance that he might actually withdraw from medicine voluntarily, she urged him to give it up. "Do something else for a little while. Go for your Ph.D."

"Oh, you just don't want me to succeed," he snapped.

Pilar slammed down the receiver, yanked the roses from their vase, and tore the card that had come with them into tiny pieces. She stormed through the darkened house, throwing the roses into a trash bin and smashing the small porcelain figurines Paul had given her over the years as gifts.

When she finally fell asleep her rest was short-lived. The bedside clock read 1 A.M. when the ringing telephone brought Pilar back to consciousness. She did not recognize the man's voice on the other end of the line.

"Pilar," he said.

"Yes?" she replied.

"I miss you," he said.

"What? Paul, is that you? Are you okay?"

"I miss you," he said again.

"Well, you know, I miss you, too. What does that mean?" she asked as the lights went on in the house and her son, Erick, came into her room.

"I miss you," he repeated.

"What are you talking about, you miss me?" she said. "Paul, this is Pilar. This isn't Margaret."

There was a long silence before Paul spoke again.

"I love you, Margaret. You know I love you. I need you. You have to help me," he pleaded.

"Paul, you're very sick. You're very, very sick. And you're really frightening me," she cried, but she was speaking to a phantom.

"If you loved me, you'd be with me too," he said before hanging up.

Pilar Williams barely made it to the bathroom ten feet from her bed, where she crumpled in a puddle of tears and vomit.

In the morning, she called her parents. "I'm scared. I'm really scared," she told them. "I don't know what is happening, but he is very sick, and we need to get help. We need to get help right away."

By then, a sleepless Paul Lozano was on his way to Jane Jackson's house. The family was headed out to Mount Shadows Lake, a man-made lake east of El Paso, for a day of picnicking and play. The Jacksons had invited him along. It was spring but still chilly, so they were surprised when Paul showed up in shorts and a T-shirt. He was too stubborn to change or to borrow a jacket from John Jackson.

He was snippy all day, but Jane attributed his surly mood to exhaustion. When the wind picked up off the lake, she convinced him to slip on the hooded Boston College sweatshirt she had stashed in the trunk. While the children played, Paul talked about the end of his obstetrics rotation. He knew he did not handle transitions well, and he was conflicted about the experiences he had had in obstetrics. He loved the deliveries, but he was upset by the pain women endured in labor. It was difficult for him to watch. When one patient died of septicemia, or blood poisoning, he took it very hard. Pain of all kinds made him uncomfortable, even the Jackson children's tears over a skinned knee or a lost toy.

Jane showed him an advertisement in the *El Paso Times*. A new family practice was opening on Lee Trevino Boulevard. The doctor was a Harvard Medical School graduate with a Mexican name. "You know this Raul Marcello Rodriguez?" she asked. Paul did not know him, but he looked at the ad for a long time. Jane could not tell if his expression was one of curiosity or envy.

The next day was Easter Sunday, but the mood was anything but festive when the family gathered at Pilar and Hal Williams's house. Pilar had convinced her parents that a confrontation with Paul was inevitable. She began by telling Paul that his frightening predawn call was the last straw; it was over.

"You know I can't cover up for you anymore," she told him. "I'm sorry."

To her horror, her brother dropped to his knees and began to beg. "Please, please don't tell anyone that I'm sick. It will destroy me. I'll die," he told her. He grabbed Pilar around the waist. "Please, please," he wept. "I'm begging you. Don't turn me in. I will just die."

Marcos and Epifania looked on helplessly. Epifania began to howl, her tears mixing with her own pleas in Paul's behalf. "You can't, Pilar," she cried. "You can't do this to him."

Pilar was firm in her resolve. The next week she would speak to his supervisors at the hospital. She would make certain her brother was relieved of responsibility for the care of patients.

It was 11:42 A.M., El Paso time, on Sunday when Dr. Gault's beeper went off in his suburban Boston home. The hospital had been paging him for an hour, but the local number he had been directed to call was out of service. When the beeper screen finally flashed a Texas area code with the seven-digit number, he dialed from his kitchen telephone. Paul Lozano answered. They had an appointment on Tuesday in Boston, and Paul wanted him to know he was still in El Paso.

It was hard to tell what was going on from two thousand miles away. But Paul's speech was racing, Dr. Gault noticed. Paul was flip and sarcastic. Talking too fast. Sounding too cocky. "Are you taking cocaine or anything else?" Dr. Gault asked him. "No," Paul snapped, obviously offended. "What do you mean by that?"

Just as Jane Jackson had, Dr. Gault wondered if his patient was manifesting signs of bipolar—or manic-depressive—illness. Had he entered a manic stage? "Those were the only two things that could account for the tone I heard. He was really manicky," Dr. Gault remembered.

He was not taking his lithium, Paul conceded. "I don't need that stuff," he told Dr. Gault. He was upset with his family. They were acting like "a bunch of jerks," he said, without revealing Pilar's threat to put an end to his medical education.

As soon as he ended his conversation with Dr. Gault, with

a promise to resume his medication, Paul called Jane Jackson. He was indignant. "Can you believe he asked me that?" he sputtered about the suggestion he might be using cocaine.

"Calm down, Paul," she told him. "The guy's just worried about you. You have been pretty wound up lately."

"I'll show him. I'll prove I'm not using drugs. I'll get a urine test," he said. In the face of his planned vindication, his voice suddenly grew calmer. Getting tested was one way Paul Lozano could show he still had some control over his life.

Chapter

9

Monday, April 1, broke clear and bright in El Paso.

Epifania Lozano's older sister, Alicia, the seamstress who had taught her to sew so many years ago, was visiting from Mexico. Once a year when she came from Monterrey, she had her chronic anemia checked at the local hospital. This year her nephew, the Harvard Medical School student of whom they were all so proud, would be taking her to have her bloodwork done.

"Little Paul," as he was affectionately called by the family, already looked the part of a doctor. He came to the door of his parents' apartment in midmorning wearing his white lab coat, his pastel madras shirt, and the crimson tie he wore with everything, despite his sisters' protests that it did not match any of his shirts. His stethoscope dangled from his neck.

Alicia could not decide what to wear. She primped her gray hair and fussed with her face powder, while her nephew fidgeted. He was in a hurry. He was to begin his internal medicine studies at William Beaumont Army Medical Center the next day, so this would be the last chance he would have to take his aunt to Thomason Hospital. There would be paperwork because she was not an American citizen. He did not want to keep the hematologist waiting. And he wanted time to have his own blood and urine screened.

"Come on, Auntie," he called impatiently. "Let's go."

Jane Jackson bumped into them at the hospital just after noon. Aunt Alicia had seen the doctor, and Paul Lozano had gotten a toxicology screen. He waved the report triumphantly. He was clean. Big surprise, Jane Jackson thought. There had been people at the hospital who used cocaine but she did not believe for a minute that Paul Lozano was one of them. She had done enough work with drug abusers to know the signs, and he didn't have them. Boy, that Dr. Gault got under your skin, she thought.

In fact, he still seemed agitated. He complained about his allergies; he said he felt lousy. She offered to square it with the Graduate Education Office if he wanted to skip his first day of the new rotation. Paul thanked her and drove his aunt back to Pilot Homes.

His sister Martha and his niece Nicole were digging up cacti in the small front yard of the apartment complex when Paul slipped the lab results under his sister's nose. "Random drug test. I'm clean," he said.

"Must have been your lucky day," she joked. Her mother overheard Martha's teasing and shot her what the family calls her "sharp eyes," and Martha fell silent.

It had been a rough week for Paul, Epifania Lozano knew, and now his allergies were bothering him. She made caldo for him, the vegetable and beef soup seasoned with cilantro and lemon that was his favorite meal. She served it with her fresh corn tortillas. At dinner, Paul praised the food and reassured the family of Alicia's good health. He conceded some anxiety about beginning his new clerkship and excused himself to do some reading. He asked that his parents not wake him in the morning. He said he might sleep late if he was not feeling any better.

Martha and Nicole offered to drive up to the drugstore for the Hismanal, his allergy medicine. "You owe me," Martha teased. "I'm tired of running your errands."

He took a second to think of appropriate compensation.

"You got it," he said as he walked off to his apartment. "A lifetime of free medical care."

Nicole could hear the water running when she knocked on her uncle's door fifteen minutes later with his medicine in hand. He must be washing up, she thought.

"Just leave it on the doorstep," he shouted. Nicole propped the package against the door and scooted back to her mother in the cactus patch.

Paul telephoned Pilar's home and spoke to Erick, who for weeks had been angered by his uncle's demands on his mother. He was surprised, then, to hear Paul sounding so calm and upbeat. They had both recently misplaced their nearly identical leather bomber jackets, and there was banter about the hell they would have to pay when Pilar found out how irresponsible they had been.

Given the jovial tone of Erick's end of the conversation, Pilar was amazed to learn he had been talking to Paul.

"Relax, Mom," Erick said. "Uncle Paul's back. He's all right. He's going to make it."

Sometime in the hours after that call, Paul Lozano showered and shaved. He changed into clean white Jockey shorts and opened his internal medicine text to read. He placed the lab report, declaring his system free of illicit drugs, on the top of his desk. He then filled a hypodermic needle with the anesthetic lidocaine and numbed the skin on both hands and forearms. He refilled the syringe, this time with cocaine. In a frenzy of injections—administered either in a deliberate attempt to end his life or in a frantic response to auditory hallucinations—he pierced his skin at least seventy-five times.

At midnight, Marcos Lozano made his usual security patrol of the courtyard. When he passed number 15, Paul's studio, he saw the desk lamp on and assumed his son was still at his studies. He noticed the allergy medicine still on the doorstep, but assumed Paul would pick it up when he was ready to turn in for the night. He did not want to disturb Paul when he was studying.

In the morning, Marcos and Epifania did not notice that Paul's Honda Accord was still in its space. They simply assumed he had left for the hospital without stopping by their apartment, as was his recent habit. Just after noon Marcos gave Lupe, one of the housekeepers, the key to clean Paul's apartment.

Lupe returned a minute later. "Your son is asleep," he told Marcos, who only then saw the Honda in its usual spot.

He must be sick, Marcos thought. His allergies. As he made his way toward Paul's apartment, the sun glinted off a small white package on the doorstep. His medicine. Marcos picked up his pace. Lupe had left the door ajar. Marcos looked inside. Paul was upright in his chair, his head tilted back as if he had dozed off while reading.

Marcos Lozano knew at once that his son was dead.

The police came promptly. Marcos instructed Maria, one of the housecleaners, to keep Mrs. Lozano in their apartment, away from the windows. He could not break this news to her alone. He needed Pilar, but how could he tell his daughter what had happened by telephone? He told Maria to phone the hospital and tell Pilar only that there was an emergency and she must come.

He should have known that Pilar would demand more. When the telephone rang minutes later in Paul's room, it was she. "Dad, it's me," Pilar said. "What's wrong? What has happened?"

"Your brother is dead," Marcos Lozano told his daughter. Just like that: "Your brother is dead."

His heart ached as he heard her protest in vain that he must be wrong; he must be confused; he must summon help.

"You don't understand, the police are here. We do have help. Paul is dead," he told her.

Pilar and Hal were there within minutes. The sight of Pilar kissing her brother good-bye unleashed Marcos Lozano's own grief, and he wept silently as they walked down the courtyard to tell Epifania that her baby boy was dead.

She did not need to be told. The sight of her damp-eyed husband and daughter leaning on each other for support brought her screaming through the door. "My baby," she cried. "My baby. Let me go to him."

Pilar held her back. She needed two policemen to help her. "No, Mother, no. Paul would not want you to see him now," she shouted above her mother's wails. "You must not do this. Paul would not want this. Dad and I have been with him. He would not want you to see him like this."

With effort, they guided her back inside only to have to restrain her again when the black hearse from the El Paso County coroner's office turned into the yard. "No. No. No. My baby. My Paublo," she wept.

Breaking loose from Pilar's hold, she raised her hand in anger. "I hope you remember the look on your brother's face," she fairly spat. "I hope you remember that until the day you die that he begged you not to turn him in."

Pilar shrank back in horror. My God, she thought. How could I forget? But it wasn't even me he was talking to. I know he knew how much I loved him.

Her mother's sobs mingled with accusation. "He wanted so much for you to believe in him. And you didn't believe in him anymore," she cried. "That's why he gave up."

Part of that was true, Pilar knew. She didn't believe in him anymore. He was too dependent, too needy, too demanding. I couldn't keep going anymore, she thought.

Epifania reluctantly agreed to take a tranquilizer. She embraced her daughter as she slipped into sleep. She had spoken out of grief. She did not need to tell Pilar she had not meant to hurt her.

The next day, as they did everything else, the Lozanos went as a family to the Martin Funeral Home to select a coffin for Paul. How he would be dressed was a joint decision. The suit that his mother automatically selected was set aside. Paul had hated suits. Instead he would wear baggy blue jeans, his favorite pair of tennis shoes, the blue Perry Ellis shirt they had given him at Christmas, and his ever-present crimson tie.

Martha found the shirt in Paul's closet; it was wrinkled. As she pulled the iron from her mother's cupboard, Epifania Lozano rose groggily from her bed. "I will do that," she whispered, fingering the soft denim. "He was my son. It's my job. I can make this smooth so it won't chafe."

A Franciscan priest officiated at the funeral Mass in Spanish at Our Lady of Guadalupe Church in northeast El Paso, high in the Franklin Mountains. Desert flowers lined the whitewashed stucco walls of the Mission-style church. A pale wooden cross topped the dark wooden casket; it would later hang in his parents' home.

Around their necks, his mother and his sisters, Norma, Martha, and Pilar, wore handblown crystal lockets, each holding a small black curl of Paul's hair. His brothers, Abel and Mark, his nephews, Erick and Tyler, and his brother-in-law Hal Williams carried his body from the church to the hearse that would take Paul Anthony Lozano to his final resting place in a prairie graveyard on Montana Avenue.

During the graveside prayers, Jane Jackson kept looking past the cemetery gates toward the cars whizzing by on Montana. Just a week ago, she had driven past this place trying to lull her young friend to sleep. Now he was dead.

Dr. Raul Marcello Rodriguez, the new family practitioner in El Paso, represented Harvard Medical School at Paul's funeral. He was several years older than Paul. They had never met, but the Lozano family reminded Dr. Rodriguez so much of his own—"very close, very proud of Paul"— that he wept openly with them at the graveside.

He was thinking about Harvard as the coffin was lowered into the ground. "I thought all the world was like El Paso. You go out there to Boston and you find that the only Hispanics you run into are the few other students," he said. "You have to prove that you deserve to be there. You have to set an example for others to follow. If they falter," he said of wealthier, white students, "they always have Daddy to find them another job or another career. For us, you just come back to El Paso."

From Evergreen East Cemetery, Paul's family and friends returned to Martha's home for the postrequiem meal and the inevitable postmortems when a loved one dies by his own hand. The autopsy report had attributed Paul's death to cardiac arrest from acute cocaine intoxication. Dr. Juan U. Contin, the medical examiner for El Paso County, declared his death an accidental overdose. Why else would there be no note? Why else the multiple skin pricks? A direct injection to a vein would have brought death more certainly.

But his family and friends were convinced it was suicide. Why else had he made certain that the family saw the toxicology report declaring him drug free? Why had he deliberately numbed his skin before the fatal injections? Why had he sounded calmer and more lucid that day than he had in weeks, if not because he had resolved to end his life?

They could only speculate where Paul had gotten the cocaine. The young doctor, a resident in emergency medicine, who had done the drug screen for Paul that Monday was a known cocaine user—he himself would die a year later of a cocaine overdose. But El Paso was a border town; Paul could have gotten it anywhere.

They came together in grief, but everyone in Martha's kitchen was wrestling with a sense of guilt.

If only I had listened to him more carefully that day, thought Jane Jackson.

If only I had kept in closer touch, thought Abel.

If only I hadn't left his allergy medicine on the doorstep, thought thirteen-year-old Nicole.

If only I hadn't run my ad this week. Maybe it depressed him to see a Hispanic who had made it, thought Dr. Raul Marcello Rodriguez.

There was more than self-recrimination in their thoughts, however. If only Pilar had told us how ill he was, thought Martha.

If only she hadn't gotten on her high horse about ethics, thought Abel.

If only we'd known, thought Mark and Norma.

Pilar would not accept the blame. She knew she had done her best for her brother and her family. She had carried the burden and held Paul together when no one else could. She had just reached the limits of her endurance.

But Pilar was angry, too—at Paul, for giving up the fight; at Harvard, for turning a blind eye. But mostly at the woman she was sure had reduced her brother to the psychotic shell she buried out on Montana Avenue: Dr. Margaret Bean-Bayog. The psychiatrist who had abandoned her brother a year before because, she would later say, she could no longer carry the burden, could no longer hold him together, could no longer endure.

Two thousand miles away, Dr. Bean-Bayog was just learning that her patient was dead. The mail protruding from the gunmetal gray box at the side of her crescent driveway the day after Paul Lozano's death included the usual weekday cache of bills, catalogs, and supermarket flyers.

There, among the flotsam, was a thin white envelope from the Massachusetts Board of Registration in Medicine. In four stark paragraphs, the state panel responsible for monitoring the conduct of physicians in Massachusetts informed the forty-eight-year-old Harvard psychiatrist that she was under investigation for her treatment of Paul A. Lozano.

> Specifically, it has been alleged that you consistently counseled Mr. Lozano not to communicate with his family, that you told and wrote him over and over that you were his mother and he was your infant, that you sent him many children's books as well as numerous cards and letters in which you referred to yourself as "mom" and Mr. Lozano as the "little boy," that you composed several children's stories for him and that you gave Mr. Lozano an audiocassette in which you are reading several children's books.
>
> In addition, it has been alleged that during a number of therapy sessions you read at length to Mr. Lozano from detailed accounts of your own sexual fantasies about him and that you openly masturbated during some therapy sessions.

That the medical board did not notify Dr. Margaret Bean-Bayog that she was under investigation for substandard care and sexual misconduct until the day it learned of

Paul Lozano's death was "just coincidental," according to Alexander F. Fleming, the executive director of the board.

But, in fact, the medical board's handling of the case from the outset was a study in disorganization and delay. The board claimed it never received the letter from Dr. Gault. It also claimed to have lost the letter from his supervisor, Dr. Alvin Becker. The board insisted it never got the letter from Amy Stromsten, either, the social worker to whom Paul had confessed his sexual relationship with Dr. Bean-Bayog.

It was not until Dr. Gault contacted the disciplinary panel in February to inquire about the status of its investigation into the treatment of Paul Lozano, and then sent them a duplicate of his letter, that his two-month-old complaint against the Harvard psychiatrist was logged at all. Another two weeks passed before an investigator was assigned to the case. By then, Paul was back in El Paso, barreling toward self-destruction.

The medical board's first priority when its investigation formally began on February 26, 1991, was to determine whether Dr. Margaret Bean-Bayog posed "an immediate and serious threat" to the public. With no other complaints against her and the patient presumed to be under new and competent care, the investigator determined that the case did not warrant a summary suspension of Dr. Bean-Bayog's license.

Paul Lozano was in Texas, unavailable to meet with the medical board's investigator. Because he was due back in Boston in April, it was determined an interview with him could wait. Between February, when the complaint was logged, and April, when Paul died, the board investigator made telephone calls to Dr. Gault and Dr. Bean-Bayog. She met once with Tom O'Hare, the attorney for Newton-Wellesley Hospital, and Paul Lozano, to review the contents of the box left in his care.

In its April 3 letter, the medical board gave Margaret Bean-Bayog thirty days to reply to the allegations against her.

During those weeks, Epifania Lozano made a daily pilgrimage to her son's grave. For hours she sat on her little stool so he would not be alone out on the prairie. Paul had been afraid of the dark as a child, and Epifania wept when Pilar came to drag her away at night.

"You have to leave now, Mom," her daughter told her as the sun set.

"How can I leave him here in the dark?" she replied.

"But Mother, what about us? We need you, too," Pilar pleaded.

"You're stronger. My baby wasn't strong. I can't leave him alone," she said firmly, until her daughter would relent and wait quietly until Epifania Lozano was ready to leave.

Paul's siblings were no less consumed by grief. Martha obsessed over the delay in placing a bronze marker on his grave. She thought it made him look like a nameless pauper. She placed a cactus in a round terra-cotta planter on her brother's grave as a temporary marker, in violation of cemetery regulations banning all but artificial flower arrangements. She stood back, satisfied with her choice. There, she thought. Now we know he is here. He's a person and he is here.

That night, she tossed with nightmares until dawn. She called everyone in her family in the morning. "I saw Paul all night long in my dreams," she told them. "There is something wrong. We have to go to the cemetery first thing this morning."

There were protests; they had jobs, commitments.

"So do I," Martha said. "We have to go."

She and Pilar drove to the cemetery. The cactus was gone. Martha marched into the office of the groundskeeper and spied Paul's plant.

"How could you," she railed. Reminded of the rule prohibiting fresh plants, she insisted the cactus remain until the bronze marker, with the caduceus symbol of medicine beside Paul's name, was in place.

"I'm going to be here every day, hounding you until you call the police, unless you put that cactus or the marker on that grave site," she told him.

She and Pilar watched the groundskeeper carry the cactus back to their brother's grave.

"There," said Martha. "Now he can rest."

Peace did not come as easily to the other members of the Lozano clan. Abel stopped talking to Pilar, convinced he had been kept in the dark about the seriousness of Paul's illness and racked with guilt for not asking more questions when he visited him at Faulkner Hospital in Boston the year before. After fifty years of marriage, Epifania and Marcos became locked in a constant state of bickering. Her blood pressure shot up. She accused her seventy-year-old husband of being interested in other women. He became forgetful and tired easily. Norma's moods swung between great highs and terrible lows. Martha turned her house into a shrine to Paul, his photograph on display everywhere, the clothes he wore on the day of his death hanging in her closet, unwashed, retaining the lingering scent of her lost brother.

Hal and Pilar tried, and failed, to repair the damage Paul's illness and death had caused their twenty-year marriage. He stood by her during the next year, but they both knew the pressure had taken its toll. "I probably withdrew," Pilar said. "I was so consumed with this. I lost the ability to really share with anybody. I didn't smile anymore. I never laughed anymore. I was not myself. And maybe I hadn't been for a while. I was so preoccupied with keeping him alive. When I wasn't doing that, I was busy being a mother to my son. Our marriage basically stopped. I really couldn't feel anything anymore; I was very confused."

Only Marcos Lozano and his son Mark could face the trip to Boston to close up Paul's apartment. "He left everything. He came back with a few meager things and gave everything else away," Pilar recalled. "He didn't have the strength to touch and feel and pick up his past."

While in Boston, the Lozanos visited Dr. Alvin F. Pouissant, a psychiatrist at Harvard Medical School, who had written to express his sorrow at Paul's death. They were looking for answers Dr. Pouissant did not have; sympathy was all he could offer. "It was clear Mr. Lozano did not know what had happened to his son, and I could not tell him. I did not know either," Dr. Pouissant said.

Marcos Lozano speaks the heavily accented and fractured

English of an immigrant. He routinely asks others to speak his second language slowly. He insists he was never told by Dr. Bean-Bayog during their one brief meeting the year before that Paul's allegedly abusive childhood had caused his illness.

He devoutly wishes that he had been. He would have told her what he said a year after burying his youngest son, standing in Martha's kitchen, holding a drinking glass aloft: "My life is like this glass of water. You can see clear through from one side to the other side. You look, you won't see this thing she says we did to our boy."

Paul was gone, but his memory and his family remained. Pilar knew she had to vindicate them both. "I couldn't do anything else. I was on a vision quest," she said. "I'm responsible for all my family because they're not as strong as I am."

Within a week of Paul's death, Pilar Williams called attorney Tom O'Hare. She asked him to continue as the family's attorney in the civil lawsuit Paul had initiated against Dr. Bean-Bayog and to clear up any outstanding business Paul had at Harvard Medical School.

She was angry that the medical board had known for months of the allegations against Dr. Bean-Bayog but had done nothing until her brother was dead. O'Hare understood her frustration at the pace of the disciplinary investigation, but he also knew the medical board, so he told Pilar to be patient. Patience, however, was not Pilar's strong suit. "I wanted justice, and I was not going to rest until I got it," she remembered.

The complaint against Dr. Bean-Bayog was by no means the only one languishing in the bureaucratic bowels of the Massachusetts Board of Registration in Medicine. An audit in July 1991 found a backlog of 847 complaints awaiting action.

Chronically overworked and understaffed, the medical board has long been a lightning rod for criticism from both the consumers it is charged with protecting and the doctors it was created to monitor. The board is seen either as a rubber stamp for the profession it polices, or as a Star Chamber, which rides roughshod over the due process rights of the accused.

The polarization of views has existed since the Massachusetts Legislature established the medical board in 1975. Originally called the Board of Registration and Discipline in Medicine, the word *discipline* was quietly deleted in 1979 following complaints from doctors that the original title was "invidious" and "demeaning." Dr. Louis Alfano, president of the Massachusetts Medical Society, told his colleagues at the society's 195th annual meeting in 1976 that "the use of the word in the title of the board is an affront. That the board can discipline physicians goes without saying. Use of the word discipline only magnifies and focuses on a problem nowhere near as large as the use of the word or the title implies."

Consumers countered that, far from exaggerating the problem, the physician-dominated medical board underestimated the extent of incompetence and misconduct. With more doctors per capita than any other state in the nation, Massachusetts has had an especially bad reputation for monitoring the profession. Public Citizen Health Research Group, the Washington-based consumer group founded by Ralph Nader, consistently gives Massachusetts low marks. Based on the number of disciplinary actions taken for every 1,000 physicians, the Massachusetts medical board in 1993 ranked forty-eighth in the country.

The situation nationally is only marginally better. At most, about one-half of 1 percent of the nation's 584,900 doctors face any state sanctions each year. The figure is especially alarming when compared to the 150,000 to 300,000 people that a 1990 Harvard study estimated are injured or killed as a consequence of medical negligence in American hospitals every year.

In Massachusetts, it has sometimes been the choice of physicians singled out for sanction that has made the medical profession's attempts at self-policing open to public ridicule. In 1972, the Massachusetts Medical Society voted to censure Dr. John H. Knowles, then the director of

Massachusetts General Hospital, for undermining "mutual confidence and goodwill" in the profession. Dr. Knowles had run afoul of his colleagues by telling an interviewer that 30 to 40 percent of American doctors were making a financial killing, many by performing unnecessary surgery.

Dr. Knowles refused to appear before his peers to answer their charges. "I'm not going to diddle around with these jerks," he said before leaving Boston to become president of the Rockefeller Foundation in New York. "How is it that I'm the only man to be censured by the Society in the last half century? Who have they picked? A guy who for twenty years has run the best hospital in the country. When the John Birch Society votes to censure [then President Richard M.] Nixon for going to China, is he going to fight them about it?"

Knowles came under fire the same year that the case of a doctor convicted of more than one hundred counts of violating narcotics laws never even came before the Society's Committee on Ethics and Discipline; the same year that the Society chastised the chief of plastic surgery at Children's Hospital in Boston for "undue promotion" because his research findings had been reported in *Time* magazine.

What makes the job of disciplining doctors particularly challenging in Massachusetts is the central role that medicine plays in the economy and politics of the state. With four prominent medical schools and many of the nation's premier hospitals and research facilities, the medical field is a major employer and a powerful political influence. The Massachusetts Medical Society is widely considered the second most powerful lobby, behind the insurance industry, on Beacon Hill.

Until 1975, the state's Board of Registration in Medicine was a creature of the Massachusetts Medical Society, a physicians' trade association that has owned and published the *New England Journal of Medicine* since 1921. The Society would submit names to the governor, who selected his appointees from that list. Until 1975, a doctor's license in Massachusetts could be revoked only upon conviction for a felony. When the medical board was created, incompetence and ethical infractions were added as cause for loss of license.

The seven-member panel includes five physicians and two consumers. Overseen by the Secretary of Consumer Affairs, the medical board has the power to revoke or suspend a doctor's license, to issue reprimands, to impose fines, and to oversee the rehabilitation of doctors impaired by drug or alcohol abuse. In addition, the panel is responsible for licensing the state's 23,000 physicians.

Doctors balked immediately at the new, less collegial system of professional review. Licensing fees were resisted as an unfair tax. A move to require doctors to disclose their education and malpractice history on registration forms was denounced as a violation of a physician's right to privacy.

The resistance of the medical community to its mandate was not the panel's only challenge. From the first, it was not given the financial resources necessary to do the job. In Governor Michael S. Dukakis's first term, from 1975 to 1978, the medical board had one investigator; the state panel that regulated hairdressers, by comparison, had twelve. Conditions worsened under Governor Edward J. King, who cut the medical board's budget and moved to block public access to its deliberations. When Dukakis returned to office in 1983, he increased its resources but never to the level sought by the medical board.

Years of neglect came home to roost in 1986 when the state's abysmal record of policing its doctors came under scrutiny, first in *The Boston Globe* and then on the CBS television newsmagazine "60 Minutes." In response, the Dukakis administration attached an amendment to a medical malpractice bill, granting the medical board sweeping new authority to ferret out bad doctors. Physicians, eager for the relief in malpractice insurance rates promised by the statute, accepted more policing as the price they had to pay.

It was not long, however, before the reality of the tougher disciplinary system inspired a court challenge by eight Harvard-affiliated teaching hospitals in Boston. The new law required doctors, hospitals, and insurance companies to report suspected incidents of negligence and malpractice settlements to the medical board. Hospitals objected to providing internal reports on the performance of their medical staffs. The information was crucial to the medical board if it had any hope of intercepting incompetent doctors known as "commuters." Asked quietly to leave one hospital, such doctors would reemerge at another hospital until problems there sent them packing again.

The hospitals contended that the medical board was on a fishing expedition. The board prevailed, arguing that by withholding the information, hospitals protected negligent or incompetent physicians and that a disciplinary system that was dependent solely on voluntary reports from patients and physicians to a doctor-dominated medical board was doomed to failure.

The suspicion that government regulators were overstating the problem was understandable, said George Annas, a professor of law and medicine at Boston University School of Medicine and one of the original consumer members of the medical board. "Most doctors consort with the very best doctors. They never run across the bottom five percent," he said. "And if they do come across the worst, they step around them. After we'd revoke a license we'd hear from doctors, 'It's about time you acted on that guy.'"

Fortified by its tougher regulations and public demand for action, the medical board had some success in weeding out the worst of the profession in the mid-1980s. Under the leadership of an aggressive young executive director, Barbara Neuman, the board revoked or suspended the licenses of and accepted the resignations of a total of 117 doctors in 1987 and 1988. By comparison, only 15 doctors resigned or had their licenses revoked or suspended in 1983 and 1984.

The reaction was immediate and fierce, with physicians accusing the medical board of scalp-hunting. Disciplinary action had risen from 17 cases in 1984 to 85 in 1988, but focusing only on the increase ignored the fact that nearly 90 percent of the 500 complaints received each year were dismissed.

When the medical board slapped sanctions on two prominent doctors at Massachusetts General Hospital for prescription violations due to lax recordkeeping, an already suspicious medical community turned hostile. "I went out to talk to a local medical society in Springfield, and that was what they jumped all over me for, those two doctors," Marian Ego, then a consumer member of the medical board, recalled. "We hadn't taken their licenses. We'd just reprimanded them. But the doctors were outraged. These men were stars—how dare we!"

Physicians who had supported Michael Dukakis began to turn on him. His father had been a doctor and one of his closest friends was the head of Massachusetts General Hospital, but now the governor was the enemy. Over the vociferous objections of the Massachusetts Medical Society, which spent $337,000 to promote its cause, Governor Dukakis had signed legislation prohibiting doctors from charging patients more than the fees set by Blue Shield and Medicare. When he made a move to make a physician's license renewal contingent on complying with that law, the chairman of the medical board joined the chorus of critics and resigned his gubernatorially appointed post in protest.

Consensus was the much-ballyhooed theme of Governor Dukakis's second term, and members of his administration remember the governor and would-be president asking aides, "Why do the doctors hate me?"

"The problem was that in this arena, you can't get consensus because the public does not have an advocate," said Professor Annas. "The Medical Society is there as an organized interest to shoot down every reform, but there is no consumer group on the other side. A representative from the Society came to every board meeting; he was like a member. High-profile cases come and go, but the Medical Society is there forever."

It was there when Peter Clark, chief of the medical board's disciplinary unit, addressed the Massachusetts Bar Association in January 1989, in a speech that confirmed the medical community's worst suspicions. "We are the police. We are the prosecution. We are the grand jury and the petit jury. We are the judge and, to a certain extent, even the appellate judge," he said of the medical board.

"Any procedural rights or any benefits, which a physician who is accused of misconduct or accused of incompetence has, are truly incidental when compared to the rights of criminal defendants or civil litigants," he told the lawyers. The truth was that the medical board's procedures were grounded in administrative law and similar to those of regulatory boards across the country that repeatedly had been found by appellate courts to preserve physicians' due process rights.

But it was Clark's tone that hit a nerve among aggrieved physicians. "An aggressive, combative posture on the part of the physician is not likely to reap benefits, but a physician who is relatively supine when confronted with the board's majesty is, in fact, likely, if it's the kind of case in which the board feels it can exercise discretion, to gain some benefit from that," Clark said. The medical board chairman, Dr. Andrew G. Bodnar, disavowed the speech, calling Clark's remarks an inaccurate portrayal of members as having an "overbearing, arrogant attitude." But it was too late; the battle was on.

It was not long until the first skirmish. The same month that Clark made his ill-advised speech, the medical board revoked the license of Dr. Paul E. Bettencourt, a specialist in pulmonary disease and internal medicine at Faulkner Hospital in Boston, after a male patient accused him of sexual misconduct. Bettencourt denied the charges, but it was the doctor's word against the patient's. The case galvanized an already incensed medical community, which saw Dr. Bettencourt's treatment as emblematic of the medical board's abuse of power.

His fellow doctors united and had a bill introduced into the state legislature to reinstate his license, an effort bolstered by the affidavits of more than five hundred colleagues and patients. A Physicians Defense Fund was formed, and organizers raised more than $100,000 to bankroll Dr. Bettencourt's legal challenge of the decision. Every doctor in Massachusetts was contacted. "You could lose your medical license forever, even if the only evidence of wrong-doing against you was the word of a single patient—while your own word was ignored," the fund-raising brochure warned. The Massachusetts Medical Society filed an amicus curiae brief supporting Dr. Bettencourt.

In 1990, the Massachusetts Supreme Judicial Court sent the Bettencourt case back to the medical board for review, saying the evidence on which it had based the revocation was too thin. A year later the medical board gave the doctor his license back.

By the time Dr. Becker and Dr. Gault filed their complaints about Dr. Bean-Bayog in December of 1990, the medical board was in full retreat. Governor Dukakis had felt the pressure from physicians and backed off. The number of charges filed against doctors dropped to 19 in 1990 from 84 in 1987, and the number of disciplinary actions dropped to 40 in 1990 from 95 in 1988.

After Consumer Affairs Secretary Paula Gold left the Dukakis administration for a job in the private sector, her successor was charged with mending relations with the medical community. It was in an atmosphere of appeasement that the Massachusetts Medical Society and the defense bar won a procedural victory that Paula Gold and the medical board had staved off for years. Sympathetic lawmakers late one night tacked an amendment onto an unrelated bill, transferring disciplinary hearings from the medical board to the Division of Administrative Law Appeals, a state office already backlogged with other cases and with no experience in matters of physician discipline.

The medical board, under pressure from the administration, then fired Barbara Neuman, whose vigilance had so offended the state's powerful physicians. (Soon thereafter, Neuman became executive director of the Vermont Board of Medical Practice, whose record improved after her arrival; Vermont was ranked tenth in the country in 1993 for effective physician discipline, at a time when Massachusetts was ranked forty-eighth. When she was director of the Massachusetts board in 1987, the state was ranked twenti-eth.)

When the letters from Dr. Becker, Dr. Gault, and Amy Stromsten disappeared—the medical board posits that they might all have been lost in the mail—the board was in transition. A new executive director had been appointed to replace Barbara Neuman, and the terms of two physicians and one consumer representative had expired, creating three vacancies on the seven-member board that the new Republican governor had not yet filled.

In addition, the medical board was still plagued with budget woes. The amount of money allocated to the medical board dropped from $2.1 million in fiscal year 1989 to $1.6 million in fiscal year 1991. Staffing during the same period plunged from 56 to 39. At the time the complaint was logged against Dr. Margaret Bean-Bayog, the board had only one full-time and one part-time investigator to review almost one thousand open cases.

Even at their most active, state medical boards concentrate on the cases easiest to prove: criminal convictions, drug addiction, alcohol abuse, and, increasingly, sexual misconduct. Only 11 percent of the doctors disciplined nationwide in 1991 were sanctioned for negligence or substandard care. A 1989 Tufts University study found that even the rate of sanctions by physician-owned insurance companies was higher—13.6 percent.

The difficulty for disciplinary panels in negligence cases is similar to that faced by the comparatively resource-rich civil court system: cases often devolve into technical debates between medical experts. That complication is compounded in cases of alleged psychiatric malpractice because the credibility of a patient with a history of psychiatric problems is bound to be challenged. How many patients who complained legitimately of abuse at the hands of their psychiatrists have been dismissed as delusional, psychotic, or borderline personalities?

If the condition of a psychiatric patient deteriorates, even if it culminates in suicide, the doctor can be expected to argue that the outcome was a natural progression of his mental illness, not mismanagement of his care.

In addition, there are so many competing schools of

therapy—280 at last count by the editors of *Current Psychotherapies*—that it is next to impossible for practitioners to define a uniform standard of care in psychiatric cases. And since psychiatrists often see patients in private offices, far from the supervision of colleagues, the burden of judging what constitutes appropriate care falls on vulnerable patients.

Doctors and the defense bar have argued that most allegations of malpractice are frivolous, filed by patients or families driven by greed or an unwillingness to accept the illness or death of a loved one. But the results of a three-year medical malpractice study released by Harvard University in 1990 refutes the assertion that medical injuries are rare and that patients are litigation prone. Harvard researchers, who reviewed medical records of more than 30,000 patients in 51 hospitals in New York State, found that only a fraction of injuries are ever acknowledged. Extrapolating from the data, the researchers estimated that 4 percent of the 2.7 million people hospitalized in New York that year were injured as a result of the medical care they received. In 1984 more than 13,000 New Yorkers actually died as a result of medical injuries; more than half of those deaths involved negligence, the study reported. And yet the New York Office of Professional Medical Conduct disciplined only 16 doctors for incompetence or negligence that year.

Far from being litigious, the study found, injured patients rarely sued their doctors. Only one-eighth of the patients estimated to have been harmed through medical negligence filed suit and only one in 16 received a jury award or a settlement of their claim.

"The simple fact of the matter is that people don't sue; they don't complain. It's a myth," said George Annas, who felt that during his tenure as a consumer member, the medical board in Massachusetts was marked by "the Medical Society whipping doctors into a frenzy over the board and malpractice when, in fact, not nearly enough discipline was going on."

One area that has changed since his stint on the medical board, said Annas, is the attention being paid to allegations of sexual misconduct. "Sexual abuse cases used to be very hard," he recalled. "If a woman did not have a second complainant, they just threw it out. They didn't believe her. There had to be at least two complaints and three would be better."

Sexual activity between doctors and patients is as old as medicine itself. Freud had warned of the specific dangers posed by the intimate nature of therapy, but many of his most revered followers made no secret of their liaisons with patients: Carl Jung was known to have made mistresses of at least two patients, and Anaïs Nin, the French diarist, was both the lover and the patient of Otto Rank.

Although the exploitation of patients is by no means limited to psychiatry—studies have shown that an even greater percentage of gynecologists and general practitioners have been disciplined for such misconduct—the habits of the helping profession seem to sanction the behavior. One study by Dr. Kenneth Pope, a clinical psychologist in Los Angeles and former chairman of the American Psychological Association's Ethics Committee, found that one out of four women who had received doctorates in psychology reported having had sex with a professor or supervisor.

Professional associations for psychiatrists and psychologists did not adopt explicit prohibitions against patient-therapist sex until the mid-1970s. And even then, training programs did not address the problem. In a 1986 study, 87 percent of 587 psychologists surveyed said they had felt sexually attracted to patients, but only 9 percent said they felt adequately trained to deal with those emotions.

It was not until a study in 1986 by Dr. Nanette Gartrell, a University of California School of Medicine psychiatry professor, reported that 7 percent of male psychiatrists and 3 percent of female psychiatrists admitted having sex with their patients that the profession began to take the issue seriously. Dr. Gartrell reported that 65 percent of those surveyed had treated patients who had been sexually involved with their former therapists, yet only 8 percent had reported their colleagues to authorities.

Although the behavior of sexually exploitative therapists

had little impact on their careers, the price being paid by patients was enormous. A survey by Dr. Kenneth Pope found that 11 percent of patients who had sex with their therapists were hospitalized as a consequence and that 1 percent of the 14 percent who attempted suicide succeeded.

Barbara Noel sued instead. Noel spent nearly a decade fighting the presumption that she was a crazy patient whose transference had led her to believe that her psychiatrist had been raping her during their sessions after drugging her into a semicomatose state.

Noel's was not just any psychiatrist. Dr. Jules H. Masserman, then chairman of the psychiatry department at Northwestern Medical School, was a former president of both the World Association for Social Psychiatry and the American Psychiatric Association and one of the most revered men in his profession. Honors continued to be heaped on him even as Noel and other victims came forward to charge that he used the highly addictive drug Amytal to loosen their "resistance" in therapy and then raped them as they slept. It took years, and the settlement of several civil suits, before the American Psychiatric Association and the Illinois Psychiatric Association suspended him and he resigned his license while still proclaiming his innocence.

As an example of the profession's willingness to turn a blind eye to sexual misconduct, no case is more stark than that of the Boston psychiatrist alleged to have had sex during therapy hours with the poet Anne Sexton, who killed herself in 1974 at the age of forty-five. Sexton's friends and other therapists shared the name of the psychiatrist freely with one another. The poet's first psychiatrist, Dr. Martin T. Orne, said he even met with this colleague to try to bring an end to the affair. Diane Wood Middlebrook gave the psychiatrist a pseudonym in her best-selling biography of Sexton in 1991, but his identity is widely known in Boston psychiatric circles.

When the biography appeared, psychiatrists focused virtually no attention on the sexual conduct of Sexton's therapist. Instead, it was Dr. Orne who came under attack by his peers. They accused him of violating his late patient's confidentiality rights by giving Middlebrook access to the tapes of Sexton's therapy sessions. It was largely a theoretical debate since Sexton's family had granted her biographer use of the poet's extensive journals meticulously recounting her therapeutic experiences.

It was also a dodge for not addressing the more shocking fact that at least five psychiatrists and social workers were said to have known about the sexual misconduct, and none reported the psychiatrist to the medical board. He was still practicing psychiatry when the biography of Anne Sexton was published in 1991. No action was taken against him by the medical board in its wake.

The decision to criticize a colleague can be a costly one, as Dr. Martha Gay, a Denver psychiatrist, found in 1989 when she came to the defense of a patient who accused a former therapist of sexual abuse. It was Dr. Gay and her patient, Melissa Roberts-Henry, who were put on trial during the malpractice proceedings, not the defendant, Dr. Jason Richter. The patient won a $180,000 jury award, but not before her sexual and psychiatric history were probed by a defense team that even placed her under surveillance as part of its trial preparation. The attempt to discredit Dr. Gay was so savage that the psychiatrist relocated to another city after the trial.

And the defendant, Dr. Richter? His insurer paid the award, and he continues to practice without professional censure.

Dr. Nanette Gartrell, whose research first documented the prevalence of sexual abuse by psychiatrists, resigned from the American Psychiatric Association in support of Dr. Gay and in protest against the conspiracy of silence that perpetuates the power of exploitative psychiatrists at the expense of vulnerable patients.

In the absence of tough professional sanctions against sexual exploitation, victims began to lobby for the criminalization of sexual contact between therapists and patients. By 1990, eight states had enacted laws making sex between therapists and patients a felony and several more were weighing similar statutes.

In Massachusetts, complaints of sexual misconduct doubled in two years, from 27 in 1988 to 55 in 1989. The number of disciplinary actions also rose, from 2 in 1985 to 10 in 1989. In 1989, for the first time, the Boston Psychoanalytic Society expelled a member for sexual misconduct. And in 1990, Harvard Medical School devoted an all-day continuing education seminar for area psychiatrists to the topic.

The seminar had come too late for many of Harvard's own, however. The roll call of psychiatrists who were disciplined for sexual misconduct in Massachusetts during that period reads like a roster of Harvard faculty and alumni. Of the thirteen psychiatrists in Greater Boston who lost or surrendered their licenses in the face of sexual abuse charges from 1989 through 1992, all but one had some Harvard affiliation. These were men presumed to have been above reproach by dint of personal reputation and professional association with a great university; men whose profession, either through insufficient training or arrogant bent, put vulnerable patients at risk; men like:

Dr. Joel H. Feigon, a psychiatrist who maintained his office on campus in the Harvard University Health Service, had his license revoked for having sex for eight years with a female patient whose two children and fiancé he was also treating. He claimed to be innocent of the allegations.

Dr. Stanley S. Kanter, an assistant clinical professor of psychiatry at Harvard Medical School and nationally known for his work in group therapy, resigned his license rather than face abuse charges from three women, one of whom was hospitalized for suicide attempts after their twenty-year sexual relationship ended. Kanter denied the charges.

Dr. Edward M. Daniels, who taught at Harvard Medical School and trained a whole generation of analysts in Boston, had his license revoked for sexually abusing four female patients, a charge he denied.

Dr. Paul A. Walters, who was chief of mental health services for the Harvard University Health Service, surrendered his license while facing charges, which he denied, of having had sex twice a week for seven years with a patient in his office on the Harvard campus.

Dr. Lionel A. Schwartz, who taught at Harvard Medical School and counseled women at Wellesley College, surrendered his license on the eve of medical board hearings on the sexual abuse claims of three patients, one of whom had taken her complaint to the Boston Psychoanalytic Society, which failed to either act or forward it to the medical board, Harvard, or Wellesley. Schwartz denied any wrongdoing.

In every case, professional colleagues and Harvard officials publicly expressed shock and dismay at learning that respected psychiatrists had been charged with unethical behavior. But, privately, many of them had suspected or even known about the misconduct, according to several Boston psychiatrists. Either for lack of definitive proof, concern about confidentiality, professional loyalty, or general squeamishness, no one informed authorities.

By April of 1991, Harvard Medical School administrators had heard not only of Paul Lozano's death but also bizarre reports of his relationship with one of their own psychiatrists. One morning in April, Thomas O'Hare got a call from Dr. Eleanor Shore, dean of the faculty at Harvard Medical School. She asked if he would share with her what he knew about Paul Lozano and Dr. Bean-Bayog.

O'Hare had long wondered how much Harvard knew, how much it suspected. "I didn't tell Harvard Medical School while he was alive because he did not want me to. He could not have faced them, his shame was so great," O'Hare recalled. "He was embarrassed that this relationship had happened. He wanted to go forward with the suit to protect other patients, but he dreaded anyone knowing."

Now that Paul was dead, O'Hare said he felt some obligation to do what his client had reluctantly set out to do: "expose a gross violation of psychiatric standards."

In a meeting that lasted several hours in his Wellesley office, O'Hare laid out the details of the civil suit he was preparing against Dr. Bean-Bayog. He gave Dr. Shore copies of Dr. Bean-Bayog's explicit sexual fantasies and suggested that she pass out nitroglycerine tablets to the faculty committee that would read them.

The committee voted on May 1 to suspend Dr. Bean-Bayog quietly from her position as a clinical professor at Harvard Medical School.

Months later, still having heard nothing from the medical board, Pilar Williams was on duty in the recovery room when the telephone rang at the nurses' station. She had just hung up with a persistent representative from a credit card company that was seeking settlement of her brother's account.

"This better be important," she barked when an unfamiliar voice asked for her by name.

"Well, it's about your brother Paul," Amy Stromsten said. Pilar recognized her name immediately as that of the social worker Paul had confided in about his relationship with Margaret Bean-Bayog.

"I didn't know how to reach you when he died," Pilar said, apologizing for her snappish greeting. "He told us all about you."

Amy Stromsten had only just learned of Paul's death from a doctor who served with Margaret Bean-Bayog on the Impaired Physicians Committee of the Massachusetts Medical Society. Amy was shocked that, even after his death, no action had been taken on Dr. Gault's complaint or her own against Dr. Bean-Bayog.

She called Dr. Harrison G. Pope, the psychopharmacologist at McLean Hospital who had treated Paul's depression and collaborated with him on a research project. She told Dr. Pope, who is known informally as Skip, about Paul's death, about her experience with Dr. Bean-Bayog the previous summer in her supervision group, and about Paul's abject admission to her in January that he and his psychiatrist had had a sexual relationship.

Dr. Pope offered to call Andrew C. Meyer, Jr., a partner in Boston's largest law firm specializing in medical malpractice. The two had become friends and neighbors in Concord after Meyer bought Dr. Pope's house a few years earlier.

Amy asked Pilar if she was satisfied with her legal counsel. "I know you have a lawyer in Wellesley," she said. "Would you mind if I call him and find out how much experience he has with malpractice, because you are taking on the whole Harvard medical establishment. This is a big deal. I think you need a really heavy hitter. It's your choice because it's your family. But I really want you to call Drew Meyer." Dr. Pope had already talked to Drew, who said he would take the case if the family asked for him.

Pilar was not hard to convince. She had spent $1,200 for Dr. Larry H. Strasburger, the forensic psychiatrist, to evaluate the materials found in Paul's apartment and another $1,000 to duplicate and ship cartons of evidence. Paul had carried no life insurance, so the family bore these out-of-pocket expenses on top of the $10,000 funeral bill. She wanted faster action.

Tom O'Hare learned of his dismissal when Andrew C. Meyer, Jr., called him one morning in October to arrange for the case documents to be forwarded to his downtown office. When O'Hare called Pilar in El Paso, she confirmed that the family had decided to engage new counsel.

"That's their right. I have no argument with the Lozano family," Tom O'Hare said. "They were taking on Harvard psychiatry. They wanted a big gun, and they got one."

Chapter

10

Andrew C. Meyer, Jr., does not shy away from high-profile cases. At first blush, the medical malpractice case Skip Pope steered his way had all the elements of soap opera: sex, suicide, and Harvard psychiatry. If it was true that Paul Lozano's career was derailed by a sexually predatory psychiatrist, it would be a difficult but straightforward case to prove.

At least that was what he thought until he read Dr. Margaret Bean-Bayog's 986 pages of notes covering four years of therapy sessions with Paul. The office notes told a frighteningly different story, one of childhood torture, sexual abuse, drug addiction, alcoholism, homicidal rage, and suicidal impulses.

Hold on here, worried the wary malpractice attorney, was my victim a Horatio Alger hero or Charlie Manson?

Drew Meyer was determined to find out when Pilar Williams arrived in Boston for their first meeting on a crisp November morning, seven months after Paul Lozano's death. Meyer led her to a corner office with a grand view of the Boston Common, the Park Street Church, and the gilded dome of the Bulfinch-designed Massachusetts State House.

Known around the firm as the Trophy Room, its pale blue walls are plastered with bronzed newspaper clippings testifying to the firm's big wins. Mounted headlines scream success to potential clients: $2.2 MILLION AWARDED IN INFANT INJURY; LEAHY DOC IN COURT OVER DEATH OF WOMAN; BOSTON MAN WINS RECORD INJURY SUIT OVER BROKEN ANKLE; $1.6 MILLION AWARDED IN HOSPITAL SUIT; $660G AWARDED TO CANCER VICTIM'S SPOUSE.

Pilar noticed neither the press clippings nor the view. She was impatient with the pleasantries of introduction and annoyed by what she took to be Meyer's skeptical reaction as she detailed the harm done to her brother by his psychiatrist. She was even more alarmed when he brought in a nurse retained by the firm to evaluate potential malpractice cases.

"Were you spanked as a child?" the nurse asked.

"What's your mother like? Was she depressed?

"What's your father like? Did he drink?

"Why did Paul have this thing about being breast-fed?

"How often did he use drugs in high school?"

Pilar was reeling. "We were spanked when we deserved it," she replied. "My mother was overworked with six kids, not depressed," she answered. "No, my father is not a drunk," she said. "Paul did not have any issues around breast-feeding; he was bottle fed. He didn't use drugs in high school. He was an athlete."

What's going on here? she wondered. "What are you people driving at?" she finally asked in exasperation.

"Come on, Pilar. Let's cut the crap," Meyer said. "Your brother was a very sick man. He was tormented his whole life. He was probably even dangerous. You know he was physically abused. You know there was sexual abuse in your family."

"Now, wait a minute," Pilar interjected, drawing her five-foot frame closer to Meyer. "What I know is that you're full of shit. Who told you this? Where did you get these stories?"

"They are in the psychotherapy notes," he told her.

"Well, they're lies," she said.

"Then they are Paul's lies. He told them to Margaret Bean-Bayog, and he told them to other people, too," Meyer said.

"What?" she gasped, the wind temporarily knocked out of her. "Paul said these things?"

Meyer gave his clearly rattled client a minute to compose herself. "Why should we believe you?" he asked at last.

"Because I'm telling you the truth," Pilar replied. "Either you're interested in this case, or you're not. But I can assure you of one thing: you're not going to get to the bottom of this by interrogating me.

"Are you going strictly by her psychotherapy notes? Where are the emergency room records? Where are the social service reports of abuse? If he was an alcoholic or a drug abuser, why didn't she put him in a detox center? Why wasn't he in a drug rehab unit? He's been in and out of psychiatric hospitals. And no one identified that he was a drug addict?

"We come from a town of less than ten thousand," she continued, her anger growing and her voice rising. "I worked for the welfare department for nine years. My best friend was the head of social services. I worked with abuse cases for five years. You don't think I know the signs and symptoms of abuse and neglect?

"Let me give you our pediatrician's name. We had neighbors. Teachers. Coaches. Classmates. Go find them. Why don't you contact West Point? And the University of Texas? Don't bother talking to me. I could easily be lying to you."

Meyer was taken aback, chastened by the vehemence of her denials. "Wait a minute. Calm down. I'm on your side," he said.

"Oh, no you're not," Pilar shot back. "Let's get one thing straight here. You're not on my side. You don't even know me. What you're seeing here is a case, a potential case for yourself. And I accept that. Don't insult my intelligence by acting like you give a shit. I do, on the other hand. Now, if you're as good as you say you are, then you should be able to find out the truth. If I'm lying, then you can call me a liar.

But until that moment, you have no right to talk to me like this."

Phew! It had been a while since a client had spoken like that to Drew Meyer, whose operating principle, whether sizing up a case or a poker hand, is to believe everybody but always cut the cards. He handed Pilar Williams a pen, and she wrote down the names, addresses, and what phone numbers she could remember of everyone who knew the Lozano family in Upper Sandusky, Ohio. She put the pediatrician, Dr. Thomas Watkins, on the top of the list.

Even if her version checked out, Meyer warned her, a lawsuit could be very unpleasant for her family, especially for her mother, who stood accused of behavior toward Pilar's brother that was both morally abhorrent and criminally indefensible.

She would explain that to her parents and her brothers and sisters. They would decide as a family whether to proceed. But, for her part, this new attack only made Pilar more determined to fight.

The following night, back in El Paso, Pilar placed a plate of fresh pastries on her oak dining table, along with pots of tea and coffee. They might as well have something sweet to wash down what she was about to tell them, she thought as her mother and father and siblings took seats in her comfortable living room, its walls and mantel covered with family snapshots, a silver crucifix blessed at Paul's funeral, and a copy of the same framed print of a Native American mother and child by R. G. Gorman that hangs in Abel's home in North Carolina.

"There have been allegations of abuse—" she began.

"Spanking?" asked Mark.

"No. Beatings," she replied to stunned silence. "Being locked in a storehouse. Being whipped until welts were raised."

"This is a joke, right?" asked Norma, laughing.

"There's more," Pilar warned. "Mother is accused of sexually molesting Paul."

"Mother?" gasped Martha. "The woman who never gave us the sex talk about where babies come from?"

Pilar nodded.

"What did I do?" asked Epifania Lozano.

Pilar took a deep breath and told her family the details culled from Margaret Bean-Bayog's office notes. How Paul had reported being fondled while in diapers, how his mother was said to have played sex games under her skirt with him and Mark, how she withheld breast milk until they satisfied her sexual demands, how she was alleged to be still practicing this perversity at age seventy-one with her grandsons, how the rest of the family tolerated and even joked about their mother's behavior.

"Paul said those things?" Mark asked, incredulous. He was fourteen years older than Paul. "He wasn't even born when this stuff is supposed to have happened to me. How did he know about it?"

Pilar told him that Dr. Bean-Bayog maintained that the sexual abuse was "an open secret" in the family. Their father, the silver-haired patriarch whose stoicism had seen the Lozanos through relocations and financial crises, flinched as Pilar related how he was alleged to have taunted his boy by accusing him of "really liking your mother's breadbasket" and maybe to have engaged in an incestuous relationship with Pilar.

There was a long period of silence in the room as the gravity of their situation sank in. Dr. Bean-Bayog was not the one who would be on trial; *they* would be on trial. "First we laughed. Then we got pissed," Norma recalled. "The whole family was being painted as perverts. Now, we had to fight not just for Paul but for our mother, for our family name."

Abel, informed that night by telephone of the stories of sex games and brutal beatings, was the most astounded. He and Paul had been "joined at the hip" as children. How could any of this have happened without his knowing it?

He reviewed their childhood play, their mother's use of corporal punishment, and he recalled nothing abusive. Epifania Lozano was hardly the only parent in America to have taken a belt to her boys in that era. Child-rearing practices and social mores had changed in twenty years. As he remembered it, there were more times that they had escaped a spanking although deserving one. Like the day he and Paul had jumped hard enough on their parents' bed to splinter the frame. The boys propped up the mattress with paint cans and held their breaths. Two weeks passed before their parents made the discovery. By then, the statute of limitations must have expired: they got away with just a scolding.

The Lozanos agreed that night in Pilar's living room that one of their number be designated to receive information from Meyer and to provide it to the press, if that became necessary. The parents had too much difficulty with English to assume that role. Pilar was not the oldest sibling, but she was a nurse and, of all of them, she had been the closest to Paul. She was the obvious and unanimous choice to serve as the family's spokesperson.

They felt like David challenging the Goliath of Harvard psychiatry. It made sense to present a united front, but it was not always easy in a family of strong, vocal personalities. "I resented it, but I understood," Abel recalled. "We were afraid of what would come out if we all talked. What if I said we had played in a closet? She'd say, 'Aha!' We didn't want to say anything that would support her case. Paul wasn't this godlike figure; we weren't the perfect family, but we weren't perverts either. We wanted to speak with one voice."

Pilar hoped there would be no reporters, but if there were, she was prepared to defend her family. With the family's blessing, Pilar gave Drew Meyer the go-ahead to play the case his way. In the spring, he did. On March 26, 1992— almost one year after the death of Paul Lozano—Meyer filed three thousand pages of documentation in Middlesex County Superior Court to support the malpractice claim originally filed against Dr. Margaret Bean-Bayog the previous fall by Tom O'Hare. It was all there, every salacious detail: the sexual fantasies, the flash cards, the notes, the cards, and her office files. Taking no chance that courthouse reporters for Boston's two rival newspapers might miss it,

Meyer alerted two local television stations that he had just filed a hot one.

That night on the six o'clock news, Boston learned that one of the most respected members of the city's psychiatric community stood accused of providing "negligent, unacceptable, and unethical" psychiatric care that had led to the suicide of a promising Harvard Medical School student. The initial coverage was not about standards of psychiatric care, however. It was about sex. Dr. Margaret Bean-Bayog had "defiled, humiliated, debased, and embarrassed" her patient, Meyer's court papers alleged, by using sexually provocative language, wearing sexually provocative clothing, reading sexually explicit fantasies, and engaging in sadomasochistic sex acts.

The Boston Globe and the *Boston Herald* scrambled to catch up to TV news. In the *Globe*'s haste, the broadsheet misidentified the defendant in the civil suit as a psychologist instead of a psychiatrist. The tabloid *Herald* dubbed her the Psych Doc in screaming bold headlines. Both newspapers recounted a story of seduction and manipulation by a Medea-like sorceress who pretended to be her patient's mother at the same time that she engaged him in sadomasochistic sex. It was a story whose essence was written entirely by the plaintiff's media-savvy attorney. Dr. Bean-Bayog's more conservative lawyers, by contrast, issued "no comment" denials, with no further elaboration.

Never were two law firms more mismatched. Michael Blau, the chief defense lawyer—a dozen of his associates would assist with the case before it was over—was a partner in McDermott, Will & Emery, an old-line firm headquartered in Chicago, its four floors on venerable State Street furnished in the dark wood and heavy brocades that bespoke traditional Boston lawyering. Meyer, by contrast, was cofounder of an upstart firm formed only eighteen years before. Light and airy, the firm's suites eschewed the cordovan leather sofas and mahogany desks for blond oak conference tables and the smoky blues and soft mauves more commonly seen in trendy restaurants.

Circumspection and discretion, watchwords at McDermott, Will & Emery, held no currency at Lubin & Meyer, where the tone was boisterous and scrappy. It was the sort of bare-knuckle style that would raise nary an eyebrow in New York or Los Angeles but in terminally polite Boston it raised hackles. Meyer would win few popularity contests in the city's legal circles, where he was chided by some colleagues in the courthouse corridors for pushing the limits of aggressive representation. Envy played its part as well: in 1991 Lubin & Meyer reported to *Massachusetts Lawyers Weekly* winning close to $20 million in judgments and settlements for their clients, with 40 percent of each award typically going to the firm.

"Drew Meyer, I tip my hat to him, he really orchestrated this quite well," Blau said later. "He primed the media pump before he offered proof. Everything was ready to roll. Everything was ready to uphold justice in the terms in which Drew Meyer had cast it. Now what was Drew Meyer attempting to accomplish? He has told me that what he was principally trying to accomplish—and believe it or not I believe him—was to get the Board of Registration in Medicine to act on this case. I think he wanted them to act so that there would be a cloud cast over Dr. Bean-Bayog's license or status to enhance his opportunity for settling the malpractice case. And I think he wanted the board to do some of his investigative legwork. If the board took over the case, it would use its resources to investigate it rather than him having to do it.

"I don't think what Drew Meyer wanted to do was create a media circus. But once Drew Meyer let the genie out of the bottle, this case really took on a life of its own in the media. There wasn't really a heck of a lot you could do to stop the steamroller once it got rolling. This case pushed all of the public's hot buttons. I don't think there was a hot button that wasn't pushed by sex, the Mexican-American boy-genius, and the Harvard professor.

"What occurred was something I've never seen before: an immediate convergence of negative public opinion about

Dr. Bean-Bayog. She was crucified immediately. The national tabloids cast her as the 'Kinky Shrink' before she even had a chance to respond. She was judged guilty, and she was condemned."

Reporters descended on Dr. Margaret Bean-Bayog's Lexington home, the television sound trucks tying up traffic in the upscale neighborhood while the psychiatrist remained secluded behind the brass-handled French doors, still grieving over the death of her mother, who had succumbed to Alzheimer's disease in Iowa City at age eighty just twelve days before the malpractice case broke open in court and in the press.

Would a jury of laymen, even one drawn from the sophisticated environs of Cambridge, understand the subtleties of her innovative psychodynamic techniques? she asked her friends. It would be difficult enough to explain her mom-boy role-playing to the medical board. But what would the average juror make of the fifty-five pages of explicit sadomasochistic sexual fantasies she wrote about Paul? Would a jury believe her contention that she did not *really* yearn to be tied up, beaten, raped, and sodomized by her attractive, young patient but that she wrote such graphic stories merely to get control of the feelings he evoked in her?

What would her national network of professional colleagues make of those scrawled passages in which she imagined herself shackled, naked, and spread-eagled on the bare floor while her patient whipped her to the edge of orgasm as she proclaimed herself "ecstatic with the pleasure of it, helplessly pliant in your hands"?

What would her students make of the distinguished Harvard professor they thought they knew imagining herself the sadist, toying with her patient's sexual desire? Would they agree with her that passages like this one were nothing more than an expression of her countertransference? "I kneel over you and bring my vagina down to your mouth. You kiss it hungrily. I move my clitoris into range and you go to work on it."

In El Paso, producers from "Hard Copy" and reporters

from *People* magazine camped outside Pilar Williams's house for so long that she made them sandwiches while still, as Meyer had directed her, refusing interviews.

Following his plan to light a fire under the medical board, Meyer urged the family to pass up Diane Sawyer, Mike Wallace, and other news shows and speak only to the Boston media. His strategy worked. Within twenty-four hours the Massachusetts Secretary of Consumer Affairs demanded that the board convene to consider the case. Within seventy-two hours the board was meeting in "emergency session," although there was some question whether the emergency was medical or political.

Meyer had called Dr. Gault to warn him that the case was about to break wide open. He should expect to hear from reporters. Dr. Gault had his "no comment" well rehearsed, but nothing prepared him for the flood of media attention that washed over this case.

Klieg lights went up outside the medical board offices on the narrow downtown street said to have been laid out by Colonial-era cows en route to graze on the Boston Common. An especially brazen reporter shouted, "Do you sleep with all your patients?" as Margaret Bean-Bayog arrived to address the board behind closed doors. Accosted by more cameramen on the sixth floor of 10 West Street, Dr. Bean-Bayog was swept into a rear room, where she sipped tea and chatted confidently with staff members before meeting the medical board to argue against the summary suspension of her license.

"When the *Herald* ran her picture all over the place and she was crucified like that, I really felt sick," Dr. Gault remembered. "I had a very strong gut feeling, 'I don't want to be part of this. For all I know, her mistakes could have contributed to the patient's death. But I don't want to be a part of this.' I thought she was being denied presumption of innocence by all this smearing media. I wanted it to be taken care of quietly. I wanted the right thing to be done for this patient and for his family. I didn't want the doctor to be crucified."

The Lozano family was equally uncomfortable with the

crush of media attention. Pilar knew how private Paul had been in life and how exposed he had now become in death. She heard every thunderclap or cloudburst that punctuated an interview as a heavenly protest from Paul. You can throw the biggest temper tantrum you want up there, Paul Lozano, she would think. This is not your fight anymore. It's mine.

Meanwhile, Abel was thinking so long and so hard about the past that his wife, Sandy, began to worry about him. "I wanted to be sure in my own mind that this was as ridiculous as it seemed," he said. "I went over and over everything. We did play in a closet under the stairs sometimes. We were afraid of the dark; all kids are, aren't they?" If Paul had been damaged by the occasional use of physical punishment or the rough and tumble of a big family, Abel could say only that he saw no signs of it. There had been no abuse, no torture, no sexual games, of that much he was certain.

But had he missed something else? Had his kid brother been more sensitive than he knew? Had Paul perceived a whack on the behind from his mother as a beating? Had he heard Abel's jokes about his curly hair as something more sinister than brotherly teasing? Had Paul been harmed by their awe of his intellectual gifts? Had he interpreted encouragement as pressure?

"Why can't I remember these things?" he would ask Sandy night after night. "Why would Paul have said them if they were not true? Was he so in love with her that he just fed her what she wanted to hear?" That was the explanation that rang most true to Abel, after he recalled the conversation with Paul at Faulkner Hospital in the spring of 1990.

Paul had told his brother as they sat on a grassy hill on the hospital grounds that there was false and damaging information in Dr. Bean-Bayog's records that Paul could not change.

Paul had not gone into detail, and Abel recalled that his efforts to draw him out had made his brother anxious. Had Paul been referring that day to these allegations against the family? It made sense to Abel now. Hadn't Paul told his attorney, Tom O'Hare, that he made things up to ingratiate himself with Dr. Bean-Bayog during his daily therapy sessions? Now everything Paul had said to Dr. Bean-Bayog, true or not, would be part of the public records.

It was several days before reporters actually read all the documentation filed by Meyer, including Dr. Bean-Bayog's handwritten office notes, the nearly unintelligible scrawls that would form the foundation of her defense. Competitive pressures left little time for analysis. Rather than weigh the whole, the media digested the voluminous notes and hospital records in small bites and then coughed up "new" information as though it had been discovered through some process of investigative journalism.

When the inevitable reaction set in—within a week analysts, feminists, and the psychiatrist's friends and patients were accusing the media of a witch-hunt—the course correction merely erred in the opposite direction.

If Dr. Bean-Bayog was not evil, then the family must be. The doctor spoke through her attorneys, but Pilar Williams faced the tough questions: Your brother was not just homesick, he was psychotic, wasn't he? He tried to kill himself when he was a kid, didn't he? Your mother abused him, didn't she? When the Lozanos balked at the accusatory tone of the interrogation, more than one reporter told them they had no right to be queasy. They had filed this lawsuit, hadn't they? They had opened this Pandora's box; they had to live with the consequences.

"I never read the articles in the newspaper, and I never saw myself on TV, because it would make me sick. Every time it happened to me, I had to come home and shower. I felt like I had been rolled in the mud," said Pilar, who became a savvy advocate for her family, quickly learning what information to omit as well as what to offer in interviews.

Journalists, like lawyers, are enamored of their adversarial role. But the Lozano family was not the Gambino crime family, and Dr. Bean-Bayog was not a city councillor caught with her hand in the till. Missing in the rush to demonize one or the other of the parties were the fundamental tools of the trade: independent reporting and objective analysis.

In repentance for the initial blast of imbalanced coverage, the *Globe* reversed directions and began to treat Dr. Bean-Bayog's office notes as gospel. Hospital summaries that made mention of Paul Lozano's history of sexual abuse were cited as confirmation of Dr. Bean-Bayog's diagnosis, without establishing whether the information in the chart came from her or from the patient. The manipulative and vindictive behavior of patients with borderline personality disorder was dissected without noting that even Dr. Bean-Bayog was uncertain if Paul Lozano fit the diagnostic criteria.

Other stories quoted psychiatrists, many of them unnamed, praising Dr. Bean-Bayog for consulting senior colleagues on this case, but none questioned a consultation process that excluded meeting the patient, reading his medical records, or hearing anything about Dr. Bean-Bayog's role-playing technique or her sexual fantasies regarding the patient.

Articles painstakingly explained countertransference, a theory whose repeated invocation had the unmistakable effect of providing a scientific sheen to sexual fantasies that were too explicit for the newspapers to print and allow readers to decide whether they were a diagnostic tool or amateur pornography.

"She didn't make him psychotic; she didn't make him suicidal. He had a history of that long before she met him. Now apparently she's being blamed for trying so hard with such a sick patient," an anonymous psychiatrist with no firsthand knowledge of the case told the *Globe*. "Has anyone looked at the psychological state of his family, who is bringing these charges?"

Nancy Gertner, a prominent Boston defense lawyer, was quoted four times in *The Boston Globe* and on the evening news decrying the sexist treatment of Dr. Bean-Bayog, but not a single story noted that Gertner was acting as an informal adviser to the psychiatrist, who sought out the media-wise barrister during the initial bashing she took in the press. Dr. Thomas G. Gutheil was quoted as an expert in the field, without note being taken that he would be Dr. Bean-Bayog's expert witness before the medical board.

It was two weeks before *The Boston Globe* sent a reporter to Upper Sandusky, Ohio, to ask those who had actually known him what Paul Lozano was like as a child. What townspeople had to say to anyone who inquired cast more than a shadow of doubt over the portrait of boyhood torture, depression, and abuse painted by Dr. Bean-Bayog.

"It's sinful that someone could destroy a young person with so much promise," said Charlotte Leeth, one of Paul's high school English teachers. "I thought an awful lot of Paul. He was one of the brightest young men I ever taught. I can't imagine where she got that abuse theory. There is no one in Upper Sandusky who knows that family who believes it.

"Paul had lots of chances to escape his family if he had been traumatized by them. He loved them. Why did he go with them to Texas when he could have stayed here with one of his sisters? Sure, he left West Point. He wrote to me about how much he hated the regimentation. Two boys from Upper Sandusky who went to West Point after Paul did dropped out, too. What does that prove about any of them or their families?"

What especially galled Charlotte Leeth was the implication that she and her neighbors were such hayseeds that they must have missed the signs of abuse that Dr. Bean-Bayog said she unearthed years later. "Had there been something amiss at home, he would have confided in me," Leeth said. "We talked. And I probably know more about my kids than they know about themselves. They reveal so much of themselves in their writing.

"He was a wonderful young man. Sometimes the bright ones dominate the class. Paul would wait until after class to ask a question or make a comment. This business about the family pressuring him is nonsense. The pushing was done by Paul himself. He did want to do his very best, and he was never satisfied with less. If he was troubled later in life, maybe it was because he could see too well. Sometimes the people who don't see life as clearly are better off."

For Ralph Young, Paul's track coach, the only thing more absurd than the abuse allegations was the assertion that Paul Lozano was a regular drug user in high school. "Well, it's just not true, I would have seen it," Coach Young said. "He would have shown up late for practice; he would have been lackadaisical when he was there, not followed instructions. I would have known. I don't indulge in it myself, and I know when someone does. With the boys, you can feel it—you can sense it. They start shying away from you because they don't want their coach to pick it up."

In the view of Bethany Foltz, Dr. Bean-Bayog's mistake was in underestimating the memory of a small town and the mettle of Pilar Williams. Foltz was Pilar's friend and supervisor at the Wyandot County Social Services Department. The image of Paul as emotionally or sexually battered struck her as ludicrous. "Paul was pretty much spoiled rotten," said Foltz, a frequent guest in the Lozano home during Paul's childhood. "I think they babied him. I was there a lot and I never saw any sign of abuse, and that's my job. When you are so much more intelligent than everyone around you, I'm sure it is a burden, but he was a happy kid, and this is a lovely family."

If Dr. Bean-Bayog thought the Lozanos would be intimidated by references to esoteric psychodynamic theories or her Harvard credentials, Foltz said, it was one more way in which she was ill served by not meeting the family when Paul was alive. "I have seen Pilar on the stand in child abuse cases, and when she believes in what she's doing, look out. She doesn't give up," Foltz said. "She is not the type of person to keep quiet. It's not vindictive, though it can look like that. She's just a bulldog when she thinks she is out to right a wrong."

Pilar had displayed that trait as far back as high school. A new mother with a boyfriend slow to acknowledge paternity, Pilar Lozano went to court. She emerged the legal and moral victor, with a father publicly identified for her son.

Dr. Thomas Watkins, Paul's pediatrician, treated him thirty-eight times from age eight to seventeen. Pilar or Norma usually brought Paul and Abel in together for their regular checkups, according to the records he still retains in retirement. He understood that the mother had difficulties with English. There were the usual complaints: sore throats, earaches. The only serious illness was a bout of salmonella in 1976 after a trip to Mexico, and Dr. Watkins sent Paul to the Cleveland Clinic to be treated for ten days.

Sitting on the back porch of his house down a dirt lane in rural Tiffin, Ohio, he remembered giving Paul Lozano a physical when he was chosen to attend Boys State, the statewide mock government for high school students sponsored by the American Legion. "He was an outstanding kid, bright and funny. This psychiatrist is trying to say he was so depressed as a boy. He was so depressed he was a leader in his school! Believe me, this boy didn't get where he got in life because he was a minority. That's more likely to work against you around here. No one's trying to show the world what a big liberal they are in Upper Sandusky, Ohio."

Admittedly a little suspicious of Mexicans himself—"the migrants usually stiffed you for the bill," he said—Dr. Watkins had only fond memories of the Lozano family. "They were personable, always joking and kidding. I remember thinking, I wish my kids liked each other this much."

In the media's rush to blame either the Lozanos or Dr. Bean-Bayog, broader issues of accountability were ignored. Why didn't those consultants demand more information from her? How does Harvard Medical School choose the psychiatrists who treat its students? How reliable is the diagnosis of repressed memories of sexual abuse and personality disorders? Who decides what are acceptable standards of care in psychiatric cases? What are the limits of patient confidentiality?

Missing in much of the press coverage, as in the psychiatric treatment, was any empirical data to support the charges and countercharges. The *Globe*'s treatment of the affidavit of Thomas A. Thomson was a telling example. A sixty-year-old resident of the Harvard Medical School neighborhood, who conducted regular security patrols as part of a volunteer group, Thomson swore he intervened to prevent Paul Lozano from attempting suicide months before Paul entered therapy with Dr. Margaret Bean-Bayog.

The *Globe* ran a story on page one, describing the affidavit as "casting doubt on the assertion of Lozano's family that Lozano had become suicidal and severely depressed as a result of being sexually abused and inappropriately treated by Dr. Margaret Bean-Bayog, a Harvard psychiatrist."

In fact, the affidavit did not pertain to the effect of Dr. Bean-Bayog's treatment but only to an incident that Thomson, whom the *Globe* described as a retired electrician and a disabled Korean War veteran, said occurred in the spring of 1986. In his statement, Thomson recalled coming upon Paul Lozano, whose name he did not know then but whose picture he recognized six years later from newspaper accounts of the malpractice case against Dr. Bean-Bayog. The young man he encountered in 1986 was hanging by one hand from a chain-link fence preparing to jump into the Muddy River flats. His life was over, Paul told him, because his girlfriend had rejected him, Thomson swore in his affidavit.

For a more complete portrait of Dr. Bean-Bayog's supporting witness, readers had to consult the *Herald*. The *Herald* noted that an electrical accident, which had caused brain damage, had cut short Thomson's career as an electrician. The *Herald* noted, too, that Thomson's last address was Norfolk State Prison, where he had served time for fatally shooting an acquaintance in a bar fight. In fact, it was in prison that he met Dr. Jerome Rogoff, the chief psychiatrist at Faulkner, who had been quoted in the newspaper accounts of the Lozano case. It was in a telephone call to Dr. Rogoff that Thomson first described his encounter with Paul Lozano, and it was Dr. Rogoff who put him in touch with Dr. Bean-Bayog's lawyers.

Thomson's affidavit had a few logistical problems. For one, the location he named was an unlikely spot for a suicide. The site, which Thomson described as a drop of "fifteen to twenty feet," was no more than eight feet, by Boston Parks Department estimates, and the mud flats, which Thomson described as "like quicksand," have a firm layer of clay below the surface muck.

With these discrepancies in hand, the *Herald* conducted its own interview with the witness. He told the newspaper that Paul had never actually said he was suicidal. Thomson said he had based that conclusion on his memory of his own suicidal impulses after he shot and killed his bar mate in 1967.

Even after those details appeared in the *Herald,* the *Globe* did no follow-up reporting to give readers a more complete picture of Dr. Bean-Bayog's supporting witness.

Such apparent bias is rarely calculated. Newsrooms are too chaotic to harbor conspiracies. But even the best newspapers have a worldview, through whose sometimes distorting lens news events are filtered. Certainly there were reporters at the *Herald* who thought Dr. Bean-Bayog was being pilloried and reporters at the *Globe* who thought the Lozanos were being smeared, but each newspaper played its respective, well-established role in Boston as voice of the victim or voice of the establishment. If the *Herald* was seen as bashing the psychiatrist in some anti-intellectual identification with its newsstand readers, the *Globe* was just as surely viewed as defending her out of empathy with its more liberal better-educated subscribers.

The *Globe* published nine letters to the editor on the Bean-Bayog case, five explicitly supporting the psychiatrist and the rest commenting on broader issues of therapeutic abuse and journalistic excess. There were no letters published in support of the Lozano family's lawsuit. One of the most spirited letters in defense of the doctor was written by a woman who had been her patient for ten years. The letter, headlined DR. BEAN-BAYOG HAS BEEN RUINED BY THE MEDIA, was hand-delivered to the editorial page by her nephew— Benjamin B. Taylor, the executive vice president of *The Boston Globe* and scion of the family that had published the newspaper for 120 years.

To its credit, *The Boston Globe* recognized and reported that the media's performance in this case, including its own, was less than exemplary. In a thoughtful analysis, prominently displayed in a Sunday edition, *Globe* reporter Thomas Palmer concluded that competitive pressures had produced hasty and imbalanced coverage by both newspapers.

Part of what was at work at the *Globe,* and among the dozens of readers—most of them from the medical community—who called the newspaper in support of Dr. Bean-Bayog, was a resistance to the idea that someone with her credentials and standing in the community could have slipped so badly. That resistance was fueled, in turn, by the Harvard-centric nature of Boston and its dominant newspaper.

Annual Harvard alumni reports fill thirty-eight shelves in the library of *The Boston Globe.* By contrast, the library maintains one dog-eared, out-of-date directory of Boston College alumni. The Harvard commencement is treated as a major news event each spring. When the college celebrated its 350th anniversary in 1986, the *Globe* ran seventy stories in advance of, during, and after the celebration.

It was simply easier for much of Boston to believe that Paul Lozano's life had been destroyed by a distant, dysfunctional family of Mexican immigrants than by a familiar and well-respected Harvard-affiliated psychiatrist.

Resistance to the reality that even smart people stumble and that even fields as august as psychiatry need an occasional airing-out could also explain why so many of her colleagues were willing to stake their own reputations defending Dr. Bean-Bayog, while acknowledging that they knew no more about the case than what they read in the newspapers.

The sheer volume of what was available to be read in this case, and its sexually graphic content, certainly distinguished the disciplinary action against Dr. Bean-Bayog from the twelve others in which Massachusetts psychiatrists surrendered their licenses or had them revoked following allegations of sexual misconduct between 1989 and 1992.

"For the first time in a sexual misconduct case, the press had over a thousand pages of stuff that they don't ordinarily have," said Alexander F. Fleming, executive director of the medical board. "They had the doctor's process notes. She was a copious note taker of almost a compulsive nature. An unusual relationship, however you want to characterize it. And these sexual fantasies. My guess is, of course, sex sells. Harvard sells. Psychiatry sells. Sexual misconduct sells. Harvard-trained psychiatrist and Latino med student genius sells. They tied it all together and got the public's interest."

There were other hooks to this story as well. The patient was dead, and the psychiatrist was a woman. The other twelve sexual abuse cases involved male psychiatrists and female victims, a more typical pattern, according to researchers.

"It is inconceivable that the coverage would have been any less if genders were reversed in this tragic case, given the serious charges and access to relevant medical records," Gordon McKibbon, the *Globe*'s ombudsman, wrote in a column about the case.

But the gender disparity in the coverage was undeniable. Few of the charges against the twelve men ever made page one in the *Globe*. However, the allegations against Dr. Bean-Bayog did—twenty-two times. None of the men had to endure more than a few days of media attention, and none had his photograph in the *Globe*. Dr. Bean-Bayog did, ten times.

Many of the male psychiatrists, such as Dr. Edward M. Daniels and Dr. Sheldon D. Zigelbaum, were more prominent than Dr. Bean-Bayog and had been accused of sexual misconduct by more than one patient. Their patients were not dead, it was true, but patients' lives had been seriously damaged.

Dr. Daniels, who taught at Harvard Medical School and trained a whole generation of analysts in Boston, had been known as "the matchmaker" among local psychiatrists before his license was revoked for sexually abusing four female patients. He had made his considerable reputation, and his many friends in the analytic community, by referring patients to therapists he deemed most appropriate to their needs.

But the first of five sexual abuse complaints against Dr. Zigelbaum is a case study in the influence that the liberal elite in Boston have sometimes wielded at *The Boston Globe*. Jean Dietz, the newspaper's veteran mental health reporter, was in the newsroom on December 31, 1981, when she received a telephone tip that a civil lawsuit had been filed against Dr. Zigelbaum by a young woman who accused her psychiatrist of giving her cocaine and then having sex with her.

Dietz confirmed that the lawsuit had been filed and called Dr. Zigelbaum, who declined comment.

Minutes later, her telephone rang. It was Richard Goodwin, a former speechwriter for the late President John F. Kennedy and the husband of historian Doris Kearns Goodwin, author of *The Fitzgeralds and the Kennedys* and *Lyndon Johnson and the American Dream*. The Goodwins were close friends of Dr. Zigelbaum, a friendship that dated back to Dick Goodwin's and Dr. Zigelbaum's undergraduate days. The Goodwins were also friends with any number of senior editors and columnists at *The Boston Globe*.

As Dietz recalled it, Richard Goodwin, Harvard Law School, class of '58, asked her to kill the story, insisting that his friend, known as Ziggy, was above reproach. When she declined, Goodwin called his friend Mike Barnicle, the paper's popular local columnist, and asked him to intervene on Ziggy's behalf. "I told him, 'Geez, Dick, I can't do anything about it. I just write my column,'" Barnicle recalled. "'Call Tim Leland.'"

Goodwin took Barnicle's advice and called Timothy Leland, the managing editor and a fellow Harvard alum. "My memory is that he was a friend of this person and he argued that for a story to appear in the paper at that time, where we would nail him to the wall, would be premature," recalled Leland, later a *Globe* vice president. "Goodwin is not a fly-by-night character; he's quite big in certain circles. If I get this call from Dick Goodwin telling me this doctor is a decent individual, I would be inclined to look at it hard. The appeal he made was, 'Before you print a story that ruins his reputation and his career, you should know he's a totally above-board fellow.' I'm sure I said I would look into it. I hold Dick Goodwin in some regard, and he made a spirited defense of this man. Dick Goodwin does not call every day on a story. I wouldn't volunteer that I was the one who killed it. But I would have wanted to make sure we didn't lower the boom on a good guy."

Jean Dietz wrote her story, but it never ran. "I knew they wouldn't run it," Dietz said twelve years later. "The Goodwins got to them."

Dick Goodwin was not the only one busy working the phones in Ziggy's behalf. His wife's mission was to try to derail the civil lawsuit. Doris Kearns Goodwin had met the mother and grandmother of Dr. Zigelbaum's aggrieved patient at a luncheon the psychiatrist had arranged some time before for the family to confer with the historian about a three-generational epic the women hoped to write about their family. Dr. Zigelbaum's patient was not present.

Given her previous contact with the family, Kearns Goodwin suggested to Sheldon and Patti Levin Zigelbaum, at a dinner party at the Goodwin home, that she try to intervene. They were delighted by the offer. Kearns Goodwin telephoned the patient's mother during the Thanksgiving holiday in 1981, a month before the civil suit was filed.

Betsey Brown, the patient's mother, recalled the conversation in her deposition on November 11, 1989, to the Massachusetts Board of Registration in Medicine. "Doris said to me that Ziggy was terribly upset, just extremely distraught, almost having a nervous breakdown over this issue. She knew that my daughter had to be a really lovely person who would not wish to hurt anyone, and if I would persuade my daughter to drop the charges Ziggy would go back into therapy and agree not to treat any more women," Brown testified.

In her own deposition to the board a year later, Kearns Goodwin said, "It was my idea to say: What if I talk to [the patient's] mother and see if there is some other means of resolving this, short of a lawsuit."

The historian and Mrs. Zigelbaum both testified that it was on her own initiative that Kearns Goodwin suggested to

Betsey Brown that, as an alternative to the lawsuit, the psychiatrist would be willing to seek therapy and discontinue seeing female patients.

"Would you be upset with her [for having made that offer]?" Muriel Finnegan, the lawyer for the medical board, asked Mrs. Zigelbaum.

"Not if it had worked," Mrs. Zigelbaum replied.

It did not work, although Dr. Zigelbaum eluded public scrutiny for seven more years. But time and his misdeeds eventually caught up with Ziggy. In 1989, the slow-moving medical board formally charged Dr. Zigelbaum with sexual misconduct. By the end of its deliberations, the board concluded that Ziggy had sexually abused five female patients and used illicit drugs with at least three of them in what the board's decision called a "terrible pattern" of exploitation.

On January 22, 1992, ten years after *The Boston Globe* refused to publish Jean Dietz's original story, the Board of Registration revoked Dr. Sheldon D. Zigelbaum's license to practice medicine.

Chapter

11

The sun came out on April 29, 1992, for the first time in a week. Partygoers had to sidestep puddles on the brick path to the Harvard Faculty Club.

It was 47 degrees, chilly even for a Cambridge spring, and members of the class of '65 were bundled in their wool coats and tweed sports jackets, as they strolled past the budding magnolia on the lawn.

In the cozy lobby, its entry table graced by a blue glass vase brimming with pink and white lilies, a young man played Scott Joplin on the baby grand piano to the appreciative finger tapping of a bespectacled and bow-tied professor sitting erect in an armchair upholstered in the same muted shades of crimson and blue as the Oriental carpet under his loafered feet. He was too engrossed in the music and the latest issue of *Harvard Magazine*—its cover story headlined THE POLITICS OF CONTENTMENT—to notice the reuniongoers making their way up the winding staircase to dinner in the club library.

It was a busy evening at the Harvard Faculty Club. Marshall Goldman, the local Kremlinologist, was holding forth downstairs on the state of the former Soviet Union.

BREAKDOWN

The Classics Department was hosting its annual dinner. In a meeting room nearby, scouts for Goldman Sachs were ferreting out Wall Street prospects among the Harvard Business School students queuing up for interviews.

The lingering light of the spring evening was lost to Faculty Club members and their guests in the gloomy main dining room, its enormous Palladian windows draped in heavy crimson velvet. Chef Durr's theme for the evening—A Taste of Vienna—had an ironic Freudian flavor, given the cocktail-hour conversation upstairs at the class of '65's annual dinner, where the buzz was all about the psychiatric malpractice suit against classmate Margaret Bean-Bayog.

Dr. Bean-Bayog's Harvard and Radcliffe chums had been alerted by mail that cocktails would be extended by half an hour "to make a space in the evening's events for a gathering of those of us concerned about the recent media storm surrounding classmate Margaret Bean-Bayog. Many classmates have felt distressed and puzzled about this. There seems to be a need for contact with each other, for some perspective, and for drawing the wagons around both Margaret and ourselves."

Dr. Jonathan Kolb, a Boston psychoanalyst and classmate of Dr. Bean-Bayog's, provided that perspective by explaining the Paul Lozano case in the language of his trade: transference and countertransference, repression and regression.

It was not only in the clubby confines of Harvard that the wagons were being circled protectively around the embattled psychiatrist. Various other groups felt they had a stake in Dr. Bean-Bayog's defense: analysts under siege from biopsychiatry, feminists angered by the disparate treatment accorded a female psychiatrist accused of sexual misconduct, advocates for adult victims of childhood sexual abuse worried about doubts being cast on repressed memories. Missing in the rush to defend their ideological turf was a careful assessment of whether this was a case worthy of people's mounting the barricades.

Were Dr. Bean-Bayog's techniques really grounded in analytic theory after all? Was the issue really whether an accused woman got too much media attention or whether all those male psychiatrists got too little? Was this case really part of a backlash against victims of childhood sexual abuse or was it a red flag for therapists that the diagnosis was being made too cavalierly?

Instead of wrestling with those more difficult questions, Dr. Margaret Bean-Bayog's defenders took up arms against her critics, attacked her dead patient and his family, and defended treatment techniques that most conceded they knew little or nothing about.

One Harvard analyst opined, not for attribution, of course, that Dr. Gault was a "bit of a self-righteous fellow." Another whispered, confidentially, of course, that Amy Stromsten had a history of alcoholism, the suggestion implicit that the disease reflected on her credibility. The analyst, however, cast no such aspersions on the credibility of Dr. Bean-Bayog, herself a recovering alcoholic.

The attempt by the defense team to marginalize Amy Stromsten began as soon as the social worker submitted an affidavit recounting Paul Lozano's discussion with her about his relationship with Dr. Bean-Bayog and her memory of Dr. Bean-Bayog's comments in the supervision group about her erotic feelings for a Mexican-American medical student.

Michael Blau, Dr. Bean-Bayog's lawyer, told the *Globe* that several other therapists who attended the training session with Stromsten described Dr. Bean-Bayog's discussion as appropriate and that none recalled Amy expressing any concern about the psychiatrist's comments. However, when the four other therapists were deposed for the civil lawsuit, only Kathryn Kogan, a clinical psychologist, even remembered the discussions about the patient they would come to know through the litigation as Paul Lozano.

For her part, Kogan was committed to clearing the name of her much-admired supervisor. At times, she had trouble acknowledging that what little she knew of the case was only from Dr. Bean-Bayog's defensive perspective. Kogan argued that Dr. Bean-Bayog wrote reams of sadomasochistic sexual fantasies about Paul Lozano in order to keep her feelings "in a scientific framework," but Kogan never read the fantasies to determine if such erotica met her definition of "scientific."

She was simply trying to be supportive of her mentor, whom she described as "the most kind, moral, responsible —totally responsible—doctor and teacher; a shining light." Kogan and the other trainees continued to meet at Dr. Bean-Bayog's house on Wednesday afternoons while the litigation dominated the headlines, but they no longer talked about their patients. "This became a bunker in a way. So certainly the focus of the group changed to dealing with the crisis. And we were all very upset about it and wanting to help in any way," said Kogan, who repeated Dr. Bean-Bayog's oft-stated refrain that she was unable to publicly comment on the case because of the confidentiality bond between patients and physicians. Dr. Bean-Bayog's respect for that bond apparently was not strong enough, however, to preclude her from sharing her clinical views of Paul Lozano with her friends and colleagues and students and having them speak as surrogates for her before the television cameras.

After hearing Dr. Bean-Bayog's explanation, Kogan became convinced that Paul Lozano was a patient of "extraordinary hateful vindictiveness."

> There is a strong sense that he really set this up. He leaked information to the family. He stole information. He planted it for the family to find posthumously. And of course, they are going to pursue it legally. He had said to her at some point during the treatment, "I hope I don't have to hurt you someday." He would say things like that.
>
> He had been murderous toward other psychiatrists who had treated him. So this is a strong element in his personality, the murderousness. My feeling about it is he is one hair's length away from the criminally insane population. That's really what we're looking at. He was just together enough

not to be a murderer outright. But certainly, he had those types of wishes and sentiments and verbalized them. Whether he would have acted on them or not, I don't know. He certainly did a number on himself, with all those injections. You can see the really out-of-control destructiveness of this person. That is how I see it. It unfolds in terms of his pathology and he set this up to play out posthumously. The wish to destroy her certainly was there.

Much of the Boston psychoanalytic community got behind this line of defense. Paul Lozano was the patient from hell, reaching back from the grave to destroy a courageous, even saintly, psychiatrist who had risked everything to save him. That there is no independent corroboration of Dr. Bean-Bayog's view of Paul Lozano as a murderous sociopath is testament either to his ability to disguise those traits when not in his therapist's presence or to Dr. Bean-Bayog's ability to marshal support without evidence. Certainly, she convinced many of her colleagues of the rightness of her cause.

To read the defense documents and the newspaper coverage, one would conclude that Paul Lozano had received an unequivocal diagnosis of borderline personality disorder from the outset of his treatment. That was far from the case.

"There were a variety of opinions and speculations at different points," Dr. Bean-Bayog conceded in her eight-hundred-page deposition, even as her lawyers were portraying Paul publicly as a definitive case of an untreatable borderline. "He had five interlocking illnesses, each of which worsened the other," she said at one point. "I think I had four basic diagnoses for him," she said at another. "He had a series of revolving added diagnoses depending on who saw him and what they thought," she noted at another juncture.

Speculation rather than any hard data seemed to have been her primary diagnostic tool. Although she repeatedly characterized Paul Lozano in her defense documents as a chronic liar, Dr. Bean-Bayog accepted uncritically his account of events in making her psychiatric diagnosis.

"Why did you believe his stories of childhood suicide attempts and sexual abuse?" Meyer asked the psychiatrist during her deposition.

"Because they fit with his clinical picture," she said.

"You didn't know what his clinical picture was back then, did you? As a child of six?" Meyer asked.

"I knew what he told me," Dr. Bean-Bayog replied.

"So it fit with what he told you about his clinical condition at that time?" Meyer asked.

"It also fit with the classical diagnostic picture," she said, taking the discussion full circle.

"Which was what?" he asked.

"Of affective disorder," she said.

"Did you get his medical records?" Meyer asked.

"I didn't think there were any. I mean, maybe when he was five years old, twenty years earlier, in a Texas hospital, where he would have had his stomach pumped, somewhere, but no," she said.

In fact, Paul Lozano lived in Upper Sandusky, Ohio, until he was seventeen, and there are no medical records there of his ever having had his stomach pumped.

Dr. Bean-Bayog's confusion about how exactly to define Paul Lozano's illness underscores the tenuous nature of psychiatric diagnosis, particularly in the poorly researched area of so-called personality disorders, where diagnosis is based more on clinical experience than on empirical research, and treatment is based less on outcome studies than on ideological affinity.

"If you have a major mental disorder, like depression, one has to look at the impact of that on personality and not vice versa," said Dr. Joseph T. Coyle, chairman of the Consolidated Department of Psychiatry at Harvard Medical School. "What's changed about psychiatry is not so much defining what we know—there is knowledge about everything—but really defining the broad areas of ignorance. That is really where we get into art and you get into opinions in terms of how to manage or even diagnose someone with a borderline personality. We don't have the evidence. We know how to get the evidence. And I think we'll get the evidence. But today I can tell you only how I would approach it and why I think that's right. But that is art, not science. I'm perfectly confident to say that I would like to have a lot more evidence to determine whether that is right or not."

At the time she terminated therapy with Paul Lozano, Dr. Bean-Bayog testified, she thought he suffered from affective disorder, borderline personality, sociopathic personality, narcissistic personality, alcohol abuse, and post-traumatic stress disorder. She acknowledged, however, that her laundry list would be longer if the opinions of other psychiatrists were taken into account. In fact, the list was so long that a lay person might wonder how, given all these different illnesses, Paul Lozano had been able to function at all in his life, let alone be accepted into West Point, attend Harvard Medical School, and have a growing reputation as a researcher.

"The four basic diagnoses," said Dr. Bean-Bayog, "were affective disorder—some people thought he had schizo-affective disorder rather than straightforward affective disorder. I couldn't decide."

> The symptoms I saw in the first three years were more characteristic of affective disorder, but the symptoms in his final episodes . . . could have been either.
>
> The second was alcohol and drug abuse and possibly alcoholism. The third was personality disorder, including the main three diagnoses that were given him, borderline personality, character disorder or sociopathic personality, and narcissistic personality.
>
> And the fourth was—there isn't actually a formal term for this, but for a patient who has had an incestuous and abusive childhood, a form of post-traumatic stress disorder.
>
> He was thought by some to have multiple per-

sonality. Let's see. What else? I think Dr. Frankenberg thought he had character disorder, or dependent personality. Dr. Rogoff, I think, said he had narcissistic personality. I'm not sure what else.

It was clear he had a personality disorder. Whether it was borderline, narcissistic, it was being argued. I think he probably had aspects of all three. He definitely had borderline personality, and he definitely had character disorder. When borderlines are in treatment, they often transform from being primarily borderline to being narcissistic. But he wouldn't have had time at that point.

While Dr. Bean-Bayog's defenders championed her posthumous view of Paul Lozano, the psychiatrist's own deposition could not have demonstrated more clearly just how imprecise an art is diagnosis of a personality disorder in a severely depressed patient.

Dr. Bean-Bayog testified after Paul's death that she did not remember when she first diagnosed him as borderline but that she agreed with Dr. Frankenberg, who came to that conclusion in May of 1987, during Paul's second admission to McLean Hospital. But Dr. Bean-Bayog's own office notes contradict that testimony. "Borderline Personality Disorder and Character Disorder have been suggested," she wrote. "I don't think so because of his capacity for empathy and his moral character: his superego is enormous and punitive, not absent."

Dr. Harrison G. Pope, the psychopharmacologist who treated Paul during his two McLean Hospital admissions, saw no evidence that Paul suffered from anything other than major depression.

"The symptoms which he displayed could be readily explained by his major depression itself, without having to postulate that he had another illness besides," Dr. Pope testified. "Some of the symptoms, such as impulsivity, are found both in patients with major depressions and in patients with borderline personality disorder. There is no doubt that he had, for example, the symptom of impulsivity; but that symptom could be explained readily by his primary illness."

Even if Paul Lozano was a borderline, it is arguable that Dr. Bean-Bayog's treatment would have exacerbated his illness. One of the characteristics of patients with the disorder is the childlike dependence that Paul Lozano exhibited. A patient's need, then, is not to regress but to orient himself to the present in order to function better as an adult. According to many experts, for a patient with a depression as severe as Paul Lozano's, a therapy so focused on the childish aspect of his personality ran the risk of merely reinforcing his bleak, self-deprecating view of himself as unworthy and incompetent.

In their attempt to portray Paul Lozano as the patient from hell, Dr. Bean-Bayog's defense team reduced a complicated and imprecise diagnostic process to a simple label. In this malignant view, accepted by many in the psychiatric community who had never met Paul, he was a borderline, a probably untreatable, crazy man. Those who did meet Paul in that last year could not know whether his dangerous, psychotic depression, his borderline symptoms, and his self-destructiveness were a natural progression of his mental illness or a consequence of four years of Dr. Bean-Bayog's intense and disorienting therapy. They chose to believe, against all available evidence, that he had always been crazy.

Not for the record, of course, several psychiatrists whispered, but Paul Lozano was really "struggling at Harvard"; he was "an affirmative action admission"; Harvard kept him only because it could "not afford to lose a Chicano."

No less an authority than Dr. Carol C. Nadelson, a former president of the American Psychiatric Association, repeated the line heard often around town. "One of the things that concerns me is why he was still in medical school. And I hate to say this but I think it was because he was a minority student. I think if he wasn't they wouldn't have bent over to keep him in school. I think he wasn't able to handle it. He certainly didn't do well. I don't know what the records say," she candidly conceded. "He may have passed those courses, but it wasn't great. It raises in my mind a dilemma that I have dealt with in physicians a lot. Most of them who later on got into trouble had trouble early. It's worrisome."

She was talking about Paul Lozano. But what about Dr. Margaret Bean-Bayog? Hadn't she gotten into trouble early on, interrupting her psychiatric training because of her alcoholism? Why was it so hard in Boston psychiatric circles to consider the possibility that it was this doctor's behavior, not the patient's, that was really "worrisome"?

This line of attack incensed those who knew or taught Paul Lozano at Harvard. "That's absolute nonsense, and just how would these people know this?" asked Dr. Harold Amos, professor emeritus of microbiology and molecular genetics and a former dean of the Medical Sciences Division, who shared many research interests with Paul. "He had been an excellent student in Texas, and he was doing quite nice work at the graduate school. And we don't make any concessions on that scene, to boot. I'm not interested in pushing someone through, and Paul Lozano did not need that."

Mark Burrowes, who worked with Paul for more than a year when both were employed as mental health aides, never saw any sign of alcoholism, sociopathology, deceitfulness, or drug abuse in his friend and coworker. "I never saw him drunk," he said. "Even in hindsight, I can't say he was anything but a friendly, studious fellow."

Even Victor Gonzalez, Paul Lozano's medical school roommate who watched him struggle with depression for two years, saw no evidence of the pathology that Dr. Bean-Bayog insists marked her patient's life at Harvard. "I never saw him drink to intoxication," Victor said, adding that he also never knew Paul to steal anything, abuse any drugs, or demonstrate "any violent tendencies."

If, indeed, Paul Lozano was a borderline, he presented a particular challenge to a psychiatrist who clearly harbored fantasies of rescuing her patient. In the September 1992 issue of *The Psychodynamic Letter,* Dr. Steven P. Gersten reviewed the pitfalls of borderlines' being treated by therapists who have their own unresolved issues. "Therapists who have insufficiently worked through their own narcissistic vulnerabilities are in greater danger of withdrawing from patients ('I don't need the patient') or from reality ('I have things under control, no problem exists, nothing can happen') or of developing overinvolved relationships with patients," he wrote.

Gersten reviewed the literature on borderlines, noting the phenomenon of the "love-sick therapist who experiences a non-psychotic loss of reality testing that allows the therapist to take great risks for self-gratification. Borderline or narcissistic character pathology may be involved, and the therapist is able to deny evidence that undue intimacy harms patients.

"A poignant example of this kind of mutually desperate and craving relationship is the 'mystical double,' in which each partner sees in the other a damaged self-representation that establishes a mutually reverberating sympathy. By using projective identification, narcissistically vulnerable therapists see in their patients aspects of themselves, both idealized/grandiose images as well as those connected to a sense of neediness, incompleteness and early damage."

Was Paul Lozano a borderline whose troubles tragically mirrored those of his psychiatrist? Or was there yet another possible explanation for the symptoms he exhibited?

Research suggests that patients who have been sexually exploited are often misdiagnosed as borderlines. In her book *Trauma and Recovery,* Dr. Judith Herman, a Harvard psychiatrist, noted that victims, usually women, who allege sexual abuse in therapy are routinely dismissed as borderlines, even though borderline and sociopathic behavior usually manifest themselves before adulthood. Since Paul Lozano was first diagnosed as a borderline in 1987, six months after he began his intense relationship with Dr. Bean-Bayog, is it not possible that he displayed those symptoms as a result of a sexual relationship with his psychiatrist? Or was that explanation not applicable to this patient because he was a man?

Even simple, undisputed facts were ignored to advance Dr. Bean-Bayog's case. One constantly repeated statement was that Dr. Bean-Bayog had taken on a patient no one else would touch and had turned to her eclectic techniques only *after* exhausting more conventional psychiatric methods.

But in fact, she was the *first* psychiatrist he ever saw. And her office notes make clear that she began the mom-and-boy role-playing as soon as Paul Lozano was released in 1986 from McLean Hospital, where, by her own admission in a letter on October 23, 1986, to Dr. Daniel D. Federman, the associate dean of students at Harvard Medical School, "his disorder has responded beautifully" to conventional treatment by medication. So how to explain the hand wringing by colleagues who insisted that the malpractice suit against Dr. Bean-Bayog would discourage the use of innovative techniques with desperately ill patients who did not respond to traditional modes of treatment?

"There are three bad lessons you can learn from this case," according to Dr. Thomas G. Gutheil, Dr. Bean-Bayog's staunchest public defender. "One: Burn your notes. Two: Don't treat sick people. Three: Never do anything for the first time."

Most of Dr. Bean-Bayog's partisans were willing to concede that by becoming too involved, she had trespassed some commonly accepted boundaries between therapists and patients. But Dr. Gutheil explained even that away, drawing a distinction between "boundary crossings" and "boundary violations."

"A boundary crossing is when you step out of your role to do something important, like get a guy who is jumping off a ledge to McLean," he said, in effect exonerating Dr. Bean-Bayog for rushing to her allegedly suicidal patient in the middle of the night and driving him to the hospital in 1987. "A boundary violation is a crossing of a boundary which exploits a patient and does not advance the therapy. Getting a suicidal guy to a hospital, keeping him alive, therefore advances the therapy—boundary crossing. Doing something which is for your gratification, sleeping with a patient, is a boundary violation."

Like the patient from hell theory, praise for Dr. Bean-Bayog's use of consultants also circulated on the basis of scuttlebutt, not fact. Margaret told her consultants all about her innovative techniques, psychiatrists insisted to one another—and to anyone who asked. Then why did those supposed consultants swear under oath, in depositions taken for the civil case, that they knew *nothing* about the role-playing, the flash cards, the stuffed animals, or the sexual fantasies?

"That is hard to say, because my impression from talking to them is that they knew what she was doing," said Dr. Nadelson. "To start with, she took on a case that a lot of people never would have touched. She got more supervision than anyone at her level ever would have got. I don't know anyone who would have talked to so many people about a case, being a senior person. You do when you are a resident or a year or two out of training. So it is clear to me that she worried about this case. She really wanted to do the right thing. And knowing her, I would expect that was her motivation. And she wanted to impress her supervisors that she was really solid. I think she probably got in over her head. But what Margaret did was get consultation and supervision from senior people—the world's best-respected people in the field. My impression was that some of her supervisors knew quite well what she was doing."

Then why would Dr. Dan Buie and Dr. Gerald Adler— the psychiatrists Dr. Nadelson cited as the world's best-respected people in the field—say under oath that they did not know?

Dr. Edward Khantzian, a psychiatrist at Cambridge Hospital who worked for almost twenty years with Dr. Bean-Bayog in the field of addictive disorders, could not imagine. But neither could he entertain the possibility that his colleague had concealed anything about her treatment techniques. "Do you think someone like Margaret, alleged to be doing what she was doing, could have gone to open-case conferences with this patient and admitted him to all these places in the metropolitan Boston area where her reputation could be sullied? Would she have called in consultant after consultant after consultant to follow Paul?" he asked. "That is not the profile of someone that would be enacting bizarre behavior toward their patient."

Although her friends might find dusty citations in the psychoanalytic literature to justify Dr. Bean-Bayog's confusing maternal role-playing with Paul Lozano, it is unlikely that Freud would have embraced her unorthodox techniques. In his paper "Fragment of an Analysis of a Case of Hysteria," the founder of psychoanalysis ruminated in 1905 about why Dora, one of his early patients, abruptly ended treatment with him.

"Might I perhaps have kept the girl under my treatment if I had acted a part, if I had exaggerated the importance to me of her staying on, and had shown a warm personal interest in her—a course which, even after allowing for my position as her physician, would have been tantamount to providing her with a substitute for the affection she longed for?" Freud wrote. "I have always avoided acting a part, and have contented myself with the humbler arts of psychology."

Psychiatrists who were usually incensed when female victims of sexual abuse in therapy were treated by the profession as "crazy" or not credible for accusing a well-respected male psychiatrist were silent when Dr. Bean-Bayog's friends and defense team treated Paul Lozano the same way. There were no protests when the process put him on trial posthumously. His life was dissected, in search of any scrap of evidence to support the patient from hell theory. What did that brief marriage mean? Immaturity or a personality disorder? What did his withdrawal from West Point mean? Unhappiness or alcoholism? What about his imaginary playmates as a preschooler? Innocent childhood fantasies or hallucinations?

Reporters and private investigators for Dr. Bean-Bayog combed through the lives of the Lozano family, sifting the sands for any sign of pathology. The Lozanos invited the search. "We have nothing to hide," Pilar promised.

But no newspaper dispatched a reporter to Iowa to pore over the past of Margaret Harvey Bean and her family. Certainly, she did not encourage such inquiries. Her brothers, a sculptor in New Jersey and an education professor in Indiana, refused comment. Her friends declined to be interviewed, citing their aversion to the "media circus." Her parents' friends were skittish, fearful that Margaret's troubles would reflect badly on the memory of Bill and Gail Bean. Her prep school headmaster would not even show a visitor a copy of her high school yearbook without the written authorization of her attorney.

In contrast to the wild suppositions about the Lozanos, there was no speculation at all about Dr. Margaret Bean-Bayog. No one asked, for instance, whether it was narcissism or simple self-absorption that had prompted Dr. Bean-Bayog, a recovering-alcoholic-stepmother-in-the-midst-of-adoption-efforts-with-her-Filipino-husband, to list her top research interests on her résumé as "the psychology of alcoholism, step-families, adoption and interracial families."

The lack of scrutiny extended back through two generations. "Do you *know* who her family is?" more than one psychiatrist asked in annoyed response to inquiries about Dr. Bean-Bayog, as if the fact that her family was well-respected and well-educated should exonerate her. Some of her supporters had known Bill Bean from her father's brief tour at Harvard, others from his years as editor of *Annals of Internal Medicine*. They knew her grandfather to have been the much-published chairman of the Department of Anatomy at the University of Virginia in Charlottesville. But none had any familiarity with Robert Bennett Bean's theories of racial development, nor his book *The Races of Man*, the underlying premise of which is the inherent superiority of the white race.

It was all reflexive, this deification of the Beans and demonization of the Lozanos. One of their own was under assault, and her colleagues came to Dr. Bean-Bayog's defense out of some instinctive fear that there, but for the grace of God, go I. It happens in most professional circles, said Dr. Khantzian. "I think many of us have some good ideas or have people gather around us that we know will support or reinforce them. I don't think Margaret was any different in that respect. On the other hand, she was one of the female leaders. And she was very, very assertive."

Her female colleagues, in fact, were among the first to protest her gender-biased treatment by the media and the Board of Registration in Medicine. Their complaint rang a little hollow, however. Dr. Bean-Bayog, after all, was not the only woman accused of sexual misconduct in this case. There was far less substantiation for allegations that Epifania Lozano had committed vile—not to mention felonious—sexual acts against her son in childhood than for the charges that Dr. Bean-Bayog had an erotic relationship with him in adulthood.

Where were the feminist complaints about the rush to judgment against Epifania Lozano? Where was the righteous indignation about the smearing media that circulated unproven claims against *this* woman of impeccable reputation? Or did the good name of a Mexican-American housewife carry less weight than that of a Harvard psychiatrist?

Ironically, in her handwritten sexual fantasies about Paul Lozano, Dr. Bean-Bayog did not maintain the same level of commitment to the cause as the women who rushed to her defense. She forswore sisterhood for the pleasures of sexual passivity:

> This is not what I expected. It had simply never occurred to me that I wouldn't remain in control. This wasn't part of my plan.
>
> Without realizing it, I had locked off the part of me that was the most private and soft and helpless inside of me. I had never, ever planned to share it with anyone. I don't know how you knew she was in there, or how you got her out, but there's no going back now.
>
> I suddenly grasp what you have been doing and understand what I need to do. I am bottomlessly grateful. Bit by bit, I relinquish my will, my autonomy, my control. This is hard to do after years of practice, but I am determined. I become totally open to you. I trust you utterly. I renounce each

shred of resistance, one by one. I understand that I do not exist separate from your will for me, and I submit fully to it.

A voice in the back of my head says, "Christ, whatever happened to the women's movement?"

Nothing. All that is still there. I'm still competent and driving and smart. But maybe I'm luckier than all those angry, lonely, embittered women. And, maybe I know something they don't know. Maybe a man is helping me to let go of myself, to know myself as a woman so I can really love.

It was a man who led the cheerleading squad for Dr. Bean-Bayog. All the brouhaha was not about therapy, in Dr. Gutheil's view. It was about sex. "This is about society's difficulty tolerating women's sexuality, if you want my bottom line on all this," he said. "People would not like to say, 'I'm very upset with these fantasies.' They would say, 'I'm very upset by this bad therapy.'"

From his perspective, there was nothing amiss about either Dr. Bean-Bayog's fantasies or her therapy. Nor did he see anything amiss in his own role as an expert witness for the defense, even though he had served as a consultant to Dr. Bean-Bayog when Paul Lozano was alive. He saw no conflict, but the Lozanos' lawyer did, as did many of Dr. Gutheil's colleagues, who saw the roles of consultant and expert witness as incompatible. Dr. Dan Buie and Dr. Gerald Adler, for instance, refused to serve as expert witnesses, as did Dr. Jerome Rogoff.

"I didn't see how I could be an expert and a material witness at the same time. Besides, I had been somewhat critical. She was overinvolved," said Dr. Rogoff. "I don't accept that on its face her treatment was injurious. But if you are going beyond what are the normative bounds and design a treatment plan, you'd better get consultation up front. You don't go off on your own, Don Quixote style, and tilt at windmills.

"What in the hell was Margaret doing writing down these fantasies? I don't know any reason why you would but, if you do, put them someplace they can't be stolen. That's just plain stupid. Go talk to someone, get supervision, or if your attraction is that deep and that much, you can't treat the patient any longer."

Dr. Gutheil had no reservations about being an expert, even though he had been an adviser on the case at Faulkner Hospital in 1987 and to Dr. Bean-Bayog when she was ending the therapy in 1990. In addition, he was a longtime acquaintance, having dated Dr. Bean-Bayog's Harvard Medical School roommate. When this case began leading the evening newscasts, Dr. Gutheil was one of the first to telephone Dr. Bean-Bayog to express his condolences. "The initial stuff was, I would say, critical to the point of being abusive, and I feel sorry if anybody gets that," he said, in explaining his call.

Dr. Gutheil is something of a professional witness, spending 10 percent of his work hours evaluating cases for lawyers at a rate of $300 an hour or $3,000 a day. He threw himself eagerly into that role in this case, often appearing as a public commentator on the issues raised by the lawsuit. He was a guest on the ABC news program "Nightline," discussing sexual abuse in psychotherapy. To a reporter he explained the psychodynamic perspective on the treatment of victims of childhood abuse.

"If a patient brings up alleged memories or even false memories, as a treater, not as a forensic assessor, you have to take them as true, otherwise you can't treat a patient," Dr. Gutheil said, his feet propped up on his paper-strewn desk at the Massachusetts Mental Health Center. "If a patient says, 'I was butchered and beaten with chains and branded with hot irons,' you don't say, 'That doesn't sound plausible.' You say, 'That must have been terrible.' If you are treating a victim, you have to start with a victimization. Later, five years later, they may retell their story. But you've got to take it at face value. So, it doesn't matter from a clinical viewpoint whether he was telling the truth or not. You start by assuming it's true."

But what if the evidence suggests that it was the doctor who promoted the idea that the patient had been sexually abused and the patient, infatuated or sexually involved with the doctor, served up details he thought she would want to hear? How does one separate fact from fiction?

"Let's say he was telling that to her just because he thought she would want to hear it, because it would make her right. That it was part of an ingratiation strategy, let's assume. So, a) he is still a liar and b) that's his unconscious, anyway. Again, from a clinical viewpoint even if he 'made it up' it's like, 'I'm going to fool my doctor; I'm not going to tell her my real dream, I'm just going to make up one.' The paradox is that it is the same unconscious that is dictating your fantasy that is dictating an actual dream you might have had. So, you can't fool anybody by making up stuff. It's of interest, but you can't have it both ways. Either you really had this experience, in which case she is right and everything is cool. Or he is a liar, in which case she is right and everything is cool."

It was not clear to Dr. Gutheil that the Lozano family even understood what was meant by sexual abuse, let alone whether all those incensed neighbors in Upper Sandusky were sophisticated enough to follow the subtleties of Dr. Bean-Bayog's thinking.

"They're bringing in these senile pediatricians who say, We examined him and he didn't have any scars on him," he said of Dr. Thomas Watkins, the Lozano family pediatrician, who appeared to be in full command of his mental faculties in his videotaped deposition in the civil case and impressed a visitor the same way during a two-hour conversation at his Tiffin, Ohio, home. "The point is, we are not talking about whipping. We're talking about overstimulation beyond what a child at that developmental stage can handle."

But, in fact, Dr. Bean-Bayog did claim in her deposition that Paul Lozano and his siblings had been beaten. "Yeah, there is that, too. And that is the direct abuse. But the sexual abuse we are talking about doesn't mean rapes with instruments. It means overstimulation. Okay? So we have to be very careful about this and portraying the parents as being very violent. That may be true, too, and that a pediatrician might or might not see. But the sexual stuff, no one is going to see because people are always very private about that, number one. Number two, it's not abuse in the sense of damage—it's flooding. It's overstimulating a person beyond their ability to handle and modulate the feelings that get stirred up."

Dr. Gutheil proposed a cultural, and characteristically speculative, explanation for the sexual overstimulation Paul Lozano was alleged to have suffered at his mother's hands. "Some Hispanic families—Brazilians and rural area folks—routinely masturbate children of both genders as a soothing device. It is not seen as deviant behavior. So there is a possibility that when they say sexual abuse, and you say it to the family, they really don't get it. They don't connect a standard pacifying model in rural Hispanic realms as a problem which we now call abuse. There may be something lost in the translation."

An interesting theory. Except, of course, that Marcos and Epifania Lozano are Mexicans, not Brazilians, and they raised their six children not in a rural South American village but in a middle-class farming community in the heartland of the United States of America.

"I knew that it would happen and that's why I'm not bitter about it," Pilar Williams said of the battering her family took by suing the prominent Harvard psychiatrist.

> I knew that was the price I would have to pay to reveal, to show. But I felt the evidence that I had was not word-of-mouth. It was not hearsay. It was not the sort of sick speculation made about our family. It was concrete. In black and white. In her handwriting. Her pictures. So I felt that she could throw all the mud she wanted, I was completely without a doubt, knowing that we were innocent, that no matter who looked where, they would find nothing. We felt that the sacrifice was worth it because we had already suffered the ultimate. And my brother had paid. For any wrongdoing he may have done, for any misjudgments, for any weakness

in his character by believing in her, by delivering the lies about us to keep her happy—he paid the ultimate price with his life.

I don't blame the other idiots who defended her so much. Because they don't know. They really don't know. They only know what she's told them. And what they read in the papers and the theories they dream up about dirty little ignorant Mexicans who masturbate their babies.

Similar psychobabble was employed in the effort to market Dr. Bean-Bayog's explicit sexual fantasies about Paul Lozano as pseudoscience. The fifty-five handwritten pages full of orgasms and erections, passionate kisses and mutual bondage, were not sex stories, the public was told, they were countertransference.

It was only after the case was resolved that Michael Blau, the defense counsel, acknowledged that "these fantasies are not your typical Victorian or Gothic romance. These were very direct. Very explicit. Hard-core kind of documents. Not the kind of material that one would expect to find among psychiatric materials in a box maintained by the patient."

While the case was still active, however, these documents were scientific, not pornographic. Transference occurs when a patient unconsciously projects onto his therapist feelings and attitudes that were originally associated with important figures from childhood, such as parents or siblings. Countertransference is the psychiatrist's emotional reaction to the patient. The concept has its roots in psychoanalysis, but few psychiatrists of competing schools would dispute the basic soundness of its main tenet: that a patient's problems often provoke intense reactions in the psychiatrist and the doctor would be wise to manage those feelings or end the therapy.

What nonanalytic therapists have difficulty with is the notion that these countertransference feelings exist separate and apart from the psychiatrist who is having them. Laymen have trouble with that idea as well, as this exchange between

Dr. Bean-Bayog and Andrew C. Meyer, Jr., the Lozano family's attorney, during her deposition, demonstrates:

Meyer: Were you sexually attracted to Paul Lozano?

Dr. Bean-Bayog: Me, myself? No.

Meyer: Did you have sexual fantasies about Paul Lozano?

Dr. Bean-Bayog: Not as me, myself, no.

Meyer: As who did you have sexual fantasies about him?

Dr. Bean-Bayog: In a countertransference sense.

Meyer: Who was that?

Dr. Bean-Bayog: I beg your pardon?

Meyer: Who was that that had that fantasy if it wasn't you, yourself?

Dr. Bean-Bayog: It was in a countertransference sense.

Meyer: When countertransference occurs such as in the case of Paul, was that sexually arousing to you?

Dr. Bean-Bayog: To me personally, or in the countertransference?

Meyer: Are there two different people? Maybe I'm losing something here, but, if you are sexually aroused, are you sexually aroused as a person or in the countertransference mode? I mean, if your body reacts physically, does it happen? How does it happen?

Dr. Bean-Bayog: You can make the separation in the same way that you don't murder a patient that you want to murder in the countertransference.

Meyer: Right. I understand that. But if you end up committing a murder, you raise your hand and do it. Now, does this countertransference person do that or does your person do that if you actually do the murder?

Dr. Bean-Bayog: I didn't do the murder.

Meyer: Maybe I'm losing the amount of people we're dealing with here. There is only one person sitting in the room with the patient, is that right?

Dr. Bean-Bayog: Yes.

Meyer: And that's you?

Dr. Bean-Bayog: Me, and myself in many other roles.

Meyer: Your role is really placed there in regard to help Paul?

Dr. Bean-Bayog: Yes.

Meyer: And in that role, as the role you are in when you're working with Paul and you become sexually aroused, what happens to the real you, as opposed to the role? Does that person become sexually aroused?

Dr. Bean-Bayog: I think I've tried to specify that this is an experience in the countertransference.

Meyer: I understand that. And if you become sexually aroused, what happens to the real you? That person doesn't become sexually aroused; is that what you're telling me?

Dr. Bean-Bayog: Well, that person maintains some distance and understanding of what's going on.

Meyer: Do they stand across the room or something?

Depending on one's point of view, this frustrating exchange demonstrated either the lawyer's lack of sophistication about psychoanalytic theory or the psychiatrist's adherence to cant over common sense.

The problem with this case, as Dr. Gutheil saw it, was that nonpsychiatrists on the medical board and a civil court jury were being asked to understand psychodynamic concepts they could not possibly comprehend. "Look, remember the Hyatt walkways that fell down and injured all those people?" he asked, a reference to the accident in Kansas City, Missouri, in 1981 that killed 114 people. "Was the engineering used innovative or mainstream? How the hell would you know? How the hell would I know? It assumes that you know the underlying principles. We can't sit here and say, 'Oh yeah, that's mainstream. That's state of the art.' How would you know that? We'd have to practically take a course in engineering even to get a feeling for what they're talking about. And this is what we are talking about. How would the average person know whether these approaches are some variations of those which are commonly used?"

Maybe that was the problem: there were no articulated, comprehensible standards by which the public could judge psychiatric practice. The notion that the field was simply too complicated for the public to be able to distinguish between legitimate and misguided therapy struck Dr. William Barry Gault as nothing more or less than professional hubris.

"When I would read this or that psychiatrist in the newspaper kind of theoretically commenting on the treatment that she gave Paul Lozano, I'd think, 'They couldn't have read the material that I read," Dr. Gault recalled. "Pages of sexual stories. Plus the 'you're my baby, I'm your mother' stuff. This young man seemed to be the object both of a yearning to be a good mother and intense sexual desire. I mean, the sexual writings were a pretty convincing account of an experience of sexual desire. You can't read all that and think that this psychotherapy was okay."

He knew he would be vilified in some quarters for turning Dr. Bean-Bayog in to the medical board. He himself was sickened by the media's frenzied coverage of the case. But for him and many other psychiatrists in Boston who chose to keep silent during the publicity, the case raised larger issues about psychiatry's standards. They looked expectantly to the medical board and civil court jury to rise above the field's internecine battles to address those issues, however complicated.

As for Dr. Gutheil's objection to laymen sitting in judgment: if the collapse of the walkways at the Kansas City Hyatt Regency really was analogous, he and Dr. Bean-Bayog's defense team would have been well advised to note the aftermath of that tragedy.

Without benefit of a degree in engineering, the judge for Missouri's Administrative Hearing Commission found evidence that the chief project engineer was guilty of "a cavalier attitude" and "a conscious indifference to his professional duties."

On November 15, 1985, Judge James B. Deutsch filed a 442-page ruling that found the two structural engineers guilty of gross negligence, misconduct, and unprofessional conduct.

Chapter

12

Jack Fabiano was busy drafting questions for former president Gerald Ford, a party to a civil suit he was preparing that July, when the telephone rang in his spacious twenty-sixth-floor law office overlooking the Boston waterfront.

The Tall Ships were set to sail into Boston the next morning and, from his high-rise perch, the masts of barkentines could be seen at anchor in the outer harbor. From the park below came the sound of musicians tuning up for the jazz concert that would kick off Boston's biggest tourist weekend of the summer of 1992.

The telephone roused Fabiano from details of the pension fund on whose board the former president served. It was Steven Wallace, the assistant secretary of consumer affairs, calling. If Fabiano was still interested, Wallace said, the medical board would like him to serve as special prosecutor in the Dr. Margaret Bean-Bayog case.

Fabiano was delighted. He liked his pro bono work with a public service angle just as he liked his coffee with cream. And, like everyone else in Boston, Jack Fabiano had been following with fascination the unfolding tale of the Harvard psychiatrist and the Mexican-American medical student.

The saga was gripping enough as melodrama, but the high-profile case also offered a lawyer the prospect of litigating the limits of psychiatry on the national stage.

He had been intrigued to watch the wagons circle around the embattled psychiatrist. He had seen it before. It was standard operating procedure in Boston, a town that is nothing if not parochial, where political and professional allegiances, like ethnic and religious ties, are tribal in their intensity. Five years earlier, Fabiano had served as special prosecutor for the Judicial Conduct Commission, building a disciplinary case against a politically connected judge accused of having a dangerous habit of browbeating battered women who sought the court's protection from their abusive spouses. The judge denied the charges and, in the end, strolled back to the bench with only a warning about his bad temper.

Fabiano knew that the record for disciplining errant doctors in Massachusetts was even worse than that for intemperate judges. But it seemed to him that public accountability was the only antidote to the arrogance of the powerful and powerfully entrenched.

Fabiano was an obvious choice for the medical board. Chief of litigation for Hale & Dorr, he projected the polish of his white-shoe firm. He was a Harvard man himself—the college and the law school. Although they had never met, he and Margaret Harvey Bean as undergraduates had even been in the same science lecture class.

The medical board's formal charges against Dr. Bean-Bayog did not include sexual misconduct and responsibility for Paul Lozano's death, so Fabiano would focus instead on broader allegations of substandard care.

Her treatment harmed Paul Lozano, the medical board said, and "did not conform to accepted standards of medical practice." In addition to inappropriately encouraging her patient to think of her as his mother, the medical board charged that Dr. Bean-Bayog failed to deal professionally with her own explicit sexual fantasies about Paul Lozano. "Her failure to terminate or otherwise address these fantasies did not conform to the standards of accepted medical practice."

In addition, the panel alleged, Dr. Bean-Bayog "failed to perform a proper initial evaluation and formulation of Paul Lozano's psychiatric illness, failed to devise an appropriate treatment plan, failed to manage the care of the patient properly, improperly conducted and utilized psychotherapy sessions, failed to use consultants properly, continued therapy after termination had become necessary, and when she did terminate, did so improperly."

The medical board had allowed Dr. Bean-Bayog to continue practicing, under the supervision of another psychiatrist, because there was no evidence of improper treatment of any other patients. In fact, her attorneys had submitted letters from a number of Bean-Bayog's patients testifying to their high regard for their psychiatrist.

Fabiano's task was difficult but far easier than the one facing Andrew C. Meyer, Jr., in civil court. To win the malpractice suit Meyer would need to prove not only that the psychiatrist had mismanaged the case but also that Margaret Bean-Bayog's sexual exploitation of Paul Lozano had caused his death.

It would be a difficult case to prove and by no means typical of psychiatric malpractice suits. A psychiatrist in the United States faces a one-in-twenty chance of being sued in any given year, but lawsuits usually address such narrow issues as medication management or the failure to hospitalize a suicidal patient. Sexual abuse accounts for less than 10 percent of the claims filed against psychiatrists covered by Massachusetts's largest malpractice insurer. It is even more rare for a psychiatrist to be sued for negligent psychotherapy, because the standards are so subjective and the patient's mental state so vulnerable to legal attack.

As a result, malpractice premiums for psychiatrists are among the lowest paid by any specialist. Only 2 percent of the claims against psychiatrists insured by the American Psychiatric Association ever go to trial. The vast majority end in settlements. The average settlement is a relatively modest $50,000, but million-dollar settlements are not unprecedented. In some cases, patients have recovered more than a policy's annual limit, usually between $1 million and $2 million, when they proved that the malpractice spanned more than a single year.

Meyer knew that his civil case turned on the medical board's action. It was unlikely that the Massachusetts Malpractice Joint Underwriting Association, Dr. Bean-Bayog's insurance carrier, would want to defend a doctor in civil court who had been disciplined by the state agency responsible for monitoring physician conduct. If Fabiano won, the malpractice case would settle.

Even though he did not have to prove a direct link between Dr. Bean-Bayog's treatment and Paul Lozano's death, Fabiano had his work cut out for him. For one thing, there were no clearly defined standards of psychiatric practice against which to measure her conduct. If he was going to argue that she deviated from accepted psychiatric guidelines, he would need to identify those guidelines. Proving even her procedural failures would be a challenge. Massachusetts law required psychiatrists in publicly funded mental health clinics to file detailed treatment plans every four months for peer review. But no such requirement existed for psychiatrists in private practice.

The more he looked at his case, the more Jack Fabiano realized he would be putting psychotherapy itself on trial.

The hiring of a special prosecutor enraged Dr. Bean-Bayog's supporters even more than the media frenzy had. Her attorney, Michael Blau, noted that 1992 was the three hundredth anniversary of the Salem witch trials. Massachusetts was at it again, he implied.

The medical board had used a special prosecutor only once before, to investigate the practices of a cardiac team whose surgical outcomes showed a higher than average mortality rate. "Truly unprecedented," Blau would fume later. "One allegation of malpractice in a single case and we have a special prosecutor!"

But the medical board was engaged less in witch-hunting than derriere-covering. Stung by criticism about case backlogs and inaction against incompetent or impaired physicians, the medical board had been targeted for reform a year before by Governor William F. Weld. In January a special task force had concluded that the panel lacked adequate staff and financial resources to protect the public from bad doctors. The task force urged the medical board to seek outside legal counsel in complicated cases.

If anything, the medical board's need for assistance was dramatized by its initial fumbling in the Dr. Bean-Bayog case. First, the board claimed to have lost or never received the letters of complaint. It then waited thirteen months to issue charges against the psychiatrist, a delay that Consumer Affairs Secretary Gloria Larson huffily attributed to the failure of the Lozanos' lawyer to turn over relevant documents. Her buck-passing backfired a day later when Meyer produced a receipt from the medical board, establishing that the panel had the key documents in hand on March 8, 1991, three weeks before Paul Lozano died by his own hand.

Alexander F. Fleming, the executive director of the medical board, took one look at the resources Michael Blau's firm was devoting to Dr. Bean-Bayog's defense and knew that this case called for a special prosecutor. Otherwise, the medical board would have to depend on its lone in-house prosecutor, who was already burdened with hundreds of other cases and had a support staff so thin that the prosecutor routinely typed his own pleadings and did his own photocopying.

As vociferous as they were, protests about the appointment of a special prosecutor were tame, however, compared to the howls that greeted the news that the proceedings would be held in Gardner Auditorium, a 600-seat hearing room in the basement of the Massachusetts State House, a space more commonly used for state budget deliberations. The medical board had arranged to use the auditorium after Court TV, the national cable television channel that had aired the William Kennedy Smith rape trial the year before, announced plans to televise the hearings live and requested permission to place a satellite dish atop the Saltonstall Building, where the medical board is headquartered.

Blau denounced the disciplinary process as a media

circus. But despite all his public protests, Dr. Bean-Bayog's attorney never filed a motion with the Division of Administrative Law Appeals either to close the hearings or to restrict the number of cameras or reporters in the room.

Christopher Connolly, the chief magistrate of the division, said he would not have agreed to close the hearings in a case that had generated so much public interest, but he had planned to partition the auditorium to blunt the cavernous effect, and he would have considered requests to limit press coverage. "They never asked," he said of Dr. Bean-Bayog's lawyers.

Nor was this the first high-profile medical board case to necessitate a move to larger quarters. Marian Ego, a former consumer member of the medical board, recalled the staff scrambling to find a bigger hearing room in 1986 to accommodate the busloads of mostly elderly patients who descended on the proceedings to protest disciplinary action against Dr. Archie D. Kiegan, a suburban general practitioner who had admitted prescribing narcotics to his addicted patients.

"Do you suppose that one wasn't a circus because the crowd was on the doctor's side?" Ego asked rhetorically.

The flap about the auditorium was a red herring, diverting attention from substantive questions about the propriety of Dr. Bean-Bayog's therapy. By focusing on the venue for the hearings, her defense team reinforced the image of the doctor as victim, targeted by a sexist and sensation-seeking press, a head-hunting medical board, and an anti-intellectual public eager to bring down a successful woman psychiatrist from Harvard.

What Fabiano needed was an expert witness who could cut through the cant. The medical board had run up against The Club in its search for a local psychiatrist to take on the case, not because there were no psychiatrists in Boston who objected to Dr. Bean-Bayog's methods—Dr. Larry H. Strasburger had rejected her methods in the strongest terms in an affidavit in the civil case—but because most of those who privately disapproved hesitated to break ranks publicly.

The medical board found its man in the pages of an upcoming edition of *The American Scholar*. An essay by Dr. Paul R. McHugh about the arrogance and trendiness of modern psychiatry seemed to capture the essence of the problem with Dr. Bean-Bayog's conduct.

> Psychiatry, it needs always to be remembered, is a medical discipline—capable of glorious medical triumphs and hideous medical mistakes. We psychiatrists don't know the secret of human nature. We cannot build a New Jerusalem. But we can teach the lessons of our past. We can describe how our explanations for mental disorders are devised and develop—where they are strong and where they are vulnerable to misuse. We can clarify the presumptions about what we know and how we know it. We can strive within the traditional responsibilities of our profession to build a sound relationship with people who consult us—placing them on more equal terms with us and encouraging them to approach us as they would any other medical specialists, by asking questions and expecting answers, based on science, about our assumptions, practices, and plans. With effort and good sense, we can construct a clinical discipline that, while delivering less to fashion, will bring more to patients and their families.

Exactly right, thought Fabiano. That Dr. McHugh was chairman of the Department of Psychiatry at the Johns Hopkins University School of Medicine sealed his unimpeachable credentials. That he was also a Harvard man—the college and the medical school—would short-circuit any suggestion that he had an ax to grind.

However, Fabiano underestimated the enmity between competing schools of thought in American psychiatry. The selection of Paul McHugh provoked a collective groan in Boston's analytic community. "His choice is a very revealing one. It would be kind of like getting a Christian Scientist to discuss a surgical operation," sniffed Dr. Thomas Gutheil, who described Dr. McHugh as an "observational, descriptive pharmacologic psychiatrist. He is not really into people having inner experiences."

Dr. Edward J. Khantzian, a Cambridge psychoanalyst tired of defending Freudians against the advancing army of biopsychiatrists, was appalled by the choice. To him, Dr. McHugh was part of a cabal that chants empiricism like a mantra, as if proof of anything could ever be pure.

It was not that Dr. Khantzian did not recognize the pomposity of some of his own peers. He had seen it himself for years at seminars at the Boston Psychoanalytic Society and Institute. "I thought the Institute was going to be a place of enlightenment. I have seen the most narrow-minded, arrogant professional so-called dialogues go on in those forums. Even though I am a card-carrying psychoanalyst and I'm in good standing and all of that, I grow weary and impatient with it," he said.

But was the deification of the scientific method any less a tyranny than the worship of the unconscious? "Who proves anything without a guiding principle?" he asked. "It was Einstein, by the way, who said, 'Our theories help us to identify the facts.'

"I grew up in an age of a brainless mind and now we are living in an age of a mindless brain," Dr. Khantzian said. "These folks have taken the same arrogant turn because things have happened that are so empowering—they're breakthroughs. It has empowered them like the psychoanalysts were empowered a generation ago. And you see these people get up and speak in the same arrogant way, and turn on major whole-life views and conclusions about what life is about based on some subtle, absolutely esoteric, scientific, methodologic, or empirical issue. It is just as obscure and arrogant as any of my psychoanalytic colleagues a generation ago."

Maybe. Maybe it was all just a battle between branches of psychiatry. But Jack Fabiano did not think so. At some level, it seemed to him, such debates sounded suspiciously like an evasion, a way to escape accountability. Maybe psychiatry was a softer science than oncology, but shouldn't it be subjected to similar rigorous standards? How else would patients be protected from the latest fad or dogmatic adherence to untested ideology?

Common sense told him that Dr. Bean-Bayog's treatment was a syllabus of errors. He needed a psychiatrist to put on the stand who talked sense, not psychobabble. Paul McHugh made sense.

The Johns Hopkins psychiatrist had learned good sense as a boy from his father, a high school teacher in the mill city of Lowell, Massachusetts. At age sixty-one, Paul McHugh still ranked his father as the smartest man he had ever met, not so much because of his knowledge of American history or his command of a classroom but because of his intuitive good sense about his fellow human beings.

Paul's father, Francis P. McHugh, applied those instincts in dealing with his eleven-year-old son, a good boy and smart enough but inclined, maybe, to work only as hard as was necessary. He took young Paul for a drive one afternoon in 1943, and walked him around the bucolic grounds of Phillips Academy, Andover.

"What do you think of this school?" he asked his son.

"Oh, it's a fabulous place," Paul replied.

"Too bad you have to be so smart to get in here. You'd never make it," his father told him.

"I think I could get in," snapped Paul, rising to the bait.

Paul did get in, although he hung on by his fingernails that first year, all the time feeling isolated and insecure as an Irish day student among all those well-heeled boarders. But he stuck it out, every year managing to do better than the year before.

"That was my Paul Lozano experience. It was awful, but it was great. It made me," says Dr. McHugh, a handsome man, his impish face crowned by a mass of hair as white as the lab coat he wears to emphasize psychiatry's connection to medicine.

Andover prepared him for Harvard, where his experience as a freshman composition student might well have set him on his antianalytic course in psychiatry. English Composition was required of all entering students in order to ensure proficiency in writing. Paul McHugh loved the nuts-and-bolts nature of that class, grammar and word order and the vigor of the active voice. So he was taken aback one day when the poet John Ciardi, an academic known for his translations of Dante, came to class as a visiting lecturer.

Ciardi took for the day's text Sigmund Freud's monograph on Leonardo da Vinci. The professor recounted a recurring dream that the Renaissance painter, inventor, and scholar had had. "It's all about this big bird that landed in his cradle and hit him around the face," Dr. McHugh recalled. " 'That explains everything,' this guy tells us. 'It's his homosexuality he's hiding from in the dream.' It's coming out in the symbol, all that long tail stuff, see?"

"I listen to this. I'm seventeen. I say to myself, It's a lousy idea. I read some book about Leonardo when I was in high school that I had liked so I said, 'Excuse me, but that's a lousy idea.' He says to me, 'You must have some sexual hang-ups.' Now, that makes me mad because presumably I did have some sexual hang-ups, but it's neither here nor there. We're talking about da Vinci and metaphors. Oh boy, he got so mad! I try to talk to him about metaphor, and he is trying to tell me about the secrets of human sexuality. I go away wondering to myself, Why is it that this guy wants to give such a shabby argument? It would be one thing if he had said, Look, here's a metaphor. Maybe it's right, maybe it's wrong. Maybe it's illuminating, maybe it isn't. Instead, he insists he has a lock on truth and he spoils this class for me."

Paul McHugh left Boston after Harvard Medical School and postgraduate training in psychiatry for much the same reason. The town was too dominated by analysts. He wanted to be at a place where science and evidence mattered more than ideological allegiance.

Dr. McHugh found that place at the Johns Hopkins University School of Medicine. For the past eighteen years he has presided over a staff of analysts as well as biopsychiatrists as chairman of the Department of Psychiatry. Different perspectives on the human condition define those in the department, but a commitment to empiricism unites them. "Hopkins is a grand place," he said, his enthusiasm ironically mirroring that of the late Dr. William Bennett Bean, who had been the Sir William Osler Professor of Medicine at the University of Iowa. Osler had been at the Johns Hopkins medical school at the turn of the century and is still revered as one of the heroes of American medical education.

"You know, terrible things happen to human beings," Dr. McHugh reflected one autumn afternoon in his small, neat office on the Johns Hopkins campus. "We are shipped to concentration camps. We are born poverty stricken. We lose our father and mother in a disaster. And still some of us make it. Not only survive. Triumph. We triumph because we are free. Unless we are ill. And if we are ill, it is up to our counselors to help us to see the real story in ourselves—not the Marxist story, not the psychoanalytic story, not the feminist story—our story, your story, my story, and how it has come to an impasse, demoralized us, and how we can get back on course. The victim story helps no one."

It was a generic, and unsubstantiated, victim story that Dr. McHugh read in Dr. Bean-Bayog's records of Paul Lozano. A story written by the doctor, not the patient, a story that distracted Paul Lozano from identifying and coping with his real troubles.

The only thing Dr. McHugh and Dr. Bean-Bayog agreed on about Paul Lozano was that he had a major depression. "Paul Lozano was a tough case. No question. Tough case. He had a very serious depressive disorder. You know, when he called Barry Gault from El Paso he was a little manicky. That's a mixed state. And they are tricky cases. You've got to be right on top of it. But not impossible. We take care of them all the time. I mean, this is Harvard Medical School psychiatry. For God's sake, they are supposed to take care of tough cases!"

The problem, as Dr. McHugh saw it, was that the psychiatrist failed first to evaluate her patient properly and to monitor his underlying illness before plunging into a course of intensive psychotherapy against the advice of her colleagues at McLean Hospital. Maybe Paul Lozano did have a personality disorder, but if he did, it was secondary to his depression. "She blew it because she didn't do the basics. What it comes down to is just a continuing absence of common sense, shown in every aspect of this case, in the commitment to first impressions and in the rashness with intimacy," he said.

You don't go to a dermatologist and have him say, "Well, we're going to take your face off because of this little basal cell cancer you've got." If he does, you say, "Well, wait a minute. I know it's funny, but it's the only face I've got. Where is the evidence that this radical thing has to be done to me?" And he'd tell you, "This is what a basal cell cancer is. This is how you treat it. Here is the evidence. If you want, we'll get a second opinion. Have a little conference." You'd listen. You'd be on the same footing with the guy. But not in psychiatry! You go to a psychiatrist and say, "Listen, I'm feeling depressed," and he says, "Tell me everything about your mother." The patient ought to ask, "How is this helping me with the depression? What do you know about depression? Are all depressions the same? Are there differences in therapy? By the way, have we gotten into therapy yet, or are we just talking about diagnosis?" All of those things, they don't happen in psychiatry. You put yourself in the psychiatrist's hands and assume he just knows the truth. It's nonsense. And it's dangerous.

When Paul Lozano turned up in her consulting room full of doubt and depression, pessimism and self-hatred, Dr. McHugh says, Dr. Bean-Bayog should have tried to determine whether his condition was provoked by his circumstances—Harvard Medical School being a very stressful place—or whether it rested on a constitutional tendency toward the illness. "The major problem in the therapy was that instead of addressing his depression directly and teaching him about it, she produced this evocative, emotionally charged therapy that was tied to a fundamentally vile accusation about the people he came from," said Dr. McHugh, noting that neither sexual abuse nor a familial tendency toward depression was ever confirmed through consultation with the family. "If one of my residents failed to do the basic fact-checking that she failed to do, I'd rap his knuckles."

Dr. McHugh was certain after reading the 986 pages of office notes that Dr. Bean-Bayog had suggested the sexual abuse notion to a susceptible, dependent patient and reinforced it with the books she gave him to read and the frequency with which she saw him. She might well have believed her theory, but her work with Paul Lozano focused on selling it, rather than confirming it.

"It makes me irritated that she is prepared to talk about her expertness in psychotherapy and yet what you see here is a serious psychotherapeutic mistake—promoting a resistance to discussing the real issues of this boy by distracting him. The distraction about his mother. And the distraction of the erotic atmosphere that Margaret Bean-Bayog produced every time that kid walked in the office, permitting this sex talk to run on and on, while she's licking her lips and posing for pictures," he said.

Arguing that she was not sexually attracted to her patient but felt aroused only in her countertransference role is just double-talk, he said.

"This stuff about 'it wasn't me in the real sense. It was me in the countertransference sense' is garbage. Pure garbage! The problem in discussing these terms is that they are moving targets. They can always say, 'Oh, you don't really understand.' But that's an emperor's new clothes approach. Fundamentally, transference emotions are our emotions. They just happen to have been generated in a therapeutic situation. You don't have to be a rocket scientist to understand this stuff. To say that she wrote down fantasies that would make Caligula blush as a way of learning more about them, that's a new one to me!"

Similarly, to argue that Dr. Bean-Bayog's unorthodox methods grew out of her desperation to save an untreatable patient implies that she had no resources to draw on to help her. "She was in Boston! At Harvard! If she did not know what to do, why didn't she ask someone honestly for some guidance, not for self-justification, but for real guidance?"

Whether Paul Lozano was a borderline or a manic-depressive, he was certainly suffering from a major depression. "You'd find psychiatrists who'd say that regression would be legitimate for some patients. But I don't think you'll find any psychiatrist who'll say it is legitimate for a delusional depressive, which Paul certainly was. His depression caused him to take on a self-blaming, guilt-ridden view of himself and the world. He needed someone to help him see the distortion in that view, to help him see himself as competent and accomplished, not dependent."

If she was determined to risk regressive techniques, in Dr. McHugh's view, Dr. Bean-Bayog should have consulted her colleagues and conducted her therapy in a controlled setting, with care taken to ensure there was no misunderstanding: this is role-playing and ends at the close of the fifty-minute hour.

Paul Lozano had real problems, "probably simpler problems: issues of advancing himself, separating himself. Common enough. It's called life. But if you throw in an illness like depression on top, it can be terrible," said Dr. McHugh, who expressed no patience for Dr. Gutheil's insistence that the objective truth about sexual abuse allegations is less important than a trusting relationship with a patient.

"I never heard anything so crazy in my life. If someone said to you, as a psychiatrist, 'I was lacerated by my father,' you'd say, 'Where? Show me the wound.' If a patient says, 'You can't talk to my family,' you'd say, 'That puts an obstacle in our way because I want to know the kind of person you were and I also want to have an alliance with someone who can help me.'

"I believe in confidentiality, but if a case was the toughest I ever handled, as Dr. Bean says Paul was, I'd tell him we need to keep you alive. Refusing to speak to the family on principle is just an old psychoanalytic idea. Dead as a doornail. It's just not psychiatry in the contemporary era."

It was the adherence to shopworn notions combined with the concoction of her own bizarre reparenting techniques, Dr. McHugh suspects, that prevented Dr. Bean-Bayog from heeding the early warnings of her colleagues at McLean Hospital.

Psychoanalysis is a therapy. It's a not a mode of diagnosis. Margaret Bean is a psychiatrist and should know that her first responsibility was to do a full and adequate evaluation of this patient, to lay out a treatment plan with all the alternatives that would relate to the different diagnoses that she had formed. She didn't do any of that.

When she decided on psychotherapy as the program of choice, she should have told him what was appropriate and what was going to be inappropriate in their relationship, what psychotherapy really was, and how he and she would behave together.

Once she had decided that this was a patient who had major depression and asked a psychopharmacologist to manage the medicine, she should have explained to Skip Pope what else she was going to do and get his input. She didn't do that. In the process of laying out that treatment plan, she should have put time limits on how long she was going to continue. If the person was still jumping off of bridges, she should have called together her consultants to reconsider her plan.

To pass off conversations with her personal analyst in her own therapy sessions as a consultation "just won't stand up to honest scrutiny from straightforward people," continued Dr. McHugh. A letter from her consultant, Dr. Gutheil, in 1990 about Paul Lozano's suicide risk is a perfect example of the pitfalls of analytic thinking.

"Mr. Lozano was able to identify, in relation to his

injecting himself with toxins and various risky drugs, an element of thrill seeking and a kind of 'rush' of excitement similar to that he experienced when he was skydiving," Dr. Gutheil wrote. "Through our conversation he and I were able to relate this to masturbatory excitement in which one retains and maintains control of one's own pleasure, thrill and sexual excitement: control over life and death (related to his equally thrilling experience of saving a new mother from death on his obstetrical rotation) and freedom in the sense of having his own life in his hands and no one being able to stand between him and taking it."

The letter astounded Dr. McHugh. "Paul held his life in his hands and his penis in his hands. Get it? A fellow looks suicidal, and Tom Gutheil produces a masturbatory metaphor for him! Does that tell you about Paul Lozano? No, it tells you about Tom Gutheil. If you go to them, they'll shape you according to their metaphors. They have a language and thought process that keeps them from seeing the obvious: Paul Lozano is dead. Nothing is real to them, not even death itself. Death is not a metaphor. Death is real."

For Dr. McHugh, the errors in treatment were only compounded by Dr. Bean-Bayog's refusal to be accountable for a therapy gone terribly wrong. "She should have sat down with the doctors who were picking this patient up—some of them called her for help, for goodness' sake—and explained what she had done. She should have come clean about it all, explained why she was transmitting his care and how things had run off the track. She did none of those things. And that is indefensible."

In public, Dr. Bean-Bayog's attorneys insisted that she would fight Dr. McHugh's interpretation of this case and win. In his first encounter with Michael Blau, Jack Fabiano was told "this case will never settle. She won't give up." But privately, the doctor and her family were wearing down. The insurance company would bear the cost of the civil trial, but preparing her defense before the medical board had already cost her well over $100,000, the hearings were still weeks away, and the meter kept running at McDermott, Will & Emery.

Public hearings were a gamble. They would drag on for weeks—on national television—and after the cameras were gone, it could be years before a decision was rendered, years when the ghost of Paul Lozano would be hanging over Dr. Bean-Bayog's practice. Since the medical board had been stripped of its power to conduct its own disciplinary hearings, the Division of Administrative Law Appeals would hear the case and refer it back to the medical board with a recommendation for resolution.

Speed was not a hallmark of the division, which held more than one thousand hearings a year on issues ranging from construction contract disputes to civil service jobs. Medical board cases were supposed to receive priority treatment, but in the first two years of division oversight, the backlogged agency returned only five of twenty-five cases to the medical board for final action.

The unflagging interest of the supermarket scandal sheets and tabloid television programs in the "Kinky Shrink" story was taking a toll. Dr. Bean-Bayog brought a new attorney, Michael Mone, into the case to negotiate a settlement and to resolve a dispute with McDermott, Will & Emery about her legal bills. Mone was well respected in Boston legal circles— six months later he would be named president of the Massachusetts Bar Association. Mone had enough experience as a plaintiff's attorney in malpractice suits to assess Dr. Bean-Bayog's prospects for a more private resolution of the case. In a roomful of defense and prosecution lawyers itching to go to trial, Michael Mone's goal was to wrap up the civil action and disciplinary proceedings at once.

Mone called Fabiano on July 28 to say that Dr. Bean-Bayog could not afford, emotionally or financially, to go forward. What were the prospects for a settlement? When the call came, Fabiano was meeting with Dr. McHugh in his office, getting an education in the fundamentals of psychotherapy. Fabiano made clear to Mone that he would require an admission on the psychiatrist's part of errors made and of boundaries crossed. They could debate the specifics, but she would have to be held accountable.

Mone asked Fabiano to draft a settlement. That night,

when all the other lights flickered out on the twenty-sixth floor of 60 State Street, those in Fabiano's office continued to burn. He spread out the flash cards, the sexual fantasies, the photographs, and the depositions from the civil case on a long conference table. He sat on the carpet, surrounded by even more material, and he drafted an outline of a settlement. It took hours.

"Our notion was that everything that went in there, every fact that we put into the brief, would be what we thought we could prove," Fabiano remembered, noting that a sexual relationship between psychiatrist and patient was not one of them. There was not enough evidence to prove that Margaret Bean-Bayog had had sex with Paul Lozano. It would be her word against his, and Paul was dead.

But there was no question in Fabiano's mind that she was responsible for the erotic atmosphere that permeated their therapy sessions, and that somewhere along the way she had lost control of the relationship. "We would try to make it factual. Not to humiliate her or force her to admit things just for the sake of demeaning her," said Fabiano. "Our goal was to be fair. He was harmed by her care. I wanted to say that."

When the draft was completed, Fabiano sent it to Dr. McHugh and to the prosecutorial staff at the medical board. It called for a suspension that would have allowed Dr. Bean-Bayog to resume her practice in as little as a year, but it also required her to admit that she had lost control of her treatment of Paul Lozano and never regained it. "They said, 'Oh, it's wonderful. It's terrific. She'll never sign,'" Fabiano recalled.

They were right. Any suggestion of impropriety or misjudgment or deviation from psychiatric standards was unacceptable to Dr. Bean-Bayog. The public needed to understand that she was the victim in this case, of an insane and vindictive patient, of a politically motivated medical board, of an unsophisticated and hostile press, of a greedy, dysfunctional family. She would take no responsibility for mistakes she did not make.

Dr. Bean-Bayog rejected the first proposal, counter-offering a suspension, to be immediately lifted so that she could continue to see her twenty private patients, and no admission of wrongdoing. Dr. McHugh pronounced the proposal "nauseating," and Fabiano began packing psychiatry texts along with his blue jeans for his family's vacation in Wyoming. If that was the defense team's idea of compromise, this case was going to trial.

Fabiano met with Michael Blau a few days before leaving for vacation on August 14. "This is not like an auto insurance case," Fabiano told him. "I'm not going to say twenty thousand dollars and you say ten thousand dollars and we settle at fifteen thousand dollars. I'm saying twenty thousand dollars and that's what it's going to be. If you want to change the payment schedule, that's one thing. But I'm not going to move off what I think has to be done."

Dr. Bean-Bayog was equally inflexible. She had three colleagues—Dr. Gutheil and Dr. Robert J. Waldinger and Dr. John T. Maltsberger of Harvard Medical School—willing to testify that she had conformed to accepted psychiatric standards. Why should she submit to the prosecution's view of the case? An oddly arrogant position, Fabiano thought, given that she was the party seeking the settlement.

Back from Wyoming, having written his opening remarks, Fabiano met with Blau to discuss one of Dr. Bean-Bayog's strongest objections to the settlement statement: the suggestion that she knew Paul Lozano had copies of her sexual fantasies. "She was sticking to her story of the burglary—a story I find absolutely incredible," Fabiano recalled. "Her lawyers wanted to change the wording from 'Dr. Bean-Bayog knew he had them' to 'knew or should have surmised.' That was fine with me as long as she knew she would be held responsible."

Negotiations continued in that vein—paragraph by paragraph, word choice by word choice—for the next two weeks. But in the end, each side's intransigence precluded a settlement. Dr. Bean-Bayog could accept the proposed one-year suspension, Blau said, "but the parts of it that were particularly upsetting and unacceptable to Dr. Bean-Bayog were that the board wanted her to essentially acknowledge Paul McHugh's theories of the case. And not acknowledge at all the well-intentioned care in her attempt to save this person and to keep him from committing suicide over the four years. She could not bring herself to speak those mistruths. And she felt now that she had a choice: either to sign what she felt was a perjurious settlement agreement or to face a witch trial. Neither of those prospects was one that she wanted to face."

She decided to resign, knowing that to do so in the midst of a disciplinary proceeding would mean she could never practice medicine anywhere in the United States again. The maximum penalty the medical board could have imposed was a revocation of her license, with the right to petition for reinstatement after five years. "Once she made that decision, it fell to us to try to put the best face on. That's all that we could do. We were quite fearful that public reaction to her resignation would be—'Huh, must be guilty,'" said Blau. "And what we decided was best to do was that if there was to be a resignation that one way or another, she had to get her story out."

So, Blau set to work to find a way to circumvent the medical board's rules requiring either a hearing or an unconditional, irrevocable resignation. Could she submit her version of events to the board for its evaluation without a hearing? A violation of regulations. Could she sign a suspension agreement but attach her experts' opinion that she had done nothing wrong? Agree to the facts and then disown them, in other words.

"I had the great pleasure or privilege on my birthday, September 11, of sitting with her and drafting a resignation letter, and then over that weekend putting together an evidentiary submission which was ninety-five pages with a whole bunch of attachments which set forth her entire defense. We gave the board a choice. We said, 'Please either accept Dr. Bean-Bayog's resignation or make a decision on the record of this case that you feel is just. Do justice or accept the resignation.'"

Fabiano was furious at the tactics. Dr. Bean-Bayog was

not resigning; she was trying to cut a deal. "Look," he told Blau, "if you resign, I can't do anything about it, that's your right. But you'll resign in accordance with what the rules require. It's certainly not going to be plea-bargained because I'm not going to give you anything. I will give you the agreed statement. If she resigns it's forever. The board has to meet to accept the resignation. And if it's anything other than unconditional, then we bag it. If there is a dispute about what the facts are here, that's what trials are for: to establish the truth."

Defeated, Dr. Bean-Bayog's attorneys went back to the medical board on the afternoon of September 18. "We said, 'She meant what she said, and she said what she meant, she resigns her license one hundred percent,'" Blau remembered. "We gave the license back to the board at that time. The board accepted it. And she resigned."

It was not the resolution that anyone expected, but perhaps it should have been. In the end, the same professional arrogance that had prohibited her from reaching out for help in treating Paul Lozano kept Margaret Bean-Bayog from admitting that she had failed her patient.

"She could have faced what happened and taken her sanctions. They weren't draconian," said Dr. McHugh.

> Our profession is built on the idea that if you make a mistake, you acknowledge it, because we are all human and we all make mistakes. I'm a doctor and you can approach me like you can approach any doctor. If I have a diagnosis I should be prepared to defend it. I should be able to tell you where you can look it up. I should be able to tell you the likelihood of the treatment's success.
>
> I don't know the secret of human nature. Nobody knows the secret of human nature. I'm just a doctor. I use empirical approaches to see what seems to help. I try to use observation and experience and experiments to develop my ideas. I'm very willing to share them with you. I'm very willing to have you tell me that I'm full of baloney

and to hear why you think so. And why? Because you're the person who gives me my license to practice medicine. That's why.

Margaret Bean-Bayog should have been willing either to agree that she did something wrong or to appear before the representatives of the people of Massachusetts and explain what she did and take criticism. Instead, she gave up being a doctor and, frankly, that's appropriate. If you think it's not fair to have to explain everything about your practice and make your practice fully public, then you don't belong being a doctor.

In her letter to Dr. Dinesh Patel, the chairman of the medical board, Dr. Margaret Bean-Bayog surrendered her medical license without apologies, her indignation and her perception of herself as a heroic psychiatrist who had been victimized by a vindictive patient and his abusive, financially motivated family as secure as the bronze marker on Paul Lozano's grave:

Dear Dr. Patel:

As of today I am resigning my license to practice medicine in the Commonwealth of Massachusetts. I understand that this resignation is irrevocable, permanent, and nationwide—that is, by resigning I can henceforth never again practice medicine. This is an unspeakable loss for me and, I believe, a loss for my patients and the community at large.

I have been driven to this extreme because it is far more important that my family and patients be spared the trauma of another public assault on me than it is that I receive justice and pursue my career. To avoid this assault, I realize that I am electing an outcome that is far more severe than would ever have been imposed on me through a hearing process.

The damage inflicted by the media repetition of the false allegations against me, while the Lozano family refused to waive its psychotherapist/patient privilege and permit me to reply, was mammoth. I refuse to now subject myself to a legal but destructive hearing organized with a degree of media intrusiveness and exploitation which no other physician in the Commonwealth of Massachusetts has ever had to endure. This process is entirely out of proportion to the legitimate issues in this case.

My family, my patients and I have already suffered through an undeserved and unimaginable ordeal, and I will endure no more. I refuse to endure any further false allegations from Paul Lozano or his family; I refuse to endure any further denial of the severity of Paul Lozano's mental illness and suicidality, or the effectiveness of my treatment in keeping him alive; I refuse to endure any further gross distortions purveyed by the Lozano family's unscrupulous malpractice attorney; I refuse to endure any further the segment of the news media that reports before it investigates; I refuse to endure, at my expense, any further pandering to the public appetite for preposterous, salacious scandal; I refuse to endure any further the Secretary of Consumer Affairs' immense overreaction to the groundswell of misinformed opinion in this case; I refuse to endure any further the unprecedented procedures, employed in this case for purely political purposes (e.g., summary suspension hearings conducted without prior notice, unrealistically expedited proceedings, appointment of a Special Prosecutor, and trial in a six-hundred-seat auditorium to accommodate the press and gavel-to-gavel national television coverage); I refuse to endure any further the prejudice against "Harvard-educated", "women", "psychiatrists"; I refuse to endure any further the burden of overcoming common fears and misconceptions about the practice of psychiatry; I refuse to endure any further being condemned by certain "experts" who pursue doctrinaire goals by criticizing competing but respected schools of thought; I refuse to endure any further being used as a source of precedent to sort out the diversity of standards and approaches in my profession; and I respectfully decline to serve any further as a lightning rod for all of these converging forces.

I am not resigning because I fear the potential outcome of this hearing process. It is the process itself, which has already taken a heavy toll on me and my family, and not any potential verdict, that I find daunting.

In July, I was prepared to appear at the hearing with a clear conscience and considerable serenity of spirit. And, I remain confident that if this case went to hearing I would be largely if not wholly vindicated. Top psychiatric experts have thoroughly reviewed this case and are prepared to testify that my treatment of Paul Lozano was, in all respects, within applicable standards of care. My attorneys, who have strenuously advised me not to resign, are prepared to expose the mistaken assumptions on which the prosecution's case is based, as well as the lies about my conduct which thrust this case into the public spotlight.

I emphatically deny that I engaged in any form of sexual misconduct with Paul Lozano.

What has changed since July is not my innocence, which remains, but the way this particular case is being conducted by the state. It has changed from having some semblance of fairness into a media circus.

After it was announced that the hearings would receive national television coverage, I attempted to avoid this horrible hearing process by exploring the possibility of settlement. I was offered a suspension that could be stayed after one year. But the settlement included a statement of facts and conclusions that were so outrageously false that I could not agree to them without perjuring myself. It required me to confess to conduct I did not commit and profess beliefs which neither I nor a respected segment of the psychiatric community hold to be true.

The Special Prosecutor refused to provide any reasonable alternative to an appalling hearing process. He made my integrity the price of avoiding it. I cannot relinquish that. With that settlement option foreclosed, I am forced to take the drastic step of resigning.

I am saddened to be left with no other choice. I have been able to channel all of my own life experiences into an identity as a healer. I can't imagine life without my career as a physician. It is in my bone marrow, my ancestry, and all my dreams. I loved it so.

What did I love? Caring for patients. Healing people. Making them feel better. Watching them grow. Knowing a great deal. Being skilled. Teaching. Helping develop students. Inspiring people. Making them believe in themselves. Sharing my love of my work. It was wonderfully fulfilling.

I have been very lucky. I have been fortunate enough to have done more in my truncated career than most people do in a lifetime. I have had superb teachers. I have helped some of the sickest patients. I have taught some of the best students.

I helped change the way doctors think about alcoholism. I helped nurture and develop ASAM, the American Society for Addiction Medicine, while it became a catalyst for change and a source of identity, pride and learning for doctors who work with addicted people.

I got to share people's lives. Patients took me with them into experiences they had not been able to bear alone, and we narrated our way through them to understanding and meaning. I helped people, who were determined to kill themselves, find ways to want to remain alive. And I helped a lot of people get sober, including, at last count, eighteen medical students and several dozen physicians.

But no matter how much I love the privilege and commitment to practice medicine, it is not worth the excessive price I am being asked to pay. I choose to relinquish my license before I permit any further threat and damage to my family and patients, and my personal welfare. The price is higher than the awful price of giving up my profession.

I have a story to tell, a powerful story. I believe what I did was a good faith effort to do what was right and was life saving not only for the patient who has falsely accused me, but also for the other physicians this patient intended to harm. But this story cannot receive a fair hearing in this venue. And no one should be subjected to the assault which has been prepared for me.

I know that the Board did not intend this runaway process, and will be appalled at this outcome. I believe that we have all been entrapped by the same political forces.

The only wonderful thing in this whole debacle is that I have found out how many people love me without having to wait for my own funeral, although this feels like one. I want to thank all the people who have loved and supported and written and prayed for me: my husband and children, friends and colleagues, patients and strangers. I ask you to continue to keep me in your prayers.

Sincerely,
Margaret Bean-Bayog, M.D.

Epilogue

Boston was digging out from an early blizzard a week before Christmas when members of the Lozano family arrived to wrap up their business with Andrew C. Meyer, Jr. The lawyer had called Pilar only days before with news that Dr. Margaret Bean-Bayog's insurance carrier had agreed to settle their malpractice claim against the psychiatrist for $1 million, her policy's maximum coverage.

It was over. Nine months after Meyer's three-thousand-page court filing brought a Harvard psychiatrist and a Mexican-American medical student to the center of a national debate about sexual misconduct and standards of psychiatric practice, the case had come to a quiet resolution in conference calls between lawyers.

Dr. Bean-Bayog remained secluded when the lawyers announced the settlement. Michael Mone, one of her attorneys, said only that "Dr. Bean-Bayog concurred in the decision to settle the case. This matter has been very stressful to Dr. Bean-Bayog and her family, and she is relieved that it's over." Soon afterward, she hosted a party for the people she called the "heroes and survivors" of the case, lawyers and psychiatrists, friends and students who had supported her throughout.

On Wednesday afternoons, she still ran training sessions at her home for the loyal group of junior therapists who wanted to fashion themselves in Margaret Bean-Bayog's professional image.

"It was a relief to get back to work," said Kathryn Kogan, a clinical psychologist who counted herself lucky still to have access to her mentor. "I think what is really the worst about this is we have destroyed and lost our shining light. I can't even begin to tell you how tragic that is. You know what it is like—this may sound really overly dramatic—the feelings that I have about this are really like the feelings I had about Kennedy being shot. It's sort of similar in a way. There is something in our culture where we destroy our best. To me this is in the same vein. She's not replaceable. And it's very, very sad."

Margaret Bean-Bayog paid a heavy price with the loss of her medical license. But she managed to thwart the Lozanos' primary goal: to prevent her from ever counseling patients again. True, she can no longer prescribe medication or hold herself out as a physician, but she can still practice psychotherapy. There is no law prohibiting the practice of psychotherapy by anyone who chooses to hang out a shingle anywhere in the United States.

Margaret Bean-Bayog has continued to counsel many of the same patients she treated before the Paul Lozano case claimed her medical license. In doing so, she is only following common practice. To the chagrin of the medical board and the fury of his victims, Sheldon D. Zigelbaum, the psychiatrist whose license finally was revoked in 1992 for sexually abusing five women, continues to see patients, as have at least three other Massachusetts psychiatrists recently found guilty of sexual misconduct.

"All we can do is take her license. After that, she is beyond our reach," said Dr. Alexander F. Fleming, acknowledging that the unregulated practice of psychotherapy creates "a big loophole in the system. As long as she does not call herself a doctor, Margaret Bean-Bayog is free to establish a thriving psychotherapy practice, and there is nothing anyone can do to stop her."

No states have regulations to bar such a blatant subversion of the disciplinary process. Efforts to regulate unlicensed psychotherapists have failed across the country after running into strong opposition from patients and practitioners of the hundreds of forms of therapy in the United States. Some states exercise a modicum of control by authorizing the attorney general to issue injunctions barring therapists from counseling patients after a license is revoked or surrendered. Others have made it a crime for psychotherapists to have sex with their patients, giving judges the discretion to include a prohibition on future practice as part of sentencing. Economics dissuades some from unlicensed practice, since insurance companies reimburse only those services rendered by licensed counselors.

In 1992, Colorado became the first state to create a board to oversee unlicensed therapists. One of eight states that have also criminalized sexual activity between doctors and patients, Colorado requires unlicensed therapists to register with a statewide data bank. The state tracks complaints and can remove an errant therapist from the rolls, an admittedly mild sanction, said Bruce M. Douglas, director of the program, but "it's a beginning."

As for Margaret Bean-Bayog, with her license surrendered, her academic appointments rescinded, and her psychotherapy practice reduced to a small number of patients, the resolution of the Paul Lozano case left the former Harvard psychiatrist with time on her hands. Time for her new baby.

In the midst of the acrimonious public debate about the role of her therapeutic infantilization in the death of a promising young medical student, fifty-year-old Margaret Bean-Bayog had quietly adopted the son she always wanted—a Hispanic baby boy.

Absent a trial, the issues raised by Margaret Bean-Bayog's management of Paul Lozano's psychiatric care—the personal intimacy, the self-serving use of consultants, the adoption of untested therapeutic techniques, the unsubstantiated diagnosis of sexual abuse, the isolation of the patient's family—were fodder for dinner-party conversation in Boston but not for Harvard colloquiums.

Dr. Edward M. Hundert, a psychiatrist and Associate Dean for Student Affairs at Harvard Medical School, held an open forum for students to place them at ease while the case dominated the headlines. But no formal review of the case ever occurred at Harvard.

Dr. Carol Birnbaum, who had met Paul Lozano in a clinical capacity in 1990 after Dr. Bean-Bayog had ended their relationship, expressed her personal frustration that his death was never openly addressed. Several months after he was buried, Dr. Birnbaum, a resident in psychiatry at Massachusetts General Hospital, learned of Paul's suicide from a colleague.

After hearing that Paul Lozano had died, Dr. Birnbaum approached her supervisor at the Harvard-affiliated hospital. "I remember asking him whether there would be any discussion within the department, the people who had contact with him," she recalled. "When something like that happens, it has an impact on trainees. One thing that had disturbed me about it was that I had found out about it sort of through the grapevine like that, and I didn't know any of the facts, anything about what really had happened. I was hoping that because it had an impact on me, that we could sit down at one point and talk about what was known, rather than learning it through the media."

That meeting never occurred. Instead, Dr. Birnbaum was left to sift through gossip, hearing from Dr. Gerald Adler, Margaret Bean-Bayog's therapist, that her work with Paul Lozano was "courageous" and from Dr. José Saporta, Paul's later psychotherapist, that "he couldn't be sure, but he wondered" whether Dr. Bean-Bayog had had sex with Paul Lozano.

For Amy Stromsten, the social worker and onetime member of that supervision group who turned on Dr. Bean-Bayog after Paul Lozano told her that he and his psychiatrist had had a sexual relationship, there was no question where the sympathy of the establishment lay. In rallying around Margaret Bean-Bayog, the profession had closed Amy Stromsten out. She no longer got the referrals from Harvard that were once the mainstay of her practice. Suggestions from psychiatrists in the media that she had violated patient confidentiality by revealing Paul's confession about the alleged sexual misconduct triggered an investigation by the licensing board for social workers. She was cleared, but the suggestion of unprofessional behavior clung to her. "It was the price of speaking out," she said.

Dr. Joseph T. Coyle, a psychiatry professor at the Johns Hopkins University School of Medicine, was named chairman of the Consolidated Department of Psychiatry at Harvard Medical School after Paul's death in 1991. The word *consolidated* only hints at how factionalized Harvard psychiatry was before his arrival.

Unlike other medical schools, which are usually attached to a main teaching hospital, Harvard's is linked to myriad Harvard-affiliated institutions, all of them with different, often competing, philosophical approaches toward psychiatry. Dr. Coyle was charged with bringing order out of chaos.

The Paul Lozano case "is a signal of problems" at Harvard and in psychiatry, Dr. Coyle said after the settlement. "My major reservation about the treatment was the dichotomy between his psychological treatment and his medical treatment. You cannot deal with one unless you deal effectively with the other.

"I'm empirically driven. Show me. There are a lot of things that we can't show in psychiatry. But there are an awful lot of things that we can show in psychiatry that are proven by scientific method. That's the future. It isn't about ideology; it's about proof."

But a demand for proof will be the death knell of traditional psychoanalysis, predicted Dr. Paul McHugh, the prosecution's expert witness.

> It's all over. They'll crumble. The public is not stupid. It will say to them: You only tell one story, and maybe that story wasn't right for Paul. Maybe

it isn't right for me. Maybe it isn't right for anybody. Maybe you're just telling your story and making your story run for everybody. Maybe there are a million stories out there more appropriate.

Psychiatry tries to understand the story of a person's individual life. But we need to realize that there are other things besides the life story that will shed light on mental disturbance. This case wasn't about biological versus dynamic psychiatry. The issue with Paul Lozano was how to use both dynamic and biological measures to treat him. Both had a role to play. The problem was the lack of commitment to empiricism.

We must have standards because that's the way we're going to get better. We're going to find out; we're going to go see; we're going to do a home visit. I don't care whether my residents come out saying, "I see a dynamic issue with the family" just so long as they are telling the right story. Not their imagined story, but a story that can stand the test of empiricism.

If there is no dominant scholarship, if there is no power of science, then there is no clout in the field to protect the public from anyone who comes along and says, "I put my hand on the rock and I really see the truth now." If that "truth" fits into some other idea in the culture, it takes off like crazy, and there is no force to say, "Thou shalt not do this until you prove it."

Even Dr. Bean-Bayog's defenders said the case will have been instructive if it leads to "more unambiguous standards of practice in psychiatry," in the words of her attorney, Michael Blau.

Under the auspices of the medical board, a committee of psychiatrists began meeting after Dr. Bean-Bayog's resignation to draft guidelines for the proper limits between patients and therapists. The panel did its work in secret, its very existence opposed by many psychiatrists who complained that formal standards would squelch innovation.

But Dr. Paul Applebaum, the committee chairman and president of the Massachusetts Psychiatric Association, said the Lozano case "pointed out the degree of confusion that exists in the profession. I don't presume to know what really happened between Paul Lozano and Margaret Bean-Bayog, but the subject of appropriate boundaries between patient and doctor has not been taught in a very standardized way, and that may have allowed people to go off in very idiosyncratic directions."

The impetus for change can easily be derailed, however. Within weeks of settlement of the case, legislation was filed to allow therapists to withhold medical records from patients if the therapist concluded access would "adversely affect the patient's well-being." Patients' rights groups said the effect of the measure would be to protect incompetent or errant therapists. At the same time, the Massachusetts Medical Society proposed a bill to prohibit the medical board from disciplining doctors for actions that are more than six years old, a move critics said would ensure that the panel remained one of the weakest in the nation.

The Massachusetts Medical Society, the Boston Psychoanalytic Society and Institute, and the American Society of Addiction Medicine steadfastly stood by Dr. Bean-Bayog, refusing to drop her from their rolls until she resigned her medical license. Even then, her partisans carried her banner into their meeting rooms and convention halls.

Dr. John T. Maltsberger, a Boston psychoanalyst, was to have been one of Dr. Bean-Bayog's expert witnesses at the trial she chose to forgo. He presented her case, instead, on April 15, 1993, in San Francisco in an address before the American Association of Suicidology, of which he was then president.

In a spirited 19-page defense of his colleague, Dr. Maltsberger declared that Dr. Bean-Bayog had been "brutalized without justification" and laid out her patient from hell theory to explain her decision to surrender her license.

"She had already taken an emotional beating from Paul Lozano and suffered the expectable pain of losing a patient to suicide. She was being assaulted by the press. Now she faced the prospect of public humiliation as Paul Lozano reached from the grave to fulfill his promise—that he would kill himself and ruin her career and reputation."

What happened to Margaret Bean-Bayog, he told his sympathetic colleagues, was no less a travesty of justice than the treatment of the Scottsboro Five and Captain Alfred Dreyfus.

The Boston Psychoanalytic Society and Institute was so taken with the speech, titled "A Career Plundered," that Dr. Ralph P. Engle, a former president, and Dr. Dan H. Buie, who served as one of Dr. Bean-Bayog's "consultants" on the Paul Lozano case, circulated it to every member.

In February 1994, Dr. Maltsberger gave his speech again, this time to a receptive audience at a conference sponsored by Harvard Medical School.

For the family of Paul Anthony Lozano, the legal settlement meant that Paul could be put to rest, at last. From a Cambridge boardinghouse, they set out on a December morning through snowdrifts and slushy streets to thank the psychiatrists who had supported them and the lawyers who had fought for them. They hoped never to return to Boston.

Dr. Bean-Bayog's disclaimer to the settlement, conceding no wrongdoing, stung. There would be no public forum in which to clear their family's name. Paul's mother had been ready to face her accuser. "I think so many things," Epifania Lozano said through her tears. "I believe this woman has never birthed a child of her own, so she cannot know what she has done to me. I never had a social life. My whole life was raising my children. She cannot understand what it means to lose a child, to bury my baby. This Margaret Bean, she does not know what she has done to my heart. I dreamed I would go up to Boston for a graduation, yes, a courtroom, no. I was very proud of that city of President Kennedy. Now that city, that doctor, they have broken my heart."

In the aftermath of Paul's death, Jane Jackson, his friend

and a psychiatric nurse in El Paso, arranged for evaluations and therapy for members of the Lozano family struggling with their grief. Their visits seemed to confirm the view of those who had seen Paul Lozano at McLean during his first hospitalization in 1986 that his was a classic case of biological depression, perhaps with a genetic component.

As it happened, Epifania Lozano, who Dr. Bean-Bayog had speculated suffered from psychotic depression, needed only a few visits with a Hispanic psychiatrist to pull her through a very rough patch. But Norma, plagued with mood swings all her life, was diagnosed with bipolar disorder, or manic-depression. She is responding well to lithium. And Martha, so often compared to Paul within the family because of her high standards and low self-esteem, was put on Zoloft, an antidepressant, with encouraging results.

"It explains a lot," said Abel. "Norma being so productive at work because she was manicky, but when she'd come home she'd crash. Martha's mood swings, like Paul's, and the high expectations for herself. I wonder about myself, too. I see the patterns. In Albuquerque I'd be high energy, working all the time, but when I'd come down I couldn't fulfill all the commitments I'd made. I lost my job that way once. We all have that tendency; we work so hard until we burn out."

Pattern or not, Abel had no plans to visit a psychiatrist. "You could not pay Pilar or me enough money to go to a therapist after this experience," he said. "But it is good to know there was probably a medical cause for Paul's troubles. If our family was guilty of anything, it wasn't anything worse than having vulnerable genes."

For Pilar, the psychiatrist's resignation was vindication enough. She had Margaret Bean-Bayog's medical license; she did not need her apology. "All that matters is that Paul is clean," she said. "I don't want them to have any doubt about the kind of man he was. He was sick, and he became much sicker after her treatment. For even one of those doctors in Boston to defend her, something is wrong. Because this was not defensible; it is not to be pardoned.

"Before my brother died, I just stopped believing in him,

and he knew it. That's the part I can't forgive her for. Because she doesn't know what she did. We were very close, and he died thinking that I thought he was a loser. And that's really a cruel thing to do to somebody. She never did say she made a mistake; she never did admit any responsibility for the pain she caused this family. All we ever heard was about Margaret and Margaret's reputation. It was as though my brother never existed, never had a life or dignity as a human being."

The malpractice settlement was for Paul's dignity. It was not cause for celebration. The money would pay for the lawyers and the funeral and the small house Paul Lozano had always said he would buy one day for his parents' retirement. There would be a scholarship fund for Hispanic students interested in medicine, but it would be based in the Southwest. Paul's money would not send another Mexican-American student to Harvard.

The Lozano family was not alone in the Latino community in its suspicion that the wider Anglo culture was a perilous place for their children. In 1992, the Massachusetts Institute of Technology offered spaces in its freshman class to five Hispanic students from Ysleta High School in El Paso.

The parents of the class valedictorian refused to let their daughter go. Alicia Ayala would attend the University of Texas at home in El Paso. Accusations by MIT administrators that Alicia's parents were denying their daughter a world-class education showed two cultures once again at odds.

"It's the Mexican tradition to hang onto the kids and keep them at home, but this case was severe," Joe Jasso, the MIT admissions officer who had recruited "the El Paso Five," told the press. "They love her, with a parents' love, but it was just suffocating."

Had no one in Boston learned anything from Paul's death? the Lozano family wondered. "Isn't it just possible," asked Pilar, "that the love of a Latino family deserves as much respect as the opinion of well-educated strangers?"

Notes and Sources

This is a book about families and fraternities, those we are born into and those where we forge our identities as adults.

While specifically about the Lozano family of El Paso and the psychiatric fraternity of Boston, it is also a cautionary tale about the fragility of the human mind, the imprecision of psychiatry, the cavalier diagnosis of childhood sexual abuse, and the unregulated use of unorthodox therapeutic techniques.

Exactly what happened between Dr. Margaret Bean-Bayog and Paul Lozano can never be fully known. He is dead and, taken alone, her perspective cannot stand for truth. What can be learned, however, provides a rare glimpse into the consulting room, where a patient's fear and depression and a psychiatrist's need and hubris played themselves out to fatal ends.

In researching their story, I have relied on the public record and on the recollections of those who knew the distinguished Harvard psychiatrist and the promising Latino medical student. In writing it, I have aimed for what the poet Robert Lowell once called "the grace of accuracy."

The following chapter notes are designed as an informal

guide to the research methods used to prepare this book. Published sources are cited, as well as my interviews and legal depositions taken in *The Estate of Paul A. Lozano* v. *Margaret Bean-Bayog, M.D.,* filed in 1991 in Middlesex Superior Court, Commonwealth of Massachusetts, and hereafter referred to as "the malpractice case."

In places where dialogue has been reconstructed, the sources for those exchanges are indicated, e.g., participants' recollections, Dr. Bean-Bayog's office notes, or depositions in the malpractice case.

Dr. Bean-Bayog kept unusually copious notes. In her sworn statement in the malpractice case, she said most of the notes were written during or immediately after each of Paul Lozano's therapy sessions. It appears from a careful reading of her office notes that it was Dr. Bean-Bayog's practice to record her own thoughts and/or comments in parentheses. Her notes are the source for the dialogues between psychiatrist and patient that are reproduced here. For the sake of clarity, words have been written in full in place of abbreviations used in Dr. Bean-Bayog's personal writings and office notes, but only if the substitution did not alter the meaning of the passage. For example, for clarity the pronoun *I* has been bracketed.

I spoke at length with many of Dr. Bean-Bayog's colleagues, several of whom consented to interviews only on condition of anonymity. Their comments informed my perspective, but I have confined direct quotations about her in the text to those people who agreed to be identified.

For reasons of her own, chief among them the unfair treatment she feels she received in the press, Dr. Bean-Bayog chose not to be interviewed for this book. Her perspective is well represented, however, in her public comments and those of her friends, her lawyers, hundreds of pages of defense documents filed with the Massachusetts Board of Registration in Medicine, and her 800-page sworn deposition in the malpractice lawsuit.

Prologue

The death scene was recalled in full by Pilar Williams and corroborated by her parents, Epifania and Marcos Lozano. The description of Paul Lozano's body is contained in the autopsy report of Juan U. Contin, the medical examiner of El Paso County, dated April 3, 1991. The note from Dr. Bean-Bayog to Paul Lozano, suggesting that he is her tiny baby, is part of the public record in the malpractice case.

Chapter 1

The history of the Lozano family in Mexico, Ohio, and Texas was obtained from interviews with Marcos, Epifania, Pilar, Martha, and Norma Lozano in El Paso and with Abel Lozano in Fayetteville, North Carolina. The comments of neighbors, coaches, teachers, friends, and classmates of Paul Lozano were made to the author during two visits to Upper Sandusky, Ohio, and El Paso, Texas, or in telephone interviews in 1992 and 1993. Historical information about Upper Sandusky was obtained from the Chamber of Commerce and *Pictoral Memories* by Ray D. Gottfried, published in 1976 by Watkins Printing Company. The essay Paul Lozano wrote for his Harvard Medical School application, the recommendation letters from James E. Becvar, and the license certifying the marriage of Evelyn Susan Burlingham and Paul A. Lozano are among the personal papers of the late Paul Lozano reviewed by the author.

Chapter 2

The memories of Dr. Alvin F. Pouissant, Dr. Harold Amos, Dr. Carol C. Nadelson, and Amy Stromsten were shared in interviews with the author. Statistics on the racial composition of Paul Lozano's Harvard Medical School class were provided by the medical school. Its history of minority representation is cited in a speech by Leo Eisenberg, M.D., "The Early Years," reprinted by Harvard Medical School in the fall of 1990. Paul Lozano's reaction to his depression was drawn from Dr. Bean-Bayog's office notes and interviews with those who knew him during that period. Dr. Bean-Bayog's credentials appear on her curriculum vitae, on file in the malpractice case; her approach to alcoholism treatment was gleaned from her published work, cited in the bibliography. The description of her lectures was obtained from former students who attended. The description of Paul's brief marriage to Evelyn Susan Burlingham was obtained from Dr. Bean-Bayog's notes and recollections of those who knew the couple. Evelyn Susan Burlingham did not respond to requests for an interview. Dr. Bean-Bayog's description of her life after analysis and marriage appears in the Twenty-fifth Anniversary Report of the Harvard-Radcliffe class of 1965. Her deposition in the malpractice case provided information about her miscarriages and her arrest for driving while intoxicated. Information about depression in medical students was culled from several studies, cited in the bibliography. The comments of Victor Gonzalez about Paul Lozano's state of mind are from his sworn statement to the Massachusetts Board of Registration in Medicine. The views of Drs. Frances Frankenberg and Harrison Pope are contained in the medical record of Paul Lozano's hospitalization at McLean Hospital (September 24, 1986, to November 19, 1986) and their depositions. Information about the changing view of depression came from several sources, cited in the bibliography. Dr. Thomas G. Gutheil's description of a T/A split was obtained during an interview with the author. The letter from Dr. Bean-Bayog to Dr. Daniel D. Federman on October 23, 1986, is contained in the file of the malpractice case. That Dr. Bean-Bayog consulted no one before adopting her regression techniques is stated in her deposition. The theory behind her regression techniques is contained in the Respondent's Evidentiary Summary, filed on September 17,

1992, with the Board of Registration in Medicine. Reparenting therapy is discussed in the article "Call Me Mom" by Andrew Meacham, in *Changes,* August 1992. Details of the lawsuit against Dr. Mark A. Kelley were gleaned from the opinion issued by the Court of Appeals of the State of Oklahoma, October 12, 1993. D. W. Winnicott discussed the management of regression in "Metapsychological and Clinical Aspects of Regression Within the Psychoanalytical Set-Up." Marguerite Sechehaye summarized her work in *Symbolic Realization.* Sandor Ferenczi discussed his theory of "nursery care" in *The Principle of Relaxation and Neocatharsis.* Freud's eulogy for Ferenczi is quoted in *Psychoanalysis: The Impossible Profession* by Janet Malcolm. Arnold Cooper made his comments at the Babcock Symposium at the Pittsburgh Psychoanalytic Institute in 1984. His speech was published in the *American Journal of Psychiatry* in December 1985 under the title "Will Neurobiology Influence Psychoanalysis?" Dr. Bean-Bayog's comments on Paul Lozano's failure to take his antidepressants are from her deposition.

Chapter 3

The scene leading up to Paul Lozano's hospitalization on May 3, 1987, was drawn from Dr. Bean-Bayog's office notes and his McLean Hospital records. Dr. Frances Frankenberg's impressions are contained in her deposition in the malpractice case. Dr. Bean-Bayog's reproductive history is detailed in her deposition, as is her history of alcoholism. That Dr. Buie and Dr. Adler were not told about her unorthodox techniques before Paul Lozano's death is stated in their depositions. Information about borderline personality disorder was obtained from many sources, cited in the bibliography. Bennet Simon's article "Receptivity Is the Key to Successful Treatment of Highly Traumatized Patients" was published in *The Psychodynamic Letter* in March 1992. Freud's comments on the careless use of analysis are contained in "On Beginning the Treatment," in *The Standard Edition of the Complete Psychological Works of Sigmund Freud.* The article "Psychological Damage Associated with Extreme Eroticism in Young Children," by Alayne Yates, M.D., appeared in *Psychiatric Annals* in April 1987. Dr. Bean-Bayog's comments on the Lozano family's role in Paul's stopping his medication are taken from her deposition. The need for therapists to consider cultural factors in assessing patients is described in the *Diagnostic and Statistical Manual of Mental Disorders,* Fourth Edition. Information about the Bean family was obtained from interviews by the author in Iowa City, obituaries, and the published writings of William Bennett Bean and Robert Bennett Bean, which are preserved in the Hardin Library at the University of Iowa and the libraries of the University of Virginia in Charlottesville and cited in the bibliography. Dr. Frankenberg's recollection of the meeting with Pilar and Epifania Lozano at McLean Hospital in May 1987 is contained in her deposition. Dr. Robert Gregory's assessment of Paul Lozano's relationship with Dr. Bean-Bayog is contained in the record of his hospitalization at the Faulkner Hospital (June 22 to July 28, 1987). Dr. Thomas G. Gutheil's recollection that Dr. Bean-Bayog did not disclose her therapy techniques during the case conference at Faulkner in 1987 is stated in his deposition. The social worker's notation about the relationship between Paul and his sisters is contained in his medical chart.

Chapter 4

Paul's anger at Dr. Frankenberg is recorded in Dr. Bean-Bayog's office notes. The definition of transference and countertransference is from the *Psychiatric Glossary,* published by the American Psychiatric Association. The Handy, Multipurpose Emergency and Reference Flash Card Deck is part of the file in the malpractice case. That neither Dr. Gutheil nor Dr. Adler was called in as a consultant by

Dr. Bean-Bayog to discuss her sexual fantasies about Paul Lozano is stated in their depositions. Dr. Bean-Bayog's statement that she was not charged by Dr. Susan C. Adelman for a consultation about Paul Lozano is from her deposition. Dr. Adler's commentary on the consultation process is contained in his deposition. Dr. Bean-Bayog's explanation of how Paul Lozano obtained copies of her handwritten sexual fantasies about him is from her deposition. Sources consulted for information about how psychiatrists should manage countertransference are cited in the bibliography. Dr. Bean-Bayog's comments on Epifania Lozano's alleged sexual abuse of Paul and his nephews are from her deposition.

Chapter 5

Dr. Pope's recollections of his research collaboration with Paul Lozano appear in his deposition. Mark Burrowes recalled his work with Paul at the Human Resources Institute in an interview with the author. Several sources were consulted for information about repressed memories of childhood sexual abuse. They are cited in the bibliography. Jean Piaget's observations on the suggestibility of memory are contained in *Play, Dreams, and Imitation in Childhood.* Dr. Bean-Bayog describes her role in helping Paul retrieve abuse memories in her deposition. That Dr. Bean-Bayog did not interview the Lozano family is stated in her deposition. Information about the academic habits of Harvard Medical students was obtained from Dr. Edward M. Hundert in an interview with the author. Paul's relationship with Candy Stone is described in Dr. Bean-Bayog's treatment notes. Ms. Stone's comments were made in an interview with the author. Paul Lozano's reaction to his psychiatric rotation is described in Dr. Adler's deposition and in Paul Lozano's Faulkner Hospital medical record. Dr. Adler's description of the decision to pass Paul in his psychiatry rotation is from his deposition. The description of Paul Lozano's panic at the autopsy of a stillborn baby is taken from his Faulkner medical record.

Chapter 6

The telephone call from Pilar Williams to Dr. Bean-Bayog is described in the deposition of Ms. Williams and by Dr. Bean-Bayog in the Respondent's Evidentiary Summary, filed on September 17, 1992, with the Board of Registration in Medicine. Dr. Jerome Rogoff recalled Paul Lozano in an interview with the author. Dr. Bean-Bayog's contention that sexual abuse was an open secret in the Lozano family appears in her deposition. Abel Lozano recalled his visit with Paul at Faulkner in an interview with the author. Christi Clark's memories of Paul Lozano appear in her deposition. Coral Grossman recalled living with Paul in the summer of 1990 in an interview with the author. The memories of Paul by a former patient at Faulkner were shared in an interview with the author, on condition of anonymity. Dr. Leonard Lai's assertion that Dr. Bean-Bayog did not call him about Paul Lozano appears in his deposition, which also includes his memory of conversations with Paul about Dr. Bean-Bayog's sexual fantasies. Amy Stromsten's recollections were conveyed in an interview with the author. Dr. Birnbaum's comments are taken from her deposition. Dr. Douglas F. Watt's view of Paul Lozano's termination with Dr. Bean-Bayog as "damaging and very unfortunate" appears in Paul's Malden Hospital chart. Martha Lundgren recalled her relationship with Paul Lozano in an interview with the author. Dr. Dean Solomon's comments are from his deposition. Dr. Adler's memory of calling Dr. Bean-Bayog at Paul Lozano's behest in the fall of 1990 is recounted in his deposition. Dr. José Saporta's assessment of Paul Lozano appears in his deposition.

Chapter 7

Scenes and conversations reconstructed in this chapter are based on interviews by the author with Pilar Williams, Coral Grossman, Epifania Lozano, Dr. William Barry Gault, and Thomas O'Hare. Electroconvulsive therapy is described in the deposition of Dr. Gault. Several sources were consulted on the history of psychoanalysis and the development of psychopharmacology. They are cited in the bibliography. Dr. Bean-Bayog discussed her relationship with the Boston Psychoanalytic Society and Institute in her deposition. James A. Clifton's eulogy for William Bennett Bean is on file at the Hardin Library at the University of Iowa. Paul Lozano's roommate at Newton-Wellesley Hospital's psychiatric unit discussed his memories of their hospitalizations in an interview with the author. Dr. Saporta's remarks are contained in his deposition.

Chapter 8

Amy Stromsten recalled Paul Lozano's meeting with her in January 1991 in an interview with the author. Michael Lew's comments are contained in his deposition. Dr. José Saporta's remarks are taken from his deposition. Thomas O'Hare recalled his relationship with Paul Lozano in an interview with the author. Dr. Gault's comments are from his deposition and interviews with the author. Dr. Edward M. Hundert provided the author with information about Harvard Medical School's decision to readmit Paul Lozano. Conversations and scenes reconstructed in El Paso, Texas, are based on interviews by the author with Pilar Williams, Epifania and Marcos Lozano, and Jane Jackson and a review of the record of Paul Lozano's hospitalization at Sun Valley Hospital (February 1 to February 2, 1991). Dr. Larry H. Strasburger's letter of February 14, 1991, evaluating Dr. Bean-Bayog's therapy is on file in the malpractice case.

Details of the efforts by Pilar Williams to have Candy Stone fired were obtained in interviews with Ms. Williams and Ms. Stone. Dr. Gault described in an interview with the author his sense that Paul Lozano might be in the midst of a manic episode during his March 31, 1991, telephone call from El Paso.

Chapter 9

Conversations and scenes in El Paso reconstructed here are based on interviews with Jane Jackson, Martha Tidball, Nicole Tidball, Epifania and Marcos Lozano, Pilar Lozano, Abel Lozano, Norma Grossman, Coral Grossman, and Dr. Raul Marcello Rodriguez. The cause of Paul Lozano's death is listed in the autopsy report of Juan U. Contin, the medical examiner of El Paso County, dated April 3, 1991. The letter from the Board of Registration in Medicine, dated April 3, 1991, is on file in the malpractice case. The chronology of action taken by the Board of Registration in Medicine in its investigation of the charges against Dr. Bean-Bayog is outlined in a memorandum to Consumer Affairs Secretary Gloria Larson, dated April 2, 1992. Dr. Louis F. Alfano's demand that the word *discipline* be removed from the title of the medical board was reported in *The Boston Globe* on May 27, 1976. The report "Comparing State Medical Boards" by the Public Citizen Health Research Group ranking Massachusetts forty-eighth in disciplinary actions against doctors was released on January 12, 1993. The comments of Dr. John H. Knowles about the Massachusetts medical board were reported in *The Boston Globe* on May 30, 1972. The lawsuit by eight Harvard-affiliated hospitals, challenging the authority of the medical board, was reported in *The Boston Globe* on April 12, 1987. Dr. George Annas and Marian Ego made their comments in interviews with the author. Peter Clark's speech and details of the Paul Bettencourt case were reported in *The Boston Globe* on August 14, 1989. Statistics on the number of physicians disciplined in Massachusetts were provided by the Board of Registration in Medicine. The firing of Barbara Neuman was reported in *The Boston Globe* on May 3, 1990. The strained relations between Governor Michael S. Dukakis and the state's doctors were reported in *The Boston Globe* on September 17, 1988, and confirmed by members of his administration in interviews with the author. Results of the Harvard University malpractice study were reported in *The Boston Globe* on March 9, 1990. Barbara Noel recounted her experience in her book *You Must Be Dreaming*. Anne Sexton's relationship with her therapist is discussed in *Anne Sexton: A Biography* by Diane Wood Middlebrook. The controversy over the posthumous release of her therapy tapes and her sexual relationship with her second psychiatrist is discussed by her daughter, Linda Sexton, in the introduction to *Anne Sexton: A Self-Portrait in Letters*. Melissa Roberts-Henry's suit against her psychiatrist is examined in the documentary "Doctor, My Lover," produced by Virginia Storring and John Zaritsky, that aired on the PBS series "Frontline" on November 12, 1991. The names and circumstances of psychiatrists disciplined for sexual misconduct were obtained from the files of the Massachusetts Board of Registration in Medicine. The meeting between Thomas O'Hare and Dr. Eleanor Shore was recalled by Mr. O'Hare in an interview with the author. The conversation between Amy Stromsten and Pilar Williams was recalled by Ms. Stromsten and confirmed by Ms. Williams in interviews with the author. Dr. Harrison Pope's call to Andrew C. Meyer, Jr., is discussed in Dr. Pope's deposition and was confirmed by Mr. Meyer in an interview with the author.

Chapter 10

The conversation between Andrew C. Meyer, Jr., and Pilar Williams was recalled by Ms. Williams and confirmed by Mr. Meyer in interviews with the author. The Lozano family meeting in El Paso was described by participants in interviews with the author. Abel and Sandy Lozano recalled their reaction to the allegations of abuse in interviews with the author. Michael L. Blau's comments are from his speech, "The Bean-Bayog Case," delivered to a Massachusetts Continuing Legal Education seminar on February 10, 1993. Dr. Gault and Pilar Williams discussed their reactions to the publicity in interviews with the author. The quote in defense of Dr. Bean-Bayog by an anonymous psychiatrist appeared in *The Boston Globe* on March 30, 1992. The comments of Charlotte Leeth, Ralph Young, Bethany Foltz, and Dr. Thomas Watkins were made in interviews with the author. *The Boston Globe* reported on Thomas Thomson's affidavit on April 23, 1992. The *Herald* interview with Thomson appeared on April 24, 1992. The letter defending Dr. Bean-Bayog by a former patient was published by *The Boston Globe* on September 19, 1992. The letter writer's relationship to Benjamin B. Taylor was confirmed by Mr. Taylor to the author. Alexander Fleming's comments on press coverage were made at a Massachusetts Continuing Legal Education seminar on February 10, 1993. Dr. Nanette Gartrell's study "Psychiatrist-Patient Sexual Contact: Results of a National Survey" was published in the *American Journal of Psychiatry*. Details of *The Boston Globe* coverage of Dr. Sheldon Zigelbaum's case were obtained in interviews with Jean Dietz, Mike Barnicle, and Timothy Leland. The quotes from Doris Kearns Goodwin are from her deposition in the Board of Registration in Medicine disciplinary case against Dr. Zigelbaum, taken on August 17, 1990. The comments from Patti Levin Zigelbaum are taken from her deposition in the same case.

Chapter 11

In their depositions in the malpractice case, Nancy Butters, Rita Falk, and Marguerite Ryan said they did not recall discussions about Dr. Bean-Bayog's erotic feelings toward a

Mexican-American medical student. Kathryn Kogan recalled the work of the supervision group run by Dr. Bean-Bayog in her deposition and in an interview with the author. Dr. Joseph T. Coyle spoke about the diagnosis and treatment of personality disorders in an interview with the author. Dr. Harrison G. Pope's opinion about personality disorders is contained in his deposition. Many sources consulted on borderline personality disorder are cited in the bibliography. Dr. Carol C. Nadelson's remarks were made in an interview with the author. Dr. Harold Amos recalled Paul Lozano's academic abilities in an interview with the author. Mark Burrowes discussed his work with Paul Lozano in an interview with the author. Victor Gonzalez's comments are from his statement to the Massachusetts Board of Registration in Medicine. Dr. Thomas G. Gutheil's remarks about sexual abuse, memory, Hispanic pacifying techniques, and the complexity of judging psychiatric practice were made in interviews with the author. Dr. Edward J. Khantzian discussed the case in an interview with the author. Dr. Jerome Rogoff's comments were made in an interview with the author. Dr. Gutheil discussed his fees in his deposition. Michael L. Blau's description of Dr. Bean-Bayog's sexual fantasies is from his speech "The Bean-Bayog Case," delivered to a Massachusetts Continuing Legal Education seminar on February 10, 1993. Dr. W. Barry Gault's comments were made in an interview with the author. The finding of gross negligence against engineers for the Hyatt Regency Hotel in Kansas City, Missouri, was reported in *The New York Times* on November 16, 1985.

Chapter 12

The reconstruction of the events leading to Dr. Bean-Bayog's resignation is based on interviews with Jack Fabiano, Paul R. McHugh, Christopher Connolly, Alexander F. Fleming, and Michael L. Blau's speech "The Bean-Bayog Case," delivered to a Massachusetts Continuing

Legal Education seminar on February 10, 1993. Dr. McHugh's article "Psychiatric Misadventures" appeared in the Fall 1992 issue of *The American Scholar*. Statistics on the frequency and content of psychiatric malpractice lawsuits were reported in *The Boston Globe* on April 19, 1992. Marian Ego's recollections of the disciplinary case against Dr. Archie D. Kiegan were discussed in an interview with the author. Dr. Edward Khantzian discussed the division between analysts and biopsychiatrists in an interview with the author. Dr. Thomas G. Gutheil's letter discussing Paul Lozano's risk for suicide is on file in the malpractice case. Dr. Bean-Bayog's resignation letter is in the file of the Massachusetts Board of Registration in Medicine.

Epilogue

The impact and aftermath of Dr. Bean-Bayog's resignation were gleaned from interviews with Kathryn Kogan, Amy Stromsten, Pilar Lozano, Epifania Lozano, Marcos Lozano, Abel Lozano, Martha Lozano, Jane Jackson, Joseph T. Coyle, Dr. Paul Applebaum, and associates of Dr. Bean-Bayog who requested anonymity. Information about the regulation of unlicensed therapists was provided by Bruce M. Douglas. Edward M. Hundert confirmed that Harvard had done no formal review of the case. Dr. Carol Birnbaum's comments are from her deposition in the malpractice case. Joe Jasso of MIT was quoted in the *Dallas Morning News*.

Bibliography

Many books and articles were consulted in an effort to put the relationship between Dr. Margaret Bean-Bayog and Paul Lozano in the broader context of popular and academic psychiatry. Among the most useful were:

Bass, Ellen, and Laura Davis. *Courage to Heal: A Guide for Women Survivors of Child Sexual Abuse.* New York: HarperCollins, 1988.

Bean, Margaret. *Alcoholics Anonymous.* New York: Insight Publishing, 1975.

Bean, Margaret, and N. Zinberg, eds. *Dynamic Approaches to the Understanding and Treatment of Alcoholism.* New York: The Free Press, 1981.

Bean-Bayog, Margaret, and Barry Stimmel, eds. *Children of Alcoholics.* New York: Hayworth Press, 1987.

Bean, Robert Bennett. *The Peopling of Virginia.* Boston: Chapman & Grimes, 1938.

———. *The Races of Man: Differentiation and Dispersal of Man.* New York: The University Society, 1932.

345

Eileen McNamara

————. *The Racial Anatomy of the Philippine Islanders.* Philadelphia: J. B. Lippincott Company, 1910.

Bean, William Bennett, ed. *Monographs in Medicine.* Baltimore: Williams & Wilkins Co., 1952.

————. *Sir William Osler: Aphorisms from His Bedside Teachings and Writings.* New York: H. Schuman, 1950.

Benedek, Elissa P., and Diana H. Schetky. "Problems in Validating Allegations of Sexual Abuse: Factors Affecting Perception & Recall of Events." *Journal of the American Academy of Child and Adolescent Psychiatry* 26 (1987), 912–915.

Bird, Brian. "Notes on Transference: Universal Phenomenon and Hardest Part of Analysis." *Journal of the American Psychoanalytic Association* 20 (1972): 267–301.

Clark, David C., and Peter B. Zeldow. "Vicissitudes of Depressed Mood During Four Years of Medical School." *Journal of the American Medical Association,* Nov. 4, 1988, 260: 2521–2528.

Cooper, Arnold M. "Will Neurobiology Influence Psychoanalysis?" *American Journal of Psychiatry* (December 1985).

Corsini, Raymond J., and Danny Wedding, eds. *Current Psychotherapies,* fourth edition. Itasca, IL: F. E. Peacock, 1989.

Dowling, Colette. *You Mean I Don't Have to Feel This Way?* New York: Charles Scribner's Sons, 1991.

Ferenczi, Sandor. *Final Contributions to the Problems and Methods of Psychoanalysis.* New York: Brunner/Mazel, 1980.

Fine, Reuben. *A History of Psychoanalysis.* New York: Columbia University Press, 1979.

Freud, Sigmund. *The Standard Edition of the Complete Psychological Works of Sigmund Freud,* trans. and ed. James Strachey. London: Hogarth Press, Ltd., 1961.

Gartrell, Nanette, et al. "Psychiatrist-Patient Sexual Contact: Results of a National Survey." *American Journal of Psychiatry* 143, no. 9 (1986), 1126–1131.

————. "Reporting Practices of Psychiatrists Who Knew of Sexual Misconduct by Colleagues." *American Journal of Orthopsychiatry* 57, no. 2 (April 1987), 287–295.

Gifford, Sanford. "Psychoanalysis in Boston: Innocence and Experience." In G. E. Gifford, ed., *Psychotherapy and the New England Medical Scene, 1894–1969.* New York: Academic Press, 1978.

————. "The First Fifty Years, 1933–1983." *Boston Psychoanalytic Society and Institute Newsletter* 1, no. 1 (1984), 5–8.

Gitlin, Michael. *The Psychotherapist's Guide to Psychopharmacology.* New York: Macmillan, 1990.

Goleman, Daniel. "Childhood Trauma, Memory or Invention?" *The New York Times,* July 21, 1992.

Goodwin, Donald W., and Samuel B. Guze. *Psychiatric Diagnosis,* fourth edition. New York: Oxford University Press, 1989.

Greenacre, Phyllis. "The Role of Transference: Practical Considerations in Relation to Psychoanalytic Therapy." *Journal of the American Psychoanalytic Association* (October 1954), vol. II (4), 671–684.

Gutheil, Thomas G. "The Concept of Boundaries in Clinical Practice: Theoretical and Risk-Management Dimensions." *American Journal of Psychiatry* (February 1993), 150 (2), 188–196.

————. "Medicolegal Pitfalls in the Treatment of Borderline Patients." *American Journal of Psychiatry* (January 1985), 142 (1), 9–14.

Hendrick, Ives, ed. *The Birth of an Institute.* Freeport, ME: The Bond Wheelwright Company, 1961.

Herman, Judith Lewis. *Father-Daughter Incest.* Cambridge, Mass.: Harvard University Press, 1981.

————. *Trauma and Recovery.* New York: Basic Books, 1992.

Herman, Judith, Nanette Gartrell, et al. "Psychiatrist-Patient Sexual Contact: Results of a National Survey, II: Psychiatrists' Attitudes." *American Journal of Psychiatry* 144 (1987), Feb., 144 (2), 164–169.

Jonas, Jeffrey M., and Harrison G. Pope. "Axis I Comorbidity of Borderline Personality Disorder: Clinical Implications." In J. F. Clarkin, E. Marziali, and H. Munroe-Blum, eds, *Borderline Personality Disorder,* vol. I. New York: Guilford Press, 1992.

Jones, Ernest. *The Life and Work of Sigmund Freud.* 3 vols. New York: Basic Books, 1953–1957.

Kernberg, Otto. *Borderline Conditions and Pathological Narcissism.* New York: Aronson, 1975.

Kohut, Heinz. *The Restoration of the Self.* New York: International Universities Press, 1977.

————. *The Analysis of the Self.* New York: International Universities Press, 1971.

Loftus, Elizabeth. *Witness for the Defense: The Accused, the Eyewitness, and the Expert Who Puts Memory on Trial.* New York: St. Martin, 1991.

————. "The Reality of Repressed Memories." Paper delivered at the Annual Meeting of the American Psychological Association, Washington, D.C., 1992.

Malcolm, Janet. *Psychoanalysis: The Impossible Profession.* New York: Alfred A. Knopf, 1981.

Masson, Jeffrey Moussaieff. *Assault on the Truth: Freud's Suppression of the Seduction Theory.* New York: Farrar, Straus & Giroux, 1984.

McHugh, Paul R., and P. R. Slavney. *The Perspectives of Psychiatry.* Baltimore: Johns Hopkins University Press, 1983.

Meyers, Wayne A. *Shrink Dreams: Tales from the Hidden Side of Psychiatry.* New York: Simon & Schuster, 1992.

Middlebrook, Diane Wood. *Anne Sexton: A Biography.* Boston: Houghton Mifflin, 1991.

Mondimore, Francis M., M.D. *Depression: The Mood Disease.* Baltimore: Johns Hopkins University Press, 1990.

Noel, Barbara (with Kathryn Watterson). *You Must Be Dreaming.* New York: Poseidon Press, 1992.

Piaget, Jean. *Play, Dreams, and Imitation in Childhood.* New York: Norton, 1962.

Pope, Harrison G., Jr., and James I. Hudson. "Are Eating Disorders Associated with Borderline Personality Disorder?" *International Journal of Eating Disorders* 8, no. 1, January 1989, 1–9.

———. "Is Childhood Sexual Abuse a Risk Factor for Bulimia Nervosa?" *American Journal of Psychiatry* (April 1992), 149 (4), 455–463.

Pope, Kenneth, and Jacqueline Bouhoutsos. *Sexual Intimacy Between Therapists and Patients.* New York: Praeger, 1986.

Pope, Kenneth S., and Valerie Vetter. "Prior Therapist-Patient Sexual Involvement Among Patients Seen by Psychologists." *Psychotherapy* 28, no. 3 (Fall 1991): 429–438.

Pope, Kenneth S., Barbara G. Tabachnick, and Keith Spiegel. "Ethics of Practice: The Beliefs and Behaviors of Psychologists as Therapists." *American Psychologist* 42, no. 11 (November 1987), 993–1006.

Rogers, Martha L. "Evaluating Adult Litigants Who Allege Injuries from Child Sexual Abuse: Clinical Assessment Methods for Traumatic Memories." Paper presented at the Fourth Annual Meeting of the American Psychological Society, San Diego, California, June 20, 1992.

Searles, Harold. "Oedipal Love in the Countertransference." In *Collected Papers on Schizophrenia and Related Subjects,* by Harold Searles. New York: International Universities Press, Inc., 1965.

Sechehaye, Marguerite. *Symbolic Realization.* New York: International Universities Press, 1951.

Sexton, Linda, and Lois Ames, eds. *Anne Sexton: A Self-Portrait in Letters.* Boston: Houghton Mifflin, 1992.

Stone, Elizabeth. "Off the Couch." *The New York Times Magazine.* December 6, 1992.

Styron, William. *Darkness Visible.* New York: Vintage Books, 1992.

Tavris, Carol. "Beware the Incest-Survivor Machine." *The New York Times,* January 3, 1993.

Terr, Lenore. *Too Scared to Cry: Psychic Trauma in Childhood.* New York: Basic Books, 1992.

Winnicott, Donald W. "Metapsychological and Clinical Aspects of Regression Within the Psychoanalytical Set-Up." In *Collected Papers: Through Pediatrics to Psychoanalysis,* by Donald W. Winnicott. New York: Basic Books, 1958.

———. "Clinical Varieties of Transference." In ibid.

———. "The Use of Object and Relating Through Identifications." In *Playing and Reality,* by Donald W. Winnicott. London: Tavistock, 1971.

Zimmerman, Mark, et al. "Diagnosing Personality Disorder in Depressed Patients: A Comparison of Patient and Informant Interviews." *Archives of General Psychiatry* (August 1988), vol. 45 (8), 733–737.